THE EGYPTIAN SOUDAN

THE DEATH OF GENERAL GORDON.   [*Frontispiece. See p* 19.
Khartoum, Jan. 26, 1885.
Painted by G. W. Joy.   Etched by Herbert Dicksee.   Published by Frost & Reed, Bristol.

THE
EGYPTIAN SOUDAN

ITS LOSS AND RECOVERY

INCUDING

I. —A RAPID SKETCH OF THE HISTORY OF THE SOUDAN
II. —A NARRATIVE OF THE DONGOLA EXPEDITION, 1896
III. —A FULL ACCOUNT OF THE NILE EXPEDITIONS, 1897—8

BY

HENRY S. L. ALFORD
LIEUTENANT ROYAL SCOTS FUSILIERS

AND

W. DENNISTOUN SWORD
LIEUTENANT NORTH STAFFORDSHIRE REGIMENT

*WITH NUMEROUS PORTRAITS, ILLUSTRATIONS AND MAPS
AND RECORDS OF THE SERVICES OF THE
OFFICERS (1896—8), ETC*

The Naval & Military Press Ltd

Published by

The Naval & Military Press Ltd
Unit 5 Riverside
Bellbrook Industrial Estate
Uckfield, East Sussex
TN22 1QQ England

Tel: +44 (0) 1825 749494
www.naval-military-press.com

Cover: Charge of the 21st Lancers at the Battle of Omdurman on 2nd September 1898. Picture by Harry Payne.

In reprinting in facsimile from the original, any imperfections are inevitably reproduced and the quality may fall short of modern type and cartographic standards.

THIS BOOK IS RESPECTFULLY

Dedicated

BY PERMISSION

TO HIS HIGHNESS

ABBAS II

KHEDIVE OF EGYPT

WHOSE RULE WILL BE DISTINGUISHED THROUGHOUT

HISTORY BY THE RECOVERY OF THE LOST

EGYPTIAN PROVINCES

PREFACE

ALL that has been attempted in this book has been to put before the public, in a readable and concise form, the events in the Egyptian Soudan which have led up to, and resulted in, the downfall of the Dervishes.

Every one knows that Gordon was killed at Khartoum and that Kitchener has avenged his fate, but comparatively few understand—for instance—why Gordon was ever in the Soudan at all, or why the British have reconquered that country. As for *Pasha, Bey, Sirdar, Bimbashi*—people seem to shy at the very sight of these words, and to almost wonder how an Englishman can belong to the Egyptian Army and yet retain his nationality! The sequence of events on the Nile, has extended over so long a period, in such an apparently disjointed fashion, that it is perhaps only natural there should be some vagueness on the subject.

This book is not put forward in any way as a

professional study of the Campaigns herein dealt with. Whilst endeavouring to be as complete and accurate as possible in every point that can interest the general reader, all those minor technical details which belong to a military treatise, or an official Blue-book, rather than to a popular history, have been purposely omitted.

Part II. is merely a plain unvarnished tale of our experiences during the Dongola Expedition, and we would not have ventured to intrude them on the public, were it not for the fact that we were urged to do so by friends, on the ground that an insight into the actual details of active service on the Nile would be of interest to the general reader.

With regard to the Appendices, the lists of officers who have served in the recent Expeditions forms a record which will doubtless be appreciated by those who took part in them, whilst the roll of British officers and men who lost their lives cannot fail to have a certain melancholy interest attached to it.

Our thanks are due to the following gentlemen. To Messrs. Bassano (for portraits of the Sirdar and Major-General Hunter), Russell and Sons (Major-General Rundle), Lekegian—Cairo—(the Dervish Emir and the officers of the 21st Lancers): to the proprietors of the *Graphic* and *Black and White*, for kindly allowing us the use of a number of their pictures and portraits; to Mr. Joy, the eminent artist, by whose courtesy we are enabled to reproduce his famous picture, "The Death of General Gordon;" to Messrs. Frost and Reed, owners of the copyright of this picture; to the Authorities of the Intelligence Department, War Office, to whom we are indebted for the admirable maps dealing with the campaign around the Atbara, and the final march on Omdurman, and, above all, to our numerous friends with the troops in the Soudan, who stipulated that they should be nameless, but without whose valuable assistance we could not have written so full an account of the Fall of the Khalifa.

In a book of this nature, unavoidable errors of omission and commission are bound to creep in, which we beg our readers to excuse. Any corrections will be thankfully received and acknowledged by the authors.

H. S. L. A.
W. D. S.

CHATHAM,
October 8th, 1898.

ERRATA.

THE EGYPTIAN SOUDAN.

Page 48, last line of footnote for (80th) read (94th).

,, 87, 89, 206, 264, 332, for " LAURIE " read " LAWRIE."

,, 89, third line from foot of page, for "BLUNT" read " FALKINER."

,, 323, between Ambigol and Kosheh insert

AKASHEH.

Lce.-Corpl. J. M'NAMARA, 2nd Connaught Rangers.

,, 329, index, delete BLUNT (Connaught Rangers).

,, 331, index, between "FAKRI" and "FAREIG" insert *Falkiner*, Lieut., 89.

CONTENTS

PREFACE VII

PART I

THE SOUDAN PRIOR TO ITS RECAPTURE

CHAPTER   PAGE
I.—EARLY HISTORY 1
I.—THE MAHDI 9
II.—THE KHALIFA 24
IV.—ENGLAND AND EGYPT 36

PART II

THE DONGOLA EXPEDITION, 1896

I.—THE START, CAIRO TO WADY HALFA 47
II.—PRELIMINARY SKIRMISHES 58
III.—AROUND SUAKIN 67
IV.—WADY HALFA 75
V.—THE BATTLE OF FERKET 85
VI.—THE CHOLERA 95
VII.—THE CATARACTS 104
VIII.—THE ADVANCE TO THE THIRD CATARACT 111
IX.—THE BATTLE OF HAFIR 122
X.—THE CAPTURE OF DONGOLA 133
XI.—THE CLOSE OF THE DONGOLA CAMPAIGN 143

PART III

THE OPERATIONS OF 1897

I.—The Capture of Abu Hamed 157
II.—The Reconnaissance of Metemmeh 173
III.—The Acquisition of Kassala 184

PART IV

THE NILE EXPEDITION, 1898

I.—British Regiments to the Front 195
II.—The Advance to Mutrus 205
III.—The Battle of the Atbara 214
IV.—After the Battle 225
V.—The Concentration at Wad Hamed 236
VI.—Nearing the Goal 249
VII.—The Battle of Khartoum 257
VIII.—The Capture of Omdurman 270
IX.—Khartoum—and after 280

APPENDICES

I.—Organisation of the Dongola Expeditionary Force, 1896, and the Nile Expeditionary Force, 1898.* 293
II.—Roll of British Officers, Warrant Officers, Non-Commissioned Officers, and Men Who Lost Their Lives in the Campaign on the Nile (1896—8) 321

INDEX 329

---

* With the names of the Officers serving, the Honours subsequently conferred on them, &c.

MAPS

The Egyptian Soudan (*folding*)	*To face page*	1
The Nile from Cairo to Wady Halfa	,,	47
The Nile from Wady Halfa to Dongola	,,	59
The District around Suakin	,,	67
Plan of the Battle of Ferket	,,	94
The Nile from Dongola to Metemmeh	,,	163
The Country at the Junction of the Atbara and the Nile	,,	203
Plan of the Battle of the Atbara (Mahmud's zariba)	,	215
The Nile from Metemmeh to Khartoum	,	237
Plans of the Battle of Khartoum	,,	257, 261
Plan of Omdurman and Khartoum	,,	272

ILLUSTRATIONS

"The Death of General Gordon"	*Frontispiece*	
A Dervish Emir	*To face page*	25
The Sirdar; Sir H. H. Kitchener, K.C.M.G., C.B.	,,	39
Departmental Officers attached to the North Staffordshire Regiment / Officers of the 1st North Staffordshire Regiment	,,	51
Brevet-Colonel H. M. L. Rundle, C.M.G., D.S.O. / Brevet-Colonel A. Hunter, D.S.O.	,,	58
The Intelligence Department, Egyptian Army (Colonel Wingate and Slatin Pasha)	,,	77
Landing Stores at Wady Halfa		

THE MAIN ATTACK ON THE DERVISH POSITION AT FERKET	To face page	89
THE CAMP OF THE NORTH STAFFORDSHIRE REGIMENT AT GEMAI	,,	97
A NIGHT FUNERAL AT GEMAI	,,	99
HAULING THE FIRST GUNBOAT THROUGH THE "GREAT GATE"	,,	106
THE SIRDAR'S FLOTILLA	,,	111
THE FINAL ADVANCE ON DONGOLA, SEPTEMBER 23RD, 1896	,,	136
BREVET-MAJOR "RODDY" OWEN, LANCASHIRE FUSILIERS		
CAPTAIN J. ROSE, NORTH STAFFORDSHIRE REGIMENT	,,	166
*BREVET-MAJOR H. M. SIDNEY, D.C.L.I., E.A.		
*LIEUT. E. FITZ CLARENCE, DORSET REGT., E.A.		
THE INTERIOR OF THE FORT, KASSALA	,,	190
MAJOR-GENERAL W. F. GATACRE, C.B., D.S.O.	,,	197
†MAJOR URQUHART, CAMERON HIGHLANDERS		
†MAJOR NAPIER ,, ,,		
†CAPTAIN FINDLAY ,, ,,	,,	221
†CAPTAIN BAILLIE, SEAFORTH ,,		
†LIEUTENANT GORE ,, ,,		
MAHMUD	,,	228
‡CAPTAIN CALDECOTT, ROYAL WARWICKSHIRE REGIMENT	,,	259
‡LIEUTENANT GRENFELL, 12TH LANCERS		
HERR CHARLES NEUFELD	,,	259
THE OFFICERS, AND ATTACHED OFFICERS OF THE 21ST LANCERS	,,	265
BIRD'S-EYE VIEW OF OMDURMAN	,,	271
THE MEMORIAL SERVICE AT GORDON'S PALACE	,,	281

* Killed at Abu Hamed.   † Killed at the Atbara.
‡ Killed at the battle of Khartoum.

PART I

THE SOUDAN PRIOR TO ITS RE-CAPTURE

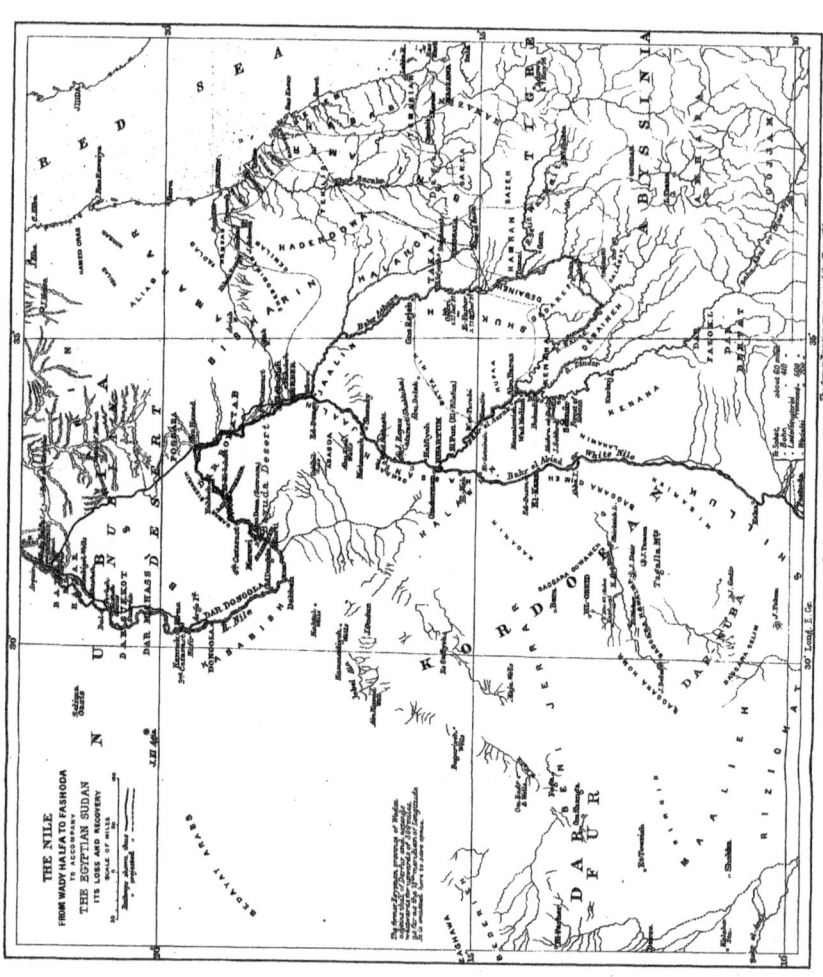

THE EGYPTIAN SOUDAN

ITS LOSS AND RECOVERY

CHAPTER I

EARLY HISTORY OF THE SOUDAN

Spread of Christianity — Conversion to Islamism — Conquest by Mahomed Ali — Khartoum founded — Growth of the slave-trade — Sir Samuel Baker — Gordon's first visit to the Soudan — Zobeir Pasha — Gessi — The prevalent discontent results in the insurrection of the Mahdi.

THE expression "Soudan" literally means "the Country of the Blacks," and includes, roughly speaking, one million square miles of trackless desert, dotted here and there with small patches of vegetation, through which flows its great artery the Nile. That part which lies within the immediate region of the Nile, and between the river and the Red Sea, is known as the "Egyptian Soudan," and it is the latter country only that is treated of in this book.

The Soudan has never, in its known history, possessed any form of rule or government—other than that practised by savage rulers and slave-dealing Arabs—unless Gordon's unsuccessful efforts be counted as such. This is due to its inaccessible position, the warlike and ungovernable qualities of its numerous tribes, and the enormous difficulty of holding in check, when subdued, the inhabitants of so vast an expanse of territory. There is no part of the world more stained with blood and oppression than the Soudan; no country where the worst passions of cruel races have had a freer vent, or where lawlessness has been more rife, or slavery more brutally practised.

Of the early history of the Soudan, designated by the ancients under the general term of Ethiopia, little is known, save of a few expeditions sent by rulers of Egypt to explore and conquer the regions of the Upper Nile. The first expedition history tells of is one sent by Amenhotep, King of Egypt, B.C. 1500. Rameses invaded Ethiopia; Cambyses, the Persian conqueror of Egypt, marched his victorious army into that country, only to be destroyed; and numerous expeditions of a like nature were made by the succeeding rulers of Egypt, with varying success.

In 24 A.D. an invasion—contrary to all precedent —was made by the Ethiopians, under Candace, Queen of Merawi, into Egypt; but, after a fierce battle at Elephantine, they were defeated by the Romans under Petronius. Merawi at this time was the principal city in Ethiopia, and, according to some writers, was mightier than the far-famed

Thebes; but to-day the only monuments left are the ruins of the ancient capital Nepata, the modern Jebel Barkal, near Merawi.

Without going into a detailed history of the numerous attempts at the conquest of the Soudan, suffice to say that up to its subjugation by Mahomed Ali, early in the present century, no Egyptian monarch had ever held the country for any length of time; and in spite of repeated invasions, the First Cataract always remained the extreme Southern boundary of Egypt.

Christianity began to penetrate the higher reaches of the Nile during the fifth century, and remained there for 800 years, when it gave way to Islamism. It was not until the thirteenth century that the green banner of the Prophet waved triumphant in Ethiopia, and then only at the point of the sword. This was brought about by the Egyptian sultan, Dhaber Bêbars, who conquered Dongola, then an independent Christian kingdom; and the inhabitants, the ancestors of those who now so fanatically perish in defence of Islamism, fell with the same fanaticism and enthusiasm for the sake of the Cross. They were out-numbered, however, and the whole of Upper Nubia was overrun with tribes of wandering Arabs, who had embraced the Koran, and now set themselves up as governors after all but exterminating the inhabitants.

The year 1821 A.D. is an important one in the history of the Soudan. MAHOMED ALI, Khedive of Egypt, despatched an expedition up the Nile under his son Ismail, and the provinces of Dongola (hitherto a separate kingdom), Kordofan and Sennâr were conquered and annexed. KHARTOUM [1] was founded and made their capital. Military stations were established on the Blue and White Niles, and the provinces were, as far as possible, brought under the rule of the Egyptians. The only result of Mahomed's conquest was to make Khartoum the great central slave-mart of the Soudan, though of course the trade itself had been long established.

During the rule of Abbas, Mahomed's grandson, who ruled Egypt from 1848 till 1854, the Soudan was in a deplorable condition. Abbas was succeeded by Said Pasha, who will always be honourably remembered in connection with the Soudan, as being the first Egyptian monarch who made any active attempt to suppress the slave-trade; but his efforts were futile, for he was powerless to enforce his wishes. Although the country had been annexed and military garrisons had been established, the Arab tribes had never been subjected to any form of rule or government, and all that could possibly be expected of them was payment of some tribute of varying amount.

In 1861 when SIR SAMUEL BAKER visited the Soudan—then governed by Musa Pasha—he found it in the same lamentable condition. In 1869 he was appointed Governor-General of the Equatorial

---

[1] "Khartoum" means an "elephant's trunk," and was probably meant to describe the narrow neck of land between the White and Blue Niles, on which the city stood.

Provinces, with control of the country south of Gondokoro. The administration by the Egyptian pashas—who had made a practice of leasing large territories to traders who used them for slave-dealing purposes—had reduced the wretched inhabitants to the lowest ebb of misery. Sir Samuel Baker made vigorous efforts to put down this execrable traffic, by which whole countries and districts in Equatorial Africa had been depopulated, and he succeeded in dealing heavy blows to the trade. Had he obtained any assistance from the corrupt Egyptian officials, Khartoum as a slave-mart would have ceased to exist.

Baker returned to Cairo in 1873, and was succeeded the following year by Charles GORDON, a colonel in the Royal Engineers, whose name has become inseverably connected with the history of the Soudan.

Gordon regarded the suppression of the slave-trade as the highest of the duties entrusted to him. The policy was adopted of bringing all the Soudanese provinces under a firm rule, and in 1874 Darfur and Harar were annexed to Egypt. This policy was absolutely necessary if any successful effort was to be taken against the slave-dealers. Some of the latter, who paid rent to the Egyptian Government, were immensely wealthy and powerful, and assumed absolute control over large territories. The most notorious of these was ZOBEIR Pasha, who lived in princely style, exercised great influence in the Soudan, and practically controlled the slave-trade. Zobeir's position may be cited as an instance of Gordon's difficulties with the Egyptian Government. Gordon had insisted that the destruction of Zobeir's gang was the turning-point in the slave-trade question, yet the Cairene officials not only ignored this fact, but created Zobeir a pasha, and treated him as an honoured guest, whilst Nubar Pasha (the Egyptian Minister) even offered to send Zobeir to assist Gordon in the suppression of the trade. He evidently believed in "setting a thief to catch a thief!"

On the 4th of August, 1877, a Convention was concluded between Great Britain and Egypt, by which all public traffic in slaves was prohibited; whilst private trade in Egypt was to be suppressed in 1884, and in the Soudan in 1889. Referring to this, Gordon wrote: "If the liberation of slaves takes place in 1884, and the present Goverment goes on, there cannot fail to be a revolt of the whole of the country. . . . It is rather amusing to think that the people of Cairo are quite oblivious that in 1884 their revenue will fall one-half. . . . Seven-eighths of the population of the Soudan are slaves, and the loss of revenue in 1889 will be more than two-thirds."

Gordon was assisted by an Italian named GESSI, Governor-General of the Bahr-el-Ghazal;[1] and in one year (March, 1878, to March, 1879) they

[1] Gessi died in 1881, and was succeeded in the Bahr-el-Ghazal by Lupton Bey. Lupton had been a mate in the P. and O. Company's service. He became a prisoner on the fall of the Soudan, and died at Khartoum in 1891.

succeeded in capturing sixty-three caravans of slaves. Needless to say their efforts were resisted in every way by the slave-dealers, and in June, 1878, a revolt, instigated by Zobeir, and led by his son Suleiman, broke out. The principal slave-dealers had apportioned out, among themselves, the provinces of the Soudan, and they gave out that they would not stop short of Cairo. They were supported by Arab tribes, and seemed powerful enough to tax the strength of all Egypt. This insurrection was suppressed by the bravery and energy of Gessi. Suleiman was shot, with eleven other ringleaders, in July, 1880.

Gordon's experiences would fill many volumes, and contain the most astounding revelations of cruelty and barbarity it is possible to conceive. He certainly broke the back of the slave-traffic, and if there had been any really honest intention to assist him on the part of the Egyptian pashas, his efforts would have put an end to it. On his departure in 1879, and the reassumption of government by the Egyptians, the trade revived with remarkable activity, and the familiar crack of the slaver's whip resounded throughout the length and breadth of the Soudan.

We are now brought to a most important period of this history, namely, the rise of the Mahdi. That the inhabitants of the Egyptian provinces of the Soudan would sooner or later rise in a body and fall upon their oppressors, was only to be expected; but no one could foresee a rebellion so rapid in its growth, so fanatical in its nature, and so far-reaching in its consequences, as that which was now to take place.

The misery and poverty of the inhabitants, the venality and oppression of the Egyptian tax-collectors, and, above all, the discontent of the Baggara tribe—the great slave-traders of the desert—rendered the Soudan in a condition ripe for open rebellion, wanting only some leader to appear who could unite all the forces under one flag. The Mahdi was that person, and his banner was that of Islam, ever a subject of overwhelming influence with the fanatical Arabs.[1]

[1] It is interesting to note the extent of the Egyptian Soudan at the time it fell into the hands of the Mahdi. It comprised : Lower Nubia (between Assouan and Dongola), Upper Nubia, which included Dongola, Berber, Shendy, Halfyieh (Khartoum), Sennâr (on Blue Nile) and other districts ; Kordofan (El Obeid), Darfur, the Equatorial provinces of Lado, Bahr-el-Ghazal, &c. ; the Suakin districts, and Harar and Galla (now provinces of Abyssinia).

CHAPTER II

THE MAHDI

Destruction of Hicks' army near El Obeid—Osman Digna—Valentine Baker—Fall of Tokar—Battles of El Teb and Tamai—Gordon returns to Khartoum—The Nile Expedition 1884-5—Fall of Khartoum and death of Gordon—Campaign around Suakin—Battle of McNeill's zariba—The Soudan evacuated by the British—Battle of Ginniss—Wady Halfa the Egyptian frontier—Death of the Mahdi.

MOHAMED AHMED—THE MAHDI—was a sheikh, the son of a carpenter, a native of Dongola. He was educated in a village near Khartoum, his principal study being religion. He was able to impress those who came in contact with him, with his deep sanctity and his virtue. Whether his life at that time was reputable or not we cannot say, but we know that his subsequent career was marked by a continuous course of sensuality. He fulfilled every condition necessary for a successful leader. To all who had grievances he promised reform; he preached universality in religion and law, and equality of goods. He appealed to the worst fanaticism of the followers of Islam by declaring (August, 1881) a

Jehad, or Holy War against the "Turk" (as all Christians are called), added to which he invested himself with divine inspiration by declaring himself to be the "Mahdi," or the "guided one": one of the prophets whom Allah periodically sends to visit the earth, as prophesied by Mohammed.

Though nearly crushed at the outset, in twelve months the influence of the Mahdi had spread from end to end of the Soudan.

Several unsuccessful attempts were made by Rauf Pasha, Governor-General of the Soudan, (at Khartoum) to capture the Mahdi. On the 9th of December, 1881 Rashed Bey was defeated by the Mahdi, and he and 1,400 men were killed. On the 7th of June, 1882 a force of 4000 Egyptians under Yussef Pasha, was surprised and massacred at Mesat, near Jebel Gedir, which disaster placed the whole of Southern Kordofan in the Mahdi's hands. At the beginning of 1883 the Mahdists captured Bara, and then, after a five months siege, El Obeid fell, and its Governor, Said Pasha, was murdered. Slatin Bey vainly endeavoured to stem the tide of revolt in Darfur. He had a force of about 8,500 men, chiefly irregulars, but at Om Waragat he sustained a severe defeat, losing nearly his whole army, and was compelled to surrender to the Mahdi.

In the middle of 1883 the Egyptian Government determined to stamp out the rebellion, and despatched all the available troops under HICKS Pasha (late of the Indian army) for that purpose. The troops were little better than an ill-fed miserable rabble. On the 9th of September Hicks started from Omdurman with 11,000 "weeping soldiers"—many of whom had been brought to the seat of war in chains!—and 6,000 camels and horses. They met with no opposition until they reached Kashgal, near El Obeid, in Kordofan. Here the Mahdi had collected a force of 40,000 fighting men, and on the 1st of November the two opposing forces encountered each other. For four days Hicks maintained an unequal struggle, but on the 5th of November a treacherous guide led the Egyptians into a wood in which the Mahdists were secreted. The latter swept down, with fanatical fury, on the ill-fated Egyptians, who, offering little or no resistance, were massacred in a little over a quarter of an hour, only some three hundred effecting their escape. Hicks was the last of the European officers to fall, after making a most heroic and desperate resistance. Twelve hundred native officers were killed, including Alla-ed-deen Pasha (Governor-General of the Soudan); so too was Mr. O'Donovan (*Daily News* correspondent). Thirty-six Krupp, Nordenfelt, and mountain guns were captured, and all the ammunition and baggage animals. This signal victory placed the Soudan at the feet of the Mahdi, and Colonel Coetlogon, at Khartoum, at once put that town in a state of defence.

The day following the disaster to Hicks, another reverse befell the Egyptian arms in the Eastern Soudan. Whilst the Mahdi was extending his power around the Nile, OSMAN DIGNA,[1] his right-hand man, was harassing the towns and villages in the extreme east, around Suakin. On the 6th of November (1883) a force sent to relieve Tokar was cut to pieces by Osman's troops, and Captain Moncrieff, the English Consul at Suakin, was killed. In December a similar attempt to relieve Sinkat resulted in 760 out of 800 of the relieving force being massacred.

The main anxiety of the Egyptians, acting under the influence of the British Government, was now for the safety of the Red Sea Littoral, and preparations were made accordingly. The Egyptian army which Sir Evelyn Wood had created, had been raised on the understanding that they would be exempt from service in the Soudan. VALENTINE BAKER[2] Pasha was instructed to raise what troops he could, and to go and pacify that region, and at the same time gunboats were despatched to defend Suakin. In February, 1884, Tokar fell, and on the 8th of February the garrison at Sinkat, under Tewfik Bey, attempted a sortie, but were all massacred. Baker's army for the relief of Tokar was signally routed on the 11th of February; out of 3,700

---

[1] Osman Digna has played such an important part in the affairs of the Eastern Soudan, that he deserves more than a passing notice. His ancestors came originally from Constantinople, settled at Suakin, and intermarried with the Hadendowa tribe of Arabs. Osman was for many years in business at Suakin, as dealer in European goods, and in slaves; but finding the slave business unprofitable—after the Anglo-Egyptian convention, and the capture of his dhows—he joined the Mahdi and was appointed Emir of the Eastern Soudan.

[2] Baker formerly commanded the 10th Hussars. He died in 1889, and is buried in Cairo.

men, 2,300 were killed, including 11 European officers (6 British). Admiral Hewett immediately landed a party of bluejackets and marines for the protection of Suakin, and the British Government sent reinforcements to that place. On the 29th of February (1884) a battle took place at EL TEB (close to where Baker's forces had been scattered), which was one of the most desperate of any fought by the British troops in the Soudan. General Graham, at the head of 4,000 men,[1] defeated 12,000 of the enemy, after fighting for over three hours, leaving 2,000 Arabs dead on the field. Our troops lost heavily; 6 officers and 24 men were killed, and 142 wounded.

On the 13th of March the force advanced to capture Osman Digna's camp at TAMAI, close to El Teb, and here almost a dire disaster occurred. The Arabs made a wild onslaught on to the British square, and a number of them creeping up, actually broke it and captured some Gatlings. A desperate hand to hand conflict ensued, until some well-timed cavalry charges of Colonel Wood's troops saved the day, and enabled the infantry to re-form the square and recover the guns.

The Red Sea Littoral was now rendered temporarily safe, and the British troops, having accomplished their purpose, returned to England.

By this time Gordon (now a Major-General) was back again at Khartoum, which, as we have seen, he had left some years before. In January, 1884,

---

[1] Consisting of the 10th and 19th Hussars, Gordon Highlanders, Black Watch, and the York and Lancaster Regiment and Marines.

whilst in England, he was requested by the British Government to return to the fields of his past labours for the purpose of securing the safe withdrawal of the beleaguered Egyptian garrisons dotted here and there in the Soudan, before they should fall before the all-conquering Mahdi. His mission was a peaceful one, for no one realised at the time what formidable power the Mahdi had acquired. Gordon was to do what he could to restore order, and, if possible, was to set up a native government in Khartoum, where the civil European and Egyptian population amounted to over 11,000 souls. Gordon assented to these proposals, on the condition that he went out under the ægis of the British Government. He arrived at Khartoum on the 18th of February, 1884, and was hailed with the greatest enthusiasm as the deliverer of the Soudan.

Gordon appeared to grasp the situation immediately, and was convinced that the Soudan was now the Mahdi's, and no longer the Khedive's. He attempted to temporise, and appointed the Mahdi Sultan of Darfur, which, if accepted, would have been a cheap method of securing the removal of that dangerous leader; but the proffered honour was contemptuously declined. Soon after his arrival he wrote to the British Government: " I shall hold out as long as I can, and if I cannot crush the insurrection I will return to the Equator, and leave to you the indelible disgrace of abandoning the garrisons of Sennâr, Cassel (Kassala), Berber, and Dongola; *with the certainty that you will be forced to smash up the Mahdi under greater difficulties if you would maintain peace in Egypt.*" The light of subsequent events has proved the truth of these prophetic words.

The revolt spread daily. On the 20th of March the Mahdists began firing into Khartoum. In May Berber fell into the hands of the Mahdists, and Debbeh was the last station to which the telegraph extended. Thus whilst British troops were embarking for home from Suakin, garrison after garrison in the recesses of the desert was being put to the sword, Khartoum was being closely invested, and Gordon, in spite of his repeated messages, was left, with Colonel Stewart and Mr. Power, to hold out as best he could. Gordon's hopeless position was beginning to be fully recognised by the majority of the English people, but the Liberal Government of Mr. Gladstone felt unequal to the task. Public feeling, however, ran so high that the Government, finding further procrastination useless, decided to make an effort to save the man they had sent out. In August, 1884, an expedition for the relief of Gordon was decided upon.

At the end of October, in the same year, Omdurman was besieged by a force sent by the Mahdi, and communication with Khartoum, on the opposite bank of the Nile, was cut off. When Gordon discovered this by signal, he sent a force for its relief, and a furious battle, in which the rebels lost heavily, was fought on the 12th of November. The rebels, however, still retained their position round Omdurman, made forts between it and

Khartoum, and kept up a continuous fire on both towns. During November Gordon wrote to Sir Evelyn Baring,[1] the British Consul in Egypt, saying he could hold out only forty days more.

In December Gordon received a signal from Omdurman that its provisions and ammunition were exhausted, and a subsequent attempt to send relief having been frustrated, he authorised Faragallah Pasha by signal to surrender to the Mahdi. After the fall of Omdurman, Khartoum fell into a dangerous state, its supplies were cut off, and it was surrounded by rebels. Poor Gordon, deserted by his country, was in despair, for the people no longer believed that a British force was coming to their assistance; the anxiety he had undergone had gradually turned his hair to a snowy white. The garrison was reduced to the last straits, his people were perishing from disease and famine, the grip of the enemy was tightening, and desertions to the Mahdi were of daily occurrence.

The NILE CAMPAIGN of 1884-5, and the heroic efforts of the British troops in the dash for Khartoum, is still in the public memory, and we will only give a brief sketch of it here. The expeditionary force, under Lord WOLSELEY,[2] consisting of nearly 14,000 British troops, pushed their way up the Nile by means of flat-bottomed

---

[1] Now Lord Cromer.

[2] Composed of the following regiments: 19th Hussars, 18th Royal Irish Regiment, 32nd Duke of Cornwall's Light Infantry, 35th Royal Sussex Regiment, 38th South Stafford Regiment, 42nd Black Watch, 44th Essex Regiment, 50th Royal West Kent, 75th Gordon Highlanders, 79th Cameron Highlanders.

boats,[1] and by Christmas, 1884, the army had concentrated at Korti, which Wolseley, who arrived there on the 15th of December, made his base.

Gordon's letters grew gradually shorter and shorter, as the closer investment of the town rendered it daily more difficult to send messages through the Mahdist lines, although his steamers still retained the command of the river. On the 14th of December he wrote on a piece of paper no larger than a postage stamp: "Khartoum all right.—C. G. GORDON. Dec. 14, 1884." This was received by Lord Wolseley on the 31st of December.

On the 30th of December, 1884, General Sir Herbert Stewart started from Korti with a force composed of a large contingent of Camel Corps (chiefly Guards) and Mounted Infantry, the 19th Hussars, and the 35th Royal Sussex Regiment; and made across the desert for Metemmeh, a distance of 185 miles. He met with no resistance until about half-way, when, on the 17th of January, 1885, at the wells of ABU KLEA, he found the enemy 10,000 strong, whilst his own troops numbered barely 1,500, and were all worn out by the privations they had undergone. The British formed a large square, with the camels in the centre of it, and advanced slowly over very broken ground towards where the enemy were drawn up, evidently determined to dispute the passage to the wells. The Dervishes then charged with their charac-

---

[1] Eight hundred boats, costing £75 each. They were navigated by 380 Canadian and Indian *voyageurs*, and by 300 Kroomen from the West Coast of Africa.

teristic fanaticism, and hurled themselves on the British bayonets. A large portion of them making a sudden rush on the left rear corner of the square, broke it, and a fierce hand-to-hand fight followed. The camels inside the square saved the day, for they checked the onward rush of the Arabs; the English rallied, and the square was re-formed.[1] The result of this action was of the most vital importance, and never was there a better instance of "do or die" than at Abu Klea, for there was no chance of retreat. The "Desert Column" pushed on next day towards Metemmeh, where they hoped to open communication with Gordon's steamers. On the following day (the 19th of January) they were attacked at GUBAT, General Stewart was mortally wounded, and Sir Charles Wilson took command. The Arabs tried their same mad rushes, but the men preserved a firm formation, and prevented them from ever reaching the square. Metemmeh was found to be in the possession of the enemy, but no attack was made upon it. On reaching the river, Wilson was joined by four of Gordon's steamers, which had come down from Khartoum and brought despatches from Gordon. One, dated the 14th of December, said: "I have done all in my power to hold out, but I own I consider the position extremely critical, almost desperate, and I say this without any feeling of bitterness with respect to her Majesty's Govern-

[1] Our loss was 9 officers (including Colonel Fred Burnaby) and 65 men killed, and 85 wounded. The Naval Brigade suffered the most, almost all the officers being killed or wounded. The Arabs lost 800 killed, and many more wounded.

ment, but merely as a matter of fact." Abdul Hamid Bey, who commanded one of the steamers, told Sir Charles Wilson that on leaving Khartoum on the 14th of January, Gordon had told him that if he did not return with English troops in ten days it would be too late.

Sir Charles Wilson was in possession of this information on the 21st, and on the 24th he, accompanied by Lord Charles Beresford and Lieutenant Montagu-Stuart-Wortley, started with the steamers. He arrived on the 28th at Omdurman, opposite Khartoum; the steamers were fired on, and had to go back. Khartoum had fallen two days before, and Gordon was dead. The expedition had arrived *forty-eight hours too late.*

The Mahdists, knowing of the rapid approach of the British troops, had made an attack in the early morning of the 26th, and had succeeded in effecting an entrance. The city was given up to pillage and massacre, and every European was put to the sword, including its brave defender.

Bordeini Bey, an eminent merchant, who willingly gave up his large stores of grain for the supply of the garrison, and an eye-witness, describes the hero's death. Some of the rebels forced their way into the palace, and to Gordon's room, outside of which they found him. He stood in the passage in front of the entrance to the office, and just at the head of the staircase.[1] On the approach of the rebels they found him standing beside the door, calm and dignified in

[1] See Frontispiece.

manner, his left hand resting on the hilt of his sword; but he made no resistance and did not fire a shot. One of the rebels, dashing forward with the curse, "Mala'oun el yom yomek" ("O, cursed one, your time is come!"), plunged his spear into his body. Gordon, making a gesture of scorn with his right hand, turned his back, when he received another spear wound, which caused him to fall forward. Then others rushed in, and, cutting at the prostrate body with their swords, killed him in a few seconds. His body was dragged downstairs and left exposed for a time in the garden, where many Arabs came to plunge their spears into it; the next day it was thrown into one of the wells. His head was cut off, sent to the Madhi at Omdurman, and exultingly shown to Slatin, then a prisoner in the Dervish camp. It was exposed in Omdurman, fixed between the branches of a tree, and all who passed by threw stones at it.

On Wilson's return from Khartoum, down the river, both vessels were lost, but the crews were safely landed, and were rescued by Lord Charles Beresford in the *Safir*.

So far we have only followed the doings of the "Desert Column." The "River Column," whose efforts were, of course, neutralised, had fought and won at KIRBEKAN, the day after Wilson reached Khartoum, and their leader, General Earle, was killed. The brunt of the fight was borne by the South Staffords (38th) and the Black Watch (42nd). The "River Column" pushed on up the Nile, and by the 24th of February, 1885, the advanced guard had reached the west end of Mograt Island, their 215 boats had gained Huella, at the head of the hitherto impassable cataracts of Dar Monassir, and there was still sixty days' food in the boats for the entire force. On that day, however, the order was given to retire to Korti; all the labour and hardships of the past few months were utterly wasted, and the attempt to save Gordon had failed disastrously.

Now followed a brief campaign around Suakin. The Liberal Ministry at home decided, under pressure, upon another expedition to Suakin to lay the Suakin-Berber railway; and in March, 1885, a force was landed, including Colonial troops from India and Australia, with General Sir Gerald Graham [1] in command. The harbour was crowded with transports of material, and the railway was begun. It was determined to establish a zariba on the route to Tamai, and on the 22nd of March, 1885, Sir John McNeill started with this object, but his force was suddenly attacked near Tofrek. A scene of terrific confusion ensued, and never did the sterling quality of the British soldier shine out more brightly than it did on this occasion. The attack lasted twenty minutes, but, owing greatly to the gallantry of the Berkshire Regiment,[2] the enemy were driven off.

[1] Now Lieutenant-General Sir G. Graham, G.C.B., G.C.M.G., V.C., .ate R.E. retired 1890.

[2] With the Berkshire Regiment were the Indian Brigade (three regiments),—Marines, Naval Brigade, a squadron of the 5th Lancers, and detachment of Royal Engineers. Our casualties numbered 550 killed, wounded and missing. The enemy lost 1,400 killed. The Berk-

The result of the action at MCNEILL'S ZARIBA, as this was called, was the death-knell of the Suakin-Berber railway; and this little campaign came to an untimely end.

A grave position now presented itself to the British Government under Mr. Gladstone. The Mahdi was in the very height of his prestige, and Egypt, whose regeneration had not as yet been commenced, was absolutely incapable of reconquering the Soudan. Either the Mahdi must be crushed at once, or the Soudan must be absolutely abandoned.

Lord Wolseley appealed to the English Government to be allowed, whilst on the spot, to crush the Mahdi once and for all. In one of his despatches he pointed out the effect of abandoning the Soudan, saying that we should have to carry on a succession of frontier affairs, harassing and vexatious to the troops, and costly in men and money; and that a large army would have to be kept on the frontier. The English Government determined on the only logical and consistent course open to them: to stamp out the rebellion immediately; but just as they were on the point of carrying out their intention, there was a scare of a war with Russia. The Government could not lock up a large force in the Soudan, under the circumstances, so they decided to evacuate it, in spite of the many warning

shire Regiment is the only one in the service with "Tofrek" on its colours. The 20th Hussars, three regiments of Foot Guards, East Surrey Regiment and Shropshire Light Infantry were in garrison at the time in and around Suakin.

voices which were raised against this half hearted policy.

Dongola was evacuated by the British troops in July, 1885, and Mohamed el Khair at once seized the province on behalf of the Mahdists. On the 31st of December he advanced with 6,000 Arabs on GINNISS, where the Frontier Field Force, consisting of the British under General Stephenson and the Egyptians under their Sirdar Grenfell, awaited them. The Egyptian army was only in the second year of its existence, but acquitted itself admirably; and a decisive blow was inflicted on the enemy, who lost over 600 killed and wounded. The losses on our side were very slight, the Cameron Highlanders losing the most men. One of the causes of the utter failure of the Dervish expedition was the dreadful character of the country lying between the frontier and Dongola,—the wild barren desert. The Dervish transport and commissariat arrangements—or rather want of arrangement—caused terrible suffering, enough to destroy the spirit of the finest troops in the world, and as a result of this, the Arabs reached the battlefield in an emaciated and worthless condition. After their defeat the Dervishes fell back on Kerma.

In April, 1886, all the British troops were withdrawn to WADY HALFA, and the Dervishes advanced and occupied Sarras. In the meantime the MAHDI had died of small-pox at Omdurman (June 22nd, 1885), and the KHALIFA ABDULLAH reigned in his stead.

CHAPTER III

THE KHALIFA

Omdurman takes the place of Khartoum—The Dervish army—The state of the Soudan—Emin and Stanley—Battle of Sarras—Osman Digna again around Suakin—Capture of Handoub—Battle of Galabat and death of King John—Menelik—Battles of Arguin and Toski—Capture of Tokar—Escape of Ohrwalder and Slatin from Omdurman.

THE Mahdi had established a kingdom from Egypt to the Bahr-el-Ghazal, and from Darfur to the Red Sea; but, as we have seen, he did not live long enough to rule it. This task was left to the Khalifa Abdullah, now generally spoken of as *the* Khalifa.[1]

One of the first things the Khalifa did was to erect an immense mosque over the Mahdi's tomb at Omdurman, and this is the tallest building in the

---

[1] An excellent description of the Khalifa is given by Father Ohrwalder in his valuable book *Ten Years' Captivity in the Mahdi's Camp*. He says that " in personal appearance the Khalifa has an intelligent face, with a long, prominent nose, a short cut beard, and a dark chocolate coloured complexion, but is much marked by small-pox. He is a man of no education, being neither able to read nor write; is now (1896) about forty-four years of age, and is energetic and ambitious. His disposition is proud, cruel, fanatical, distrustful, jealous and tyrannical. He belongs to the Baggara tribe, and speaks Arabic with a strong Baggara accent. He has won over by his influence several tribes to the Mahdi's cause. He wears the usual Dervish dress, and has 150 wives in his harem."

A DERVISH EMIR.
From a Photograph by Messrs. C. G. Lekegian & Co., Cairo.

Soudan. He also erected a large arsenal—the "Bayt-el-Amana"—in which all the necessary items of ordnance were kept stored. Khartoum was levelled to the ground in August, 1885, seven months after its capture, and two months after the Mahdi's death, and the village OMDURMAN, on the opposite side of the river, sprang into importance as the capital of the Khalifa's dominions.

The Mahdi had divided the Dervish[1] army into three parts, each under a commander-in-chief called a Khalifa. The chief of these was Abdullah, and it had long been agreed that in the event of the Mahdi's death he should succeed him. Each Khalifa had his own Jehadiah, or regular troops, a distinctive flag, and a war-drum—"naha"—made of brass instead of wood. Abdullah's flag was black, and he had also, as peculiar to his *entourage*, a powerful wind instrument—called "onbya"—made of an elephant's tusk. Each Khalifa had a number of Emirs[2] under him, and each Emir had his own banner.

It was impossible for the Khalifa to do aught else than carry on campaigns, for aggressive expeditions

---

[1] The word "Dervish" signifies "poor." Originally it denoted much the same amongst Mohammedans as "monk" amongst Christians or "fakir" with Hindoos; but now-a-days the word has quite lost its religious significance, and can only be looked upon as expressive of a fanatical slave-dealer. In fact, the Dervish army was originally a "salvation army," but—to perpetuate a pun—it took to preying instead of praying!

[2] The title "Emir" really means "chief," and is, in fact, the same word as Ameer, which we know, for instance, in Afghanistan: it is really much too high a title for the wretched officers of the Dervish army.

formed the only means of distracting the attention of his subjects from their lamentable condition, and from the broken promises of the Mahdi. Before his death the latter had, in his imagination, dreamed of the conversion of the world by force of arms, and the first step in this great war was to be the conquest of Egypt. The idea of such an enterprise was received with acclamation by the Mahdists. The young Dervish leader, WAD EL NEJUMI, was entrusted with this ambitious enterprise, but, in consequence of the numerous calls on the Dervishes for defensive operations, the expedition was postponed until a favourable opportunity might present itself. As an instance of the popularity of this project, a song was composed with a refrain "To Cairo," which was sung everywhere. The first serious frontier attack under the Khalifa's *régime* took place at Ginniss, and has been already described.[1] This reverse to the Khalifa's arms was a severe blow to him, and one that well-nigh brought about his overthrow. After the Mahdi's death the cruel despotism of the Khalifa and his Baggara had further spread discontent. The other tribes saw that it was only in the interest of the Baggara that the Khedive's rule had been overthrown; and several tribes resolved to endure this state of things no longer.

The earliest and most important revolt against the Khalifa was the rising of the Kababish Arabs. They had never been really hostile to the Egyptian Government, and proved themselves a sharp thorn

[1] P. 22.

in the side of the Khalifa. The overthrow of the latter was not so much the definite object of this rebellion as the capture of that most fertile province Dongola, to possess which had long been the ambition of this tribe. They attempted to obtain the assistance of the Egyptian Government, but it was not expedient that such assistance could be given. This rising was followed by outbreaks against the Khalifa in Kordofan and Sennâr; and the calls on the Khalifa's strength increased daily.

Abdullah might put down rebellion after rebellion, but he was only able to put the flame out, and the smouldering hidden fire still remained. Besides these internal revolts, his armies were contending in all directions on his borders. Osman Digna made his periodical assaults on the Red Sea Littoral; Wad el Nejumi was gathering together his army for the invasion of Egypt, and the Dervish army on the Abyssinian frontier was being held in check by King John.

At the end of 1886 the Soudan was in a ferment, and the condition of the natives was becoming daily more deplorable. The Khalifa compelled every available male in his vast dominions to serve in his armies, and the men being drawn away from the cultivation of the soil, the crops were not sown, with the result that food became very scarce. Famine and disease spread through the length and breadth of the Soudan, and the inhabitants were decimated.

These internal troubles restricted the aggression of the Dervishes. The only province which remained free from the Dervish yoke was the Equatorial Province (Equatoria), in which EMIN Pasha was located, and it is more than probable that, but for the circumstances explained above, the Khalifa's sway would have reached the equator. After the Mahdi's conquests, Emin found great difficulty in maintaining his position, though this was not due to external attack. A portion of his troops rebelled and occupied the country north of Wadelai. During Gordon's rule well-organised postal arrangements had been established, but on the accession of the Mahdi all means of reliable communication with Lado and Khartoum were cut off, and great anxiety was felt as to the position of Emin and his Central African province. It was not until the end of 1886 that news of Emin came, brought by a fellow-countryman, Dr. Junker. The famous Emin Relief Expedition, led by Mr. H. M. Stanley, is familiar to all readers of *In Darkest Africa*. The expedition started up the Congo on the 25th of February, 1887, and, after undergoing incredible dangers and hardships, through famine, disease, and native opposition, they fell in with Emin on Lake Nyanza, on the 18th of January, 1889. Emin remained at his post until he was compelled, through the mutiny of his officers, to retire at the end of 1889; since when the province became lost to civilising influences, and the last trace of Gordon's work was blotted out.

Whilst the Emin Relief Expedition was in progress, the vanguard of the army which Nejumi had gathered, with great difficulty, for the invasion of Egypt, pressed down the valley of the Nile, and was defeated by the Egyptians under Colonel Chermside[1] at SARRAS (April 29th, 1887). At the end of the year the Khalifa's troops, which had been victorious against the rebellion in Darfur, had to cope with a formidable rising on the Blue Nile, and with the harassing attacks of the Abyssinians.

In 1888 the district around Suakin claims our special attention, but before proceeding to describe the events of this year, it will be necessary to glance at what had been happening in that neighbourhood during the years that immediately preceded it.

After the defeat of Osman Digna in March, 1885, at McNeill's zariba,[2]—at the close of the last campaign,—Osman desisted from his attacks on Suakin. The Arabs in that neighbourhood became discontented with the rule of the Khalifa, and they combined, under the judicious advice of Colonel KITCHENER[3]— the Commandant at Suakin—to overthrow Osman Digna. The latter was compelled to retreat from his stronghold Tamai in October, 1886, and these friendly Arabs effectually kept him in check for

---

[1] Now Colonel Sir Herbert C. Chermside, R.E., K.C.M.G., C.B.
[2] P. 21.
[3] Now Major-General Sir H. H. Kitchener, K.C.B., K.C.M.G. Sirdar of the Egyptian Army.

over a year. At the end of 1887 Mahdism in the whole of the Soudan seemed on the wane. The internal troubles had well-nigh exhausted the strength of the Arabs in the Central Soudan, and Osman Digna rested at Handoub with his shattered army, whilst the tribes around Suakin were evincing the strongest hostility to him, and threatening his extinction.

This brings us to the year 1888. There was now but little trouble on the frontier near Wady Halfa, and the whole of the Dervish force available was concentrated in the neighbourhood of Suakin. In January Colonel Kitchener made a well-planned attack to capture Osman Digna at his camp, and was all but successful. Osman escaped, leaving behind his camp stores and munitions; but despite this reverse, the Dervishes commenced to draw round Suakin, and in September they assumed a threatening aspect. The Egyptian troops in Suakin barely sufficed to defend the town, and were certainly inadequate to disperse the enemy.

As a serious attack appeared imminent, warships were at once despatched, and in November strong reinforcements arrived in Suakin, under General GRENFELL (the Sirdar). On the 20th of December, the latter advanced and attacked the Dervish stronghold at HANDOUB, and after a very desperate resistance the enemy were driven from their entrenchments with great slaughter. During the month another decisive action was fought at

GEMAIZAH, near Suakin, in which the Dervishes lost heavily.

The next important battle in the Soudan was between the Dervishes and the Abyssinians. The war between these races was the outcome of a long-standing feud. The desire on the part of the Mahdi and of his successor to bring the Abyssinians under his sway, was the primary cause of the quarrel, which was intensified by the differences of religion that existed between them. This war progressed with varying success, and being of a bitter and fierce description, it taxed the Khalifa's military strength. The Dervishes having inflicted a severe defeat on KING JOHN, the Khalifa sent the latter one of his characteristic notes, which seemed to his Majesty to add insult to injury, and determined the Abyssinian King on taking his revenge. In March, 1889, King John led an army against the Dervishes, and with 150,000 met 80,000 Arabs at GALABAT. He had nearly routed them when he was killed.[1] With the death of King John the feud between the Dervishes and Abyssinians ceased. MENELIK, who was at that time King of the Shoas, a neighbouring and feudatory state to Abyssinia,

---

[1] The Dervishes saw a gorgeous tent in the distance, so they placed an old gun in position and fired a round of case-shot at it. This saved the day, for the shot killed King John, who was inside the tent, and the Abyssinians becoming discouraged retired in all directions. The Dervishes, ignorant of the cause, followed them up, and converted the threatened defeat into a decisive victory The King's retinue carried their monarch from the field of battle, but a body of Dervishes fell upon them, and seized the King's body, stripping and decapitating it. His head was buried at Wady Halfa.

and who had himself been rebellious to King John, subsequently assumed the rule of the whole of Abyssinia.

At the beginning of 1889 the Khalifa had succeeded in crushing out the rebellions against his rule, and had defeated the Sultan of Wadai—one of the far central provinces of the Dark Continent—and occupied his kingdom. Osman Digna was utterly dispirited, and required no further calls on the military strength of the Khalifa. It was therefore a seasonable moment for Nejumi to carry out his great project on Egypt.

Early in the year his forces, the pick of the Dervish army, descended the Nile on this ill-fated expedition, and on the 2nd of July his advance guard, consisting of 3,500 Dervishes, came into conflict with the Egyptian troops under Colonel Wodehouse, at ARGUIN, near Wady Halfa. A pitched battle ensued, and the Dervishes were defeated with a loss of 500, whilst the Egyptians lost 70.

Every preparation was now taken by the English and Egyptian Governments to strike a decisive blow at this long-threatened invasion, and a strong force of English and Egyptian troops was collected at Assouan. In July the opposing forces came within striking distance, and General Grenfell, who commanded the Egyptain army, despatched a messenger calling upon Nejumi to surrender. The proud Nejumi had the messenger beaten, and replied with a message couched in similar terms to the insolent letters the Khalifa had written, some time before, to the Khedive and the Sultan, and threatening Grenfell with the fate of Gordon.

On the 17th of August, after frequent skirmishes, the two forces met at TOSKI, near the great temple of Abu Simbel. Owing to their inadequate commissariat arrangements, and the dreadful country between Dongola and Wady Halfa, the Dervishes presented rather a weakly appearance; but they fought with remarkable bravery. The battle lasted seven hours, and consisted chiefly of repeated desperate charges by the Dervishes on the British troops, which were repulsed chiefly by the Hussars and Egyptian cavalry. The enemy were utterly routed: Wad el Nejumi, his principal Emirs, and half his army were killed, the other half were fugitives or prisoners, and all his standards were taken.[1] This was the most serious reverse the Khalifa's forces had sustained, and the lesson then learnt was not lost, for, although there were many raids, no serious attack on the frontier was afterwards attempted.

The next blow to the Dervish arms was dealt in February, 1891, to Osman Digna at Suakin. With the new year, the same old raids were re-commenced. Colonel Holled-Smith, Governor-General of the Red Sea Littoral, set out with a brigade composed

[1] The officers under General Grenfell were Colonel Kitchener (commanding mounted troops), Colonel Wodehouse (the infantry), Colonel Rundle (the artillery), Colonels Irwin and Breech (the English and Egyptian cavalry respectively), and Colonel Settle (the Chief Staff Officer). The British troops engaged were parts of the 20th Hussars and the Shropshire Light Infantry, York and Lancaster Regiment, and Royal Irish Rifles. The loss on our side was 17 killed (1 English, 16 Egyptians), and 131 wounded.

D

entirely of Egyptian and Soudanese troops, and on the 19th of February Osman Digna was driven out of TOKAR, and his army was routed with a loss of 700 killed, including all his chief Emirs. Osman himself fled south, accompanied by thirty horsemen.

The principal feature of this engagement was the conduct of the Egyptians. This was the first time that the Egyptian troops, unaided by British, had been employed in any serious engagement. They were commanded by English officers, and behaved splendidly. From the half-hearted cowards that they had shown themselves to be during the Mahout rebellion, the Egyptian fellaheen had been metamorphosed by the British officers into a reliable and courageous soldiery.

The Red Sea Littoral was cleared of the rebels, and many of the leading sheikhs solicited and obtained pardon. A general amnesty was proclaimed, and there was great rejoicing among the inhabitants at the prospect of peace, after the prolonged and devastating war. During the year 1892 Osman Digna attacked Tokar, but he had only a few hundred followers, and was easily repulsed.

After the defeat of the Dervishes at Toski there was no real menace to Egypt; and, except when Father OHRWALDER and two nuns escaped from Omdurman in 1891, and SLATIN appeared miraculously, a fugitive from the Khalifa's prison, four years later, no news ever came from those parts. This passiveness on the part of the Khalifa was probably due to the condition of the inhabitants, the scarcity of food, and the continuous rising of the tribes against him. His territories were threatened on all sides: on the north by the British in Egypt; on the south by the British in Uganda; on the west by the Belgians in the Congo Free State, and by the French in the Western Soudan; whilst the Italians held Kassala on the east, so that the Khalifa preferred to husband his resources until the inevitable day should arrive when he would have to fight for his position. Every day the Khalifa ruled, the condition of the wretched inhabitants grew worse and worse, and at the same time his influence and power gradually waned; but nevertheless he was still able to gather round him thousands of fanatical warriors, worthy foemen for the finest troops in the world.

CHAPTER IV

ENGLAND'S POSITION IN EGYPT

The Egyptian Soudan—The Sirdar, Sir Herbert Kitchener—The reconquest of the Soudan an imperative necessity—The Italians and Abyssinians—Battle of Adowa—Its effect on the Egyptian position—The reconquest decided on—The Caisse de la Dette—The necessity of the British Occupation.

IN order to bring this brief history to a fitting conclusion, and to better connect it with what is to follow, we must leave Omdurman and see in what light the state of affairs in the Soudan was regarded by the ministers at Cairo and Westminster. To do this, we must first understand clearly what England's position is in Egypt. This is in itself a subject on which volumes might be written, but we need only here consider the salient features of the case.

England's interest in Egypt centres in the fact that the Suez Canal is the high road to India and our Eastern possessions; consequently, England would never stand aside and allow Egypt to be controlled by any of the continental Powers, unless compelled thereto at the point of the sword. England never desires to undertake the immense responsibility of the government of Egypt, as long as that country is secure from foreign invasion;

CHAP. IV   ENGLAND'S POSITION IN EGYPT   37

but, by the force of circumstances, geographical and political, Egypt is unable to stand alone, and England has taken upon herself the *rôle* of protector. Thus when in 1882 the rising of Arabi Pasha demanded instant suppression, England was the first to come to Egypt's assistance. France was given the opportunity of joining us, but declined. Consequently, after the fall of Arabi,[1] it devolved on England alone to reconstruct the whole fabric of government in that country; and the success of England's mission constitutes the chief grievance that the French—or rather, a certain section of the French press—have against us.

One of the first measures adopted by the British after the occupation was to disband the old army (of which Arabi had been Commander-in-Chief). This was ended by a Khedivial decree of the 20th of December, 1882, which said briefly: "The army is disbanded." The nucleus of the present Egyptian army was formed in 1883, and Sir Evelyn Wood was the first Sirdar.[2] In the old army were officers of all nationalities, including many Americans. In future, with the exception of natives promoted from the ranks, the officers were to be exclusively British. The Egyptian recruits were obtained by a system

[1] Arabi was defeated by Lord Wolseley at the battle of Tel-el-Kebir, September 13th, 1882, and Cairo was occupied by the British troops the following day. Arabi's force numbered 19,000; Wolseley's 13,000. The British lost 11 officers and 43 men killed, and 22 officers and 320 men wounded. The Egyptians lost 1,000 killed and wounded, 3,000 surrendered, and the remainder dispersed.

[2] "Commander-in-Chief." The words of command in the Egyptian army are Turkish.

of compulsory service, and served for five years; the Soudanese were obtained chiefly around Suakin, and generally served for life.

At first the Egyptian army only consisted of eight battalions, and the first review took place on the 31st of March, 1883, at Abbassyieh, outside Cairo. The 9th (Soudanese) were raised in the following year, the 10th (Soudanese) in 1886, and since then the other regiments.

During the Nile Expedition of 1884, the Egyptian army was chiefly employed in guarding the line of communications along the river, and saw but little fighting; and it was not until 1886 that it was considered competent to hold Wady Halfa without the assistance of British troops. The latter indeed were kept as a kind of reserve at Assouan until 1888, by which time the young army had shown, at Ginniss and elsewhere, that it was able to take care of itself.

At the beginning of 1896 there were thirteen regiments of infantry, besides cavalry, camel corps, and artillery; and a reserve of considerable dimensions. Part of the latter (when called out in March) went to form the 14th and 15th Battalions. The battalions (or regiments, for in the Egyptian army they are the same thing) numbered nine to thirteen are Soudanese ("black") regiments; the remainder are Egyptian. With the exception of the 5th, 6th, 7th, 8th, and 14th Battalions, which had native officers only, each battalion had a couple of British officers, whilst several had three. As a general rule,

THE SIRDAR, SIR H. H. KITCHENER, K.C.M G., C.B. [*To face p.* 39.
From a *Photograph by Messrs. Bassano.*

one of these was a captain in the English army, and the other two were subalterns; but as soon as they were appointed to the Egyptian army they went up in rank.

No British officer in the Egyptian army—whatever his real rank—is lower than a *bimbashi* (major), and the captain who commands the native battalion becomes a *kaimakam* (lieutenant-colonel). Officers serve for five years with the Egyptian army, and then return to their regiments in the British army, unless specially permitted to extend their term of service under the Khedive.

The Sirdar of the Egyptian army in 1896 was Major-General Sir Herbert Kitchener,[1] who succeeded Sir Francis Grenfell in that capacity in 1892.

The soldiers of the Egyptian army have been so ably described by Sir Alfred Milner, that we need only refer those who desire further information on the subject to his invaluable book.[2] The creation

[1] In the British army, Sir H. H. Kitchener, K.C.M.G., C.B., was—at the commencement of the Dongola Expedition—a brevet-colonel on the majors' list of the Royal Engineers, and temporary major-general. He was born in 1851, obtained his commission in 1871, and was promoted captain in 1883. His war service was all in Egypt. In February, 1883, he joined the Egyptian army, and in the Soudan Campaign of 1884-5 he acted as D.A.A.G. and Q.M.G., and superintended the Intelligence Department of the Bayuda Desert Column, for which he received the brevet rank of lieutenant-colonel. He rejoined the Egyptian army in August, 1886, and was appointed Governor-General of the Red Sea Littoral until September, 1888. In this year, during the operations around Suakin, he was severely wounded at Handoub. In the Soudan Campaign of 1888-9 he commanded a brigade of the Egyptian army in action at Gemaizah; was at the battle of Toski in 1889, after which he received the C.B.; was made C.M.G. in August, 1886, A.D.C. to the Queen in April, 1888, and K.C.M.G. in February, 1894.

[2] *England in Egypt* (Arnold), p. 180.

of the present Egyptian army by a handful of English officers is one of the most successful and remarkable examples of British enterprise ever afforded in our history.

It now remains to be shown how Britain was situated with regard to the Soudan, and what led her to decide on the reconquest of that country.

It was at England's instigation that Egypt abandoned the Nile provinces in 1885. It is true that without British aid Egypt could not have held them any longer; but that does not alter the fact that the existing Ministry was responsible for the surrender of those provinces, and consequently England felt under the obligation to recover them as soon as the internal affairs of Egypt had been placed on a proper footing. It is essential to Egypt's existence that those provinces must belong to Egypt and to no other Power. In fact, the Soudan has been called the key of Egypt, for whatever civilised nation controls the waters of the Upper Nile holds Egypt at its mercy.

After the fall of Khartoum fresh dangers arose to threaten England's and Egypt's interests in the Soudan; the same dangers, in fact, as those which we pointed out (in the last chapter), as threatening the Khalifa's existence. Africa for the European Powers became the order of the day, and the quietly conceived designs of the European Foreign Offices took practical shape and developed into a greedy scramble between the Powers for the lion's share of the African continent. In the valley of the Upper Nile the race between the Powers was proceeding slowly, perhaps, but none the less surely; and the rumours which reached these shores from time to time began to attract considerable attention. The French, we found, were gradually extending their influence from the south-west, and the Belgians were sending out expeditions from the south, whilst the Abyssinians were proving themselves an important power in the south-east.

Thus it was that a certain amount of uneasiness was beginning to make itself felt, and it was generally considered by the Cabinet that some action on the part of Great Britain would be desirable as soon as a favourable opportunity should present itself.

Suddenly the news of a serious reverse to the Italians in Abyssinia brought matters to a crisis. The battle of ADOWA, on Sunday, the 1st of March, 1896, dealt a death-blow to Italy's colonial aspirations. The Italians, numbering 37,000 under General Baratieri, were defeated by 80,000 Abyssinians under Menelik, with a loss of 7,000 killed, wounded, and missing. Baratieri himself was wounded, and the Abyssinians captured 1,500 prisoners and fifty-two guns. The consternation felt in England and Egypt at this disaster deepened when it became known that KASSALA, which was held by the Italian forces, was hemmed in, and seriously threatened by 10,000 Dervishes, and that Osman Digna was marching there with reinforcements. If Kassala fell into the hands of the Dervishes, the latter would be let loose to overrun the Nile valley on the frontier of Egypt, and threaten that country itself. As if in anticipation of these reinforcements, the Dervishes suddenly assumed an offensive attitude, and it was rumoured that a large body of Dervishes were contemplating an immediate advance on Egypt, and were threatening the strategic posts of Murat Wells (near Wady Halfa), and Kokreb (between Berber and Suakin).

The British Government had, for some months previously, been in communication with the Egyptian Government and their military advisers, as to the means to be adopted in case of Dervish attacks, but there had been no intention up to then to do anything more than take measures for the defence of the Egyptian frontier, and no offensive measures had been contemplated. A totally new situation was now created, and immediate action was rendered imperative. Everything was ripe for an expedition up the Nile. Whilst creating a diversion in favour of the Italians besieged at Kassala, it afforded an opportunity of creating a stronger barrier than the Wady Halfa boundary between Egypt and the Dervishes, and it would moreover be an important step towards the long-wished-for recovery of the Soudan.

The announcement of the contemplated expedition was made in the House of Commons on the 17th of March, 1896, by Mr. Curzon, Under-Secretary for Foreign Affairs. It came as a great surprise to the whole country, which, having heard so little of the Dervishes of late years, was not prepared for a recrudescence of the Soudan question. Mr. Curzon informed the House of the pressing reasons that had determined the Government in undertaking the offensive, and mentioned that an advance had been ordered to Akasheh (one-third of the distance between Wady Halfa and Dongola); but he left it in doubt as to what the objective of the expedition was to be.

An unexpected difficulty arose in connection with the financing of the expedition. This is explained very plainly and concisely in the *Annual Register*, 1896,[1] which we quote at length :—

"In order to defray the cost of the undertaking, it being obviously desirable to impose as little strain as possible on the slowly recovering finances of Egypt, it was determined by the Egyptian Government to apply for an advance of £500,000 from the General Reserve Fund of the Caisse de la Dette, and the authorities of the Caisse obligingly handed over the money. . . . However, the French and Russian members of the Caisse de la Dette protested against the loan which the Caisse had made. The Caisse was cited, at the instance of the French bondholders' syndicate, to appear before the Mixed Tribunals, to answer for the misappropriation of its reserve funds. As the year wore on, the Mixed Tribunals pronounced against the loan. In December (1896) the International Court of Appeal required the Egyptian Government to refund to the Caisse the £500,000 which they had secured. The very next day Lord Cromer offered an English loan to make good the advance. The Egyptian Government accepted his offer, and repaid immediately the £500,000 to the Caisse, and the result of this somewhat absurd transaction is that England has thus strengthened her hold in another small point on the Government of Egypt."

The verdict of the Court of Appeal was given on the grounds that the Caisse required the *unanimous* consent of the commissioners before they could spend the money. From this it is apparent that any one commissioner has more real power than the Khedive himself, and can, no matter what be his

[1] Published by Longmans, Green and Co.

motive, prevent any progress in Egyptian affairs. That there will ever be a subject upon which the whole of the commissioners will be agreed is hard to believe; and it is clear to all who have studied the situation in Egypt that the state of affairs now existing calls for some drastic remedy. For Egypt to be at the mercy of any one Power seems as intolerable as it is unique; and it behoves England to assert her position, more than ever, as the dominant factor in Egyptian politics and administration. The benefits and blessings which the British occupation has bestowed upon Egypt, the inability of that country to stand alone amidst the dangers that beset her, and the resources that will be required to develop the Soudanese provinces which have been reconquered, are only links in the chain that binds Egypt to her powerful ally.

How the irritating and meaningless policy adopted by certain of our neighbours across the water can achieve any useful purpose from their own point of view it is difficult to conceive, and it must be apparent to any one not blinded by jealousy that it is to Egypt's interest that the day of evacuation, if it ever comes, should be a very long way off.

PART II

THE DONGOLA EXPEDITION, 1896

NOTE.—The following chapters are taken from the diaries kept by the authors during the expedition.

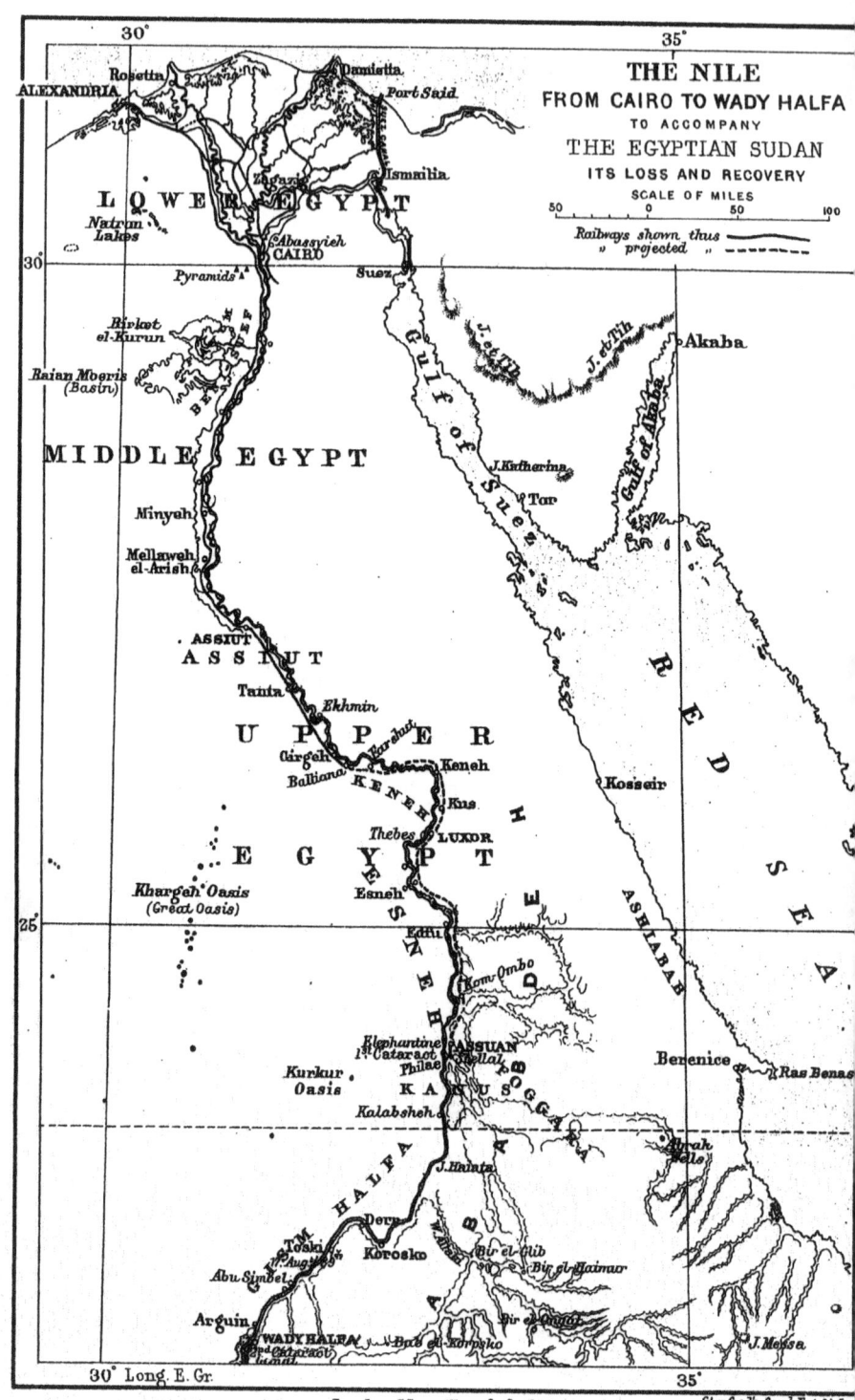

CHAPTER I

THE START. CAIRO TO WADY HALFA

Receipt of the news in Cairo—Preparations for war—Moves of the Egyptian regiments—Consideration shown by the Khedive—"Special service" officers—Departure of the Sirdar and the North Staffordshire Regiment—Departmental officers—Voyage up the Nile—Luxor and Thebes—Assouan and Philæ—Korosko and Abu Simbel—Man overboard!—Wady Halfa.

THE Cairo season of 1896 was in full swing. Every hotel was crowded with visitors who, with the garrison, were participating in the multifarious attractions afforded by this most delightful of cities. On Saturday afternoon, the 14th of March, most of them were assembled on Shepheard's verandah. The military band was playing the latest airs, the British subalterns were basking in the smiles of cosmopolitan beauty, and "all went merry as a marriage bell," when suddenly a startling rumour spread from mouth to mouth, and, unlike most rumours, it proved to be true. It was to the effect that the Sirdar had received a cablegram from London at midnight on the 12th, ordering him to proceed up the Nile at once, and commence operations against the Dervishes.

The British troops in Cairo[1] were at this time under canvas at Abbassyieh, going through the annual manœuvres. On the morning of the 14th, Colonel Beale, commanding the 1st Battalion North Staffordshire Regiment, received a telegram from General Knowles, telling him to hold his regiment in readiness to proceed to Wady Halfa in a few days. The camp was at once struck, and the troops returned to their barracks at the Citadel and Kasr-el-Nil.

The next few days were spent in active preparations for the war. All day long the thoroughfares leading to the railway station gave proof of the bustle that prevailed on all sides. Here were some Egyptian regiments marching away, here were heavy waggons creaking under the load of commissariat stores, here the machine-guns rattling down the street—all on their way to the front. The all-pervading energy seemed to reach its culminating point in the workshops of the Egyptian army. Day and night the Egyptian ordnance, under Captain Gordon (a nephew of General Gordon), turned out saddles, swordbelts, water-bottles, and the thousand and one things that go to form the equipment of an army.

The regiments of the Egyptian army were at this time distributed as follows:—

At Cairo: the 2nd, 4th, 5th and 6th battalions; and the 14th and 15th, composed of Reserves.

---

[1] Under the command of Major-General C. B. Knowles, C.B., consisted of the Queen's Bays, North Staffords (64th), and Connaught Rangers (80th).

At Suakin: the 1st, 9th and 10th.

At Wady Halfa: the 3rd, 7th, 8th, 11th, 12th and 13th.

The Reserves of the Egyptian army were at once called out, and around the various barracks and through the streets, crowds of dirty-looking fellaheen, surrounded by their sorrowing relatives, dragged themselves reluctantly along, in such numbers that the traffic was often completely blocked. Some were drafted off into various regiments, and the remainder formed, as we have already said, two new battalions, the 14th and 15th. The Egyptian regiments in Cairo received orders to move at once: the 2nd Battalion to go to Sarras, the 5th to Suakin, and the 6th to Wady Halfa; whilst the 9th (Soudanese) at Suakin were conveyed to Halfa, *via* Kosseir (on the Red Sea) and Keneh (on the Nile).

The greatest possible interest was taken by the Khedive in the expedition, from beginning to end. As an instance of this, it may be mentioned that when asked by the Sirdar for a few officers of his personal bodyguard, he at once sent him ten out of thirteen. His Highness bade farewell to each regiment as it left Cairo, and witnessed its departure from the station. We may say here that by the anxiety which he constantly showed for the welfare of his soldiers, and the kind messages which he repeatedly sent them, he endeared himself to all ranks of his army.

On the 18th a detachment under Captain Welch,

A.S.C., was sent to form a depot at Balliana, the southern terminus of the railway. Troops and stores were shipped here for Assouan, where another depot was formed under Colonel Cochrane. During the week further details were sent south. About a dozen officers of the army of occupation were placed "temporarily at the service of the Sirdar," including those of the Maxim battery, which left Cairo on the 21st. A number of so-called "special service" officers came from all parts of the army to earn decorations with the Egyptian troops, and hurried through Cairo on their way to the front.[1]

On the 22nd of March (Sunday) the Sirdar, with Major Wingate (Director of Intelligence), and Slatin Pasha, started for Wady Halfa. On the same day, the North Staffords left Cairo by two special trains. Every officer and man had undergone a close medical inspection, and, including old soldiers and boys, about 10 per cent. had been rejected, so that we now numbered 914, all told.

As the regiment marched past Shepheard's Hotel we received a great ovation from the crowd on the verandah, which was filled to overflowing; at the station all Cairo seemed to have turned out to see us off, and we steamed slowly out, with many a handshake and many a cheer, to the tune of "Auld Lang Syne."

After sleeping the night in the rather crowded carriages, we took advantage of a halt to get

---

[1] For the names of all officers, see Appendix.

DEPARTMENTAL OFFICERS ATTACHED TO 1ST NORTH STAFFORD REGIMENT.

OFFICERS OF 1ST NORTH STAFFORD REGIMENT. [*To face p.* 51.

a wash under the engine-hose on the platform; and after twenty hours in the train we reached Balliana, the southern terminus of the railway, at 2 P.M. on the 23rd. Here we found two of Cook's steamers waiting for us: the paddle-steamer *Rameses the Great* and the stern-wheeler *Ambigole*. Each steamer towed two *nuggas*, and these we began to load with live oxen, ammunition, firewood, and other stores, being impeded all the time by a violent sandstorm. All was on board by nightfall, and we started up the river next morning (the 24th).

An officer of each of the departments accompanied the North Staffords throughout the expedition, making the little British force an entirely independent one. They were, at the outset, Surgeon-Major Sloggett, A.M.S., Surgeon-Captain Carr, A.M.S., Captain Morgan, A.S.C., Captain Smith, A.P.D., and the Rev. A. W. Watson, C.F. The departmental mess was strengthened at Halfa by Lieutenant Elkington, R.E., and Surgeon-Captain Holmes, A.M.S.—these two having gone on a few days in advance—and subsequently Captain Mathew, A.O.D., Surgeon-Captains Pinches and Reily, and the Rev. Father Brindle, C.F., came up the river and joined us.

The boats [1] were crowded; the *Rameses* carried nearly 400 men, though only intended originally for 70 of Cook's tourists; but in spite of this the time

---

[1] Messrs. Cook and Son had eight of these boats on the river between Cairo and the frontier. The *Rameses the Great*—the largest of them—was 200 feet long, 28 feet beam, and had engines of 500 horse-power.

on board was quite enjoyable, and, with the aid of various games and smoking concerts, passed quickly enough. The band generally played in the evening, the "Dervish Chorus" and "To the Front" being amongst the favourite tunes.

The Nile was too low to allow us to go by night, from fear of running on the numerous sand-banks; so at dusk we used to moor up for the night off some village, where we could take in fresh provisions, and started again at daybreak. In spite of the intimate knowledge of the whereabouts of sand-banks which the *reis* (captain) possessed—or said he did—and in spite of the men in the bows who were continually sounding with their long poles, the boat made several attemps at "breaking the bank." Occasionally we *did* try to go by night, but we had never gone far on our way before the steamer would suddenly bump on a bank, and awake us—and the man at the wheel!—with a start.

The first night (24th) was spent off Farshut, which we left at daybreak.

On the 26th we reached Luxor, and as we stopped there most of the day, we were able to visit its monuments. The Temple of Luxor, by the water's edge, was the first object of interest, and then we went to Karnak and saw the gigantic Temple of Ammon, with its hall of 134 columns—a veritable forest of stone. Some of us crossed to the left bank and paid a flying visit to Thebes, whose Collossi we saw looking across the desert, five miles off.

The next day took us past Edfoo, Esneh, and Kom-Ombo, with their great temples by the river-bank.

Exactly a week after leaving Cairo we reached Assouan (29th) at the foot of the First Cataract. The latter was skirted by a light single-line railway to Shellal, which was on the upper reach of the river, opposite Philæ. The only train available was required to convey our stores, the work of transferring which was being done by gangs of convicts in chains. By 4 P.M. this was completed, and the battalion fell in to march to Shellal. As we passed through Assouan, with the band playing, crowds of natives thronged the roadway to catch a glimpse of a British Regiment, which they had not seen for eleven years. It will be remembered that the Dorsetshire regiment left a third of their number there, on their return from the Soudan in 1886, from which lamentable fact they gained the soubriquet of " Dying Dorsets."

Our way lay across the desert, and we were accompanied most of the distance by Dr. Conan Doyle, the author, who, with his friend Mr. Corbett, was about to make the journey to Halfa on camels.[1] On each side of our route lay immense blocks of syenite, many of which were covered with ancient hieroglyphics, which contrasted strangely with the white numbers painted underneath them by some

[1] Dr. C. Doyle was acting as special correspondent for the *Westminster Gazette*, but he returned to England in April.

enterprising guide-book publishers—an example of the two ages, the monumental and the practical.

After four hours in the desert, we reached Shellal, and gazed for the first time on the beautiful little island of Philæ. We had no time, however, to admire the works of the ancients, and had to embark at once on the boats.

The latter were four flat-bottomed "stern-wheelers," namely, the post-boats *Tanjore*, *Kaibar*, *Akasheh*, and the gunboat *El Teb*. They were propelled by a paddle-wheel in rear, whence their name. They only drew three feet of water, and the ease with which they could be turned was marvellous. On both sides of each boat were lashed double-decked barges, specially built for the purpose of carrying troops, the officers and the baggage being on the steamer itself. The stores were all on board by nightfall, and we started southwards again next morning.

Below the Second Cataract the Nile has been described probably more than any river in the world. We will therefore refrain from going into a lengthy account of it now, but will only give a few impressions that struck us as we journeyed on. Egypt has been described as the land of tranquil monotony, and what applies to Egypt is equally applicable to the Nile, for the two are practically synonymous. Below Assouan the country is well cultivated, and presents a fertile and flourishing aspect. Along the banks the ever-creaking sakiehs, or water-wheels turned by oxen, and the shadoufs, or water-lifts worked by the fellaheen, are constantly seen; and the scenery is largely made up of date-palms, herds of goats and sheep, and fields of dhurra.

From Assouan right up to Kosheh the scenery is quite different. The land yields nothing and supports nothing. The scenery consists only of rocks and sand, with here and there a strip of cultivation on the river-bank, only a few yards in width. Great black hillocks abound, of such exact pyramid shape that—when we first saw them—we could not help thinking they must have suggested the idea of erecting those ancient monuments. In some places there are a few palms and an occasional miserable village or so, but most of the way there is nothing but yellow sand right down to the water's edge. Yet in spite of this, as Professor Rawlinson remarks,[1] "the Nubian river is grander than the Egyptian: in the grandeur of its deserts, the sense of unending space which the mind begins to grasp when the sun sets in the western sky, in all but its temples, and these, too, are represented, though they are not so numerous. The Nile itself is too wide, as a rule, to be picturesque. Its average width is probably half a mile, but at places it is as much as two miles. The water is never clear. During the inundation it is deeply stained with the red argillaceous soil brought down from the Abyssinian highlands. At other seasons it is always

[1] *Egypt*—"Story of the Nations" series.

more or less tinged with vegetable matter, brought down from the lakes, which gives it a dull deep hue, instead of a pure translucent one." There was no lack of water-fowl: pelicans, storks, ibises, herons, cranes, and geese were plentiful enough. So too were fish, but both birds and fish had a muddy flavour about them.

We would draw attention to the fact that crocodiles are by no means "to be found in considerable numbers" at Derr and Korosko, as stated in certain guide-books, but are in fact absolutely unknown there. Some were seen at Kosheh, but the majority of us went to Dongola and back without seeing a single crocodile. Thirty years ago they were plentiful at Luxor, but in the campaign of 1884-5, they were only first seen in any numbers at Debbeh ; and now that the steamers have again invaded their peaceful haunts, there is little doubt that below the Sixth Cataract the crocodile will very soon be unknown.

We reached Korosko late on the 31st. Here the caravans start for Abu Hamed, cutting off the great bend of the Nile—or rather used to start, for at the time of our visit there was no trade in this devastated district. As soon as we had taken some coal on board we started southwards again.

The 1st of April brought a change in the weather, and we began to feel we were fairly in the tropics. The Southern Cross was now in sight—four wretched little stars forming a figure like a kite.

Abu Simbel (Ipsamboul), with its four colossal

figures at the entrance to the underground temples, was passed late in the afternoon. It is one of the grandest works on the Nile, and, as the guide-book observes, is alone worth the journey above Assouan. At the foot of one of the statues lies the tomb of Major Tidwell, R. E., who died in the Nile Expedition of 1885. The striking feature about this great ruin is that it is entirely cut out of the solid rock, with a door only fifteen feet high and eight broad. We learn from Baedeker that the ears of these colossi are six feet in length, and other similar details, but they, like all Egyptian monuments, *must* be seen to be appreciated.

After breakfast on the 2nd of April there was a cry of "Man overboard!" and we saw a close-cropped head bobbing rapidly down stream. Fortunately he fell off the leading boat, so that one of those behind was able to pick him up, none the worse for his ducking. Later in the morning, at half-past eleven, we reached Wady Halfa, having done the journey of 800 miles from Cairo in ten days.

CHAPTER II

PRELIMINARY SKIRMISHES

The concentration at the front—The objective of the expedition—Akasheh occupied—The line of communications—The "Friendlies"—Dispositions of the troops—Dervish activity—Railway and telegraph—Medical and commissariat arrangements—The first fight—Akasheh becomes headquarters.

THE Sirdar and his staff had arrived at Wady Halfa before us, on the 28th of March, and the organisation of the campaign was proceeded with.

The Chief Staff Officer of the Egyptian army was Colonel Rundle,[1] Colonel Hunter[2] taking over the command of Sarras and all the district southwards.

The expeditionary force was being hurried up the Nile to the front in every available steamer, as

[1] Brevet-Colonel H. M. L. Rundle, C.M.G., D.S.O., R.A., first saw service in the Zulu War of 1879, and was wounded in the defence of Potchefstroom in the Transvaal War. He was at Tel-el-Kebir in 1882, and joined the Egyptian army when it was re-constituted in January, 1883. In the Nile Expedition, 1884, he was on the line of communications, on special duty with the Bedouin tribes, after which he was promoted brevet-major, and received the Medjidie. Commanded the troops at the fight at Sarras (D.S.O. and Osmanieh). Commanded the Royal Artillery at Toski (promoted brevet-lieutenant-colonel). Was present in 1891 at the capture of Tokar. Was promoted brevet-colonel in 1894.

[2] Brevet-Colonel A. Hunter, D.S.O. (Royal Lancaster Regiment), joined the Egyptian army in 1888. He was promoted brevet-ma

BREVET-COLONEL RUNDLE, C.M.G., D.S.O.
From a Photograph by Messrs. Russell & Sons.

BREVET-COLONEL HUNTER, D.S.O.
From a Photograph by Messrs. Bassano.

[To face p. 58.

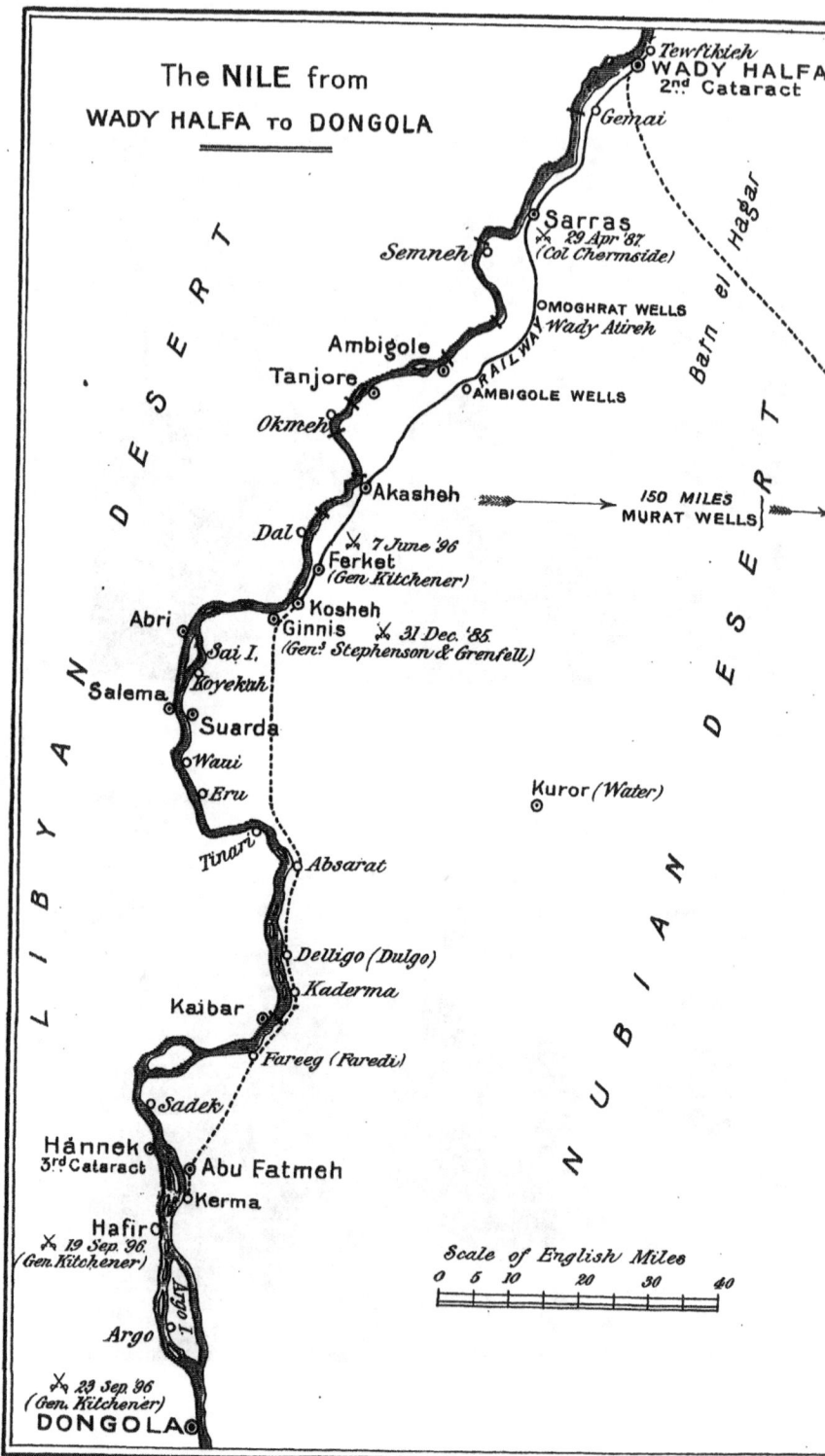

CHAP. II   PRELIMINARY SKIRMISHES   59

quickly as possible. Every day during the first week of April a battalion, squadron, or battery—to say nothing of the stores and ammunition—arrived at Wady Halfa.

It had not yet been decided what the objective of the expedition was to be. As the ostensible reason for the expedition was to draw the Dervishes from the neighbourhood of Kassala, the ultimate destination of the force could only be conjectured. Dongola was to be taken, but by Dongola was understood the province, and not merely the town, for the latter would be a very insecure frontier post.

By the beginning of April the greater part of the expeditionary force had arrived at Wady Halfa, Sarras, and Akasheh. Sarras had been for the last few years the advanced post of the Egyptian Frontier Force. On the 20th of March Akasheh had been occupied by an advanced column under Major Collinson, without any resistance being met with. A fort was at once constructed, and an entrenched camp formed. Supplies and reinforcements were pushed up rapidly to it, as Akasheh occupied a good strategic position. This was the first step of the advance.

The line of communication between Wady Halfa and Akasheh was at once strengthened, and detachments were sent to hold Sarras, Semneh, Wady

after the Nile Expedition, 1884-5, and received the Osmanieh. Was severely wounded at Ginniss (D.S.O. and Medjidie). Was present at Arguin, and wounded at Toski, where he commanded a brigade; for which services he was promoted brevet-lieutenant-colonel. Was promoted brevet-colonel in 1894.

Atireh, and Tanjore, posts about fifteen miles apart along the line. At Semneh, the old frontier of Egypt in the reign of Thothmes, the river narrows considerably. Cataracts occur here and at Tanjore and Ambigole. On the east flank the wells at Ambigole and Moghrat were secured and occupied.

The whole of the east flank was guarded against surprise by patrols of Bedouin Arabs. Each Arab received pay and a rifle, but provided his own camel and food. In the eastern desert a section of the Ababdas tribe, under four chiefs, patrolled the routes between Assouan, Korosko, Murat Wells, and Abu Hamed; and both banks of the river south of Sarras were patrolled by the Kababish and Foggara tribes.

With the exception of the troops at Suakin, nearly all the Egyptian army was now distributed along the Halfa—Akasheh line. At Suakin and its surrounding forts, Tokar, Sinkat, and Handoub, were the 1st and 5th Battalions, a squadron of cavalry, a company of Camel Corps, and other details, besides some friendly Arabs. The 9th Soudanese moving from Suakin to Halfa did the journey in remarkably fine style; they marched a distance of 120 miles through the desert, from Kosseir, on the Red Sea, to Keneh, on the river, in four days, making an average of thirty miles a day.

The news of the movement of the Egyptian army up the Nile, and the reinforcement of Suakin, soon reached the headquarters of the Dervishes at Omdurman, *via* Kassala, and in consequence they began to collect from 3,000 to 4,000 at Ferket, Suarda, and Abu Fatmeh, under the Emirs Hammuda and Osman Azrak. They were reinforced from time to time by detachments sent from Dongola by Wad el Bishara, Emir of that place. Both Bishara and Hamuda were capable men who had seen service at Ginniss, Toski, and elsewhere. The former was known to be a young general possessed of great energy, and he was the only Emir of the Dervishes who directed the movements of his troops by bugle-notes.

About the beginning of April the Dervishes began to show further signs of activity. On the 2nd they cut the telegraph line between Korosko and Murat Wells, and carried off a mile of wire. The latter place was the Egyptian outpost in the desert, 120 miles from Korosko, and formed an important point on the route to Abu Hamed. It was garrisoned by the 15th Battalion, who marched to it from Korosko in sixty-five hours, the longest halt being three hours. The fort was built in 1893, and the wells are sufficient to supply 5,000 men with water.

The construction of the railway south of Sarras was proceeded with at the rate of 500 yards a day, but sometimes as much as a mile a day was laid. Lieutenant Girouard, R.E., assisted by Lieutenants Stevenson and Polwhele, R.E., superintended the work, and the working parties were covered by the 7th Native Battalion. At the end of April the "Railhead," as the ever-changing terminus was called, was at Moghrat Wells, forty-seven miles from Halfa, at the end of May it was at Ambigole.[1]

The laying of the telegraph pole was under the direction of Lieutenant Manifold, R.E. Throughout the campaign he generally managed to have his line laid to a place by the time the troops had established themselves in it. The wire,[2] in lengths of a mile, was coiled on revolving wheels and carried on camels. As the camel moved forward the wire was unwound and trailed on the ground. The work

---

[1] Here is a copy of the first railway time-table published in the Soudan :—

DONGOLA EXPEDITIONARY FORCE ORDERS.

HEADQUARTERS,
WADY HALFA, 28*th May*, 1896.

162—The following is the approved railway time-table to take effect from the 29th of May, 1896, till further orders :—

			1st train.	2nd train.
HALFA	......dep.		5.30 a.m.	6.15 a.m.
GEMAI	....	,,	6.45 ,,	7.30 ,,
SARRAS	....	{ arr.	8.— ,,	8.45 ,,
		{ dep.	8.30 ,,	9.15 ,,
MOGHRAT	....	{ arr.	10.— ,,	10.45 ,,
		{ dep.	10.15 ,,	11.— ,,
AMBIGOLE	....	{ arr.	12.15 p.m.	1.— p.m.
		{ dep.	1.— ,,	1.45 ,,
MOGHRAT	....	{ arr.	3.— ,,	3.45 ,,
		{ dep.	3.15 ,,	4.— ,,
SARRAS	....	{ arr.	4.45 ,,	5.30 ,,
		{ dep.	5.15 ,,	6.— ,,
GEMAI	....	dep.	6.30 ,,	7.15 ,,
HALFA	....	arr.	7.45 ,,	8.30 ,,

By Order,
(Signed) *CYRIL MARTYR*
Assistant Adjutant-General.

[2] Size No. 8.—the heaviest—to guard against breakages.

of stretching and poling was of course attended to at a later date.

The medical arrangements, under Surgeon-Major Hunter, were excellent throughout. A base hospital of 340 beds was provided at Wady Halfa, a portion of the barracks being used for that purpose. A section of the movable field hospital was established at Sarras, Ambigole, and Akasheh, the latter being under Surgeon-Captain Penton. Subsequently, as the force moved forward, other sections were established at Ferket, Kosheh, and other places. Arrangements were made for the transport of the sick in native boats to the base hospital. When no boats were available the invalids were carried on camels, in padded seats fixed to the saddle, called "cacolets," one man sitting on each side.

The supplies were under the superintendence of Captain and Quartermaster Drage, A.S.C., and were sent forward with the greatest despatch to Akasheh, where a reserve of four months' supplies was to be stored. As soon as the steamers arrived at Halfa, fatigue parties were called out and proceeded to unload them immediately. Within an hour of the arrival of the steamer all the cargo was generally in the train, which conveyed it to the "Railhead," whence it was carried on camels to Akasheh.

In the middle of April news was received of fighting around Suakin, which will be described in the next chapter.

At the end of the month the Dervishes showed

signs of a forward movement, and Captain Broadwood was sent with a small body of cavalry to reconnoitre. He crossed the river, and, moving up the left bank unobserved, saw a large body of the enemy leave their camp at Ferket for the north. He returned with all haste to camp, and found that the intelligence scouts had already brought in news of the approach of a large Dervish patrol.

Major Burn-Murdoch was at once despatched (May 1st) with what cavalry was available, about 240 men. With him were Captains Whitla, Persse, and Fitton, and Lord Fincastle [1] acted as his galloper. We met the latter a few days afterwards in Halfa, and he gave us a good account of what took place. It seems that when they started they only expected to meet some seventy Dervishes, but after going about four miles from Akasheh they sighted 300 mounted Baggara, behind whom were drawn up, in support, a thousand spearmen. The ground was unfavourable for a cavalry charge, and as Burn-Murdoch had no infantry in support, he decided to retire. Some advanced scouts were to hold the enemy in check whilst the main body defiled through a khor, and more than half the party had entered the defile when suddenly the Dervishes swooped down on them. They charged very rapidly and in perfect silence, and could scarcely be distinguished on account of the dust until they were on the top of our men. As for the scouts which had been posted in advance, they came running in to the main body,

[1] Who recieved V.C. on the Indian frontier in 1898.

with shouts of " El Darweesh, el Darweesh," almost at the same moment as the Dervishes themselves. Several Egyptians were speared before the charge could be intercepted, but the little force was at once wheeled about, and charged impetuously at the Baggaras.

A hand-to-hand fight ensued. Each Dervish carried two spears, which, by the way, were very blunt, and they never threw them, as a rule, unless at some one whom they saw in the act of firing at them. For about twenty minutes the struggle lasted, and then the Dervishes wheeled about, and galloped off to the rear of the spearmen who were supporting them. The ground would not admit of another charge, so the Egyptians dismounted and poured volleys into them. The 11th Soudanese (Major Jackson) were just arriving in support when the Dervishes drew off.

The fight had lasted from noon till three, and the heat had been terrific. The losses were not heavy : of the Dervishes 18 were killed and 80 wounded, whilst on our side 2 men were killed and 10 wounded, including Captain Fitton very slightly. The Dervishes showed in this day's work that their old courage had not deserted them. In the charge most of them came on, never flinching, but going to almost certain death, though, of course, there were some who hung back, waiting for their bolder comrades to give them a lead. Every Dervish who got inside the *melée* was killed. Their marksmanship, on the other hand, was abominable. They could have

F

shot down half our men when caught in the defile, but they did not understand the use of the "sights," and most of their shots went too high.

The second week of May the camp at Sarras was broken up, and the troops were moved on to Ambigole Wells (old name Ambuko), which the railway reached on the 27th of May.

During the month Major Viscount Trombi was sent by the Italians as their representative in the Soudan, and was attached to the Sirdar's personal staff, but he only remained about a month.

On the 17th of May Captain Broadwood and a small party set out from Akasheh to ascertain what the enemy were doing. They struck the river south of Ferket, where the Dervishes were found to be mustered in force, and they thoroughly reconnoitred the position.

Twelve days afterwards a party of Dervish camelmen were reported to be in the neighbourhood of Akasheh, but though the Camel Corps set out in chase, they were unable to catch them.

On the 1st of June the headquarters were moved to Akasheh, and during the first few days of the month nearly all the Egyptian army was concentrated in camp there, awaiting the order to advance against the enemy.

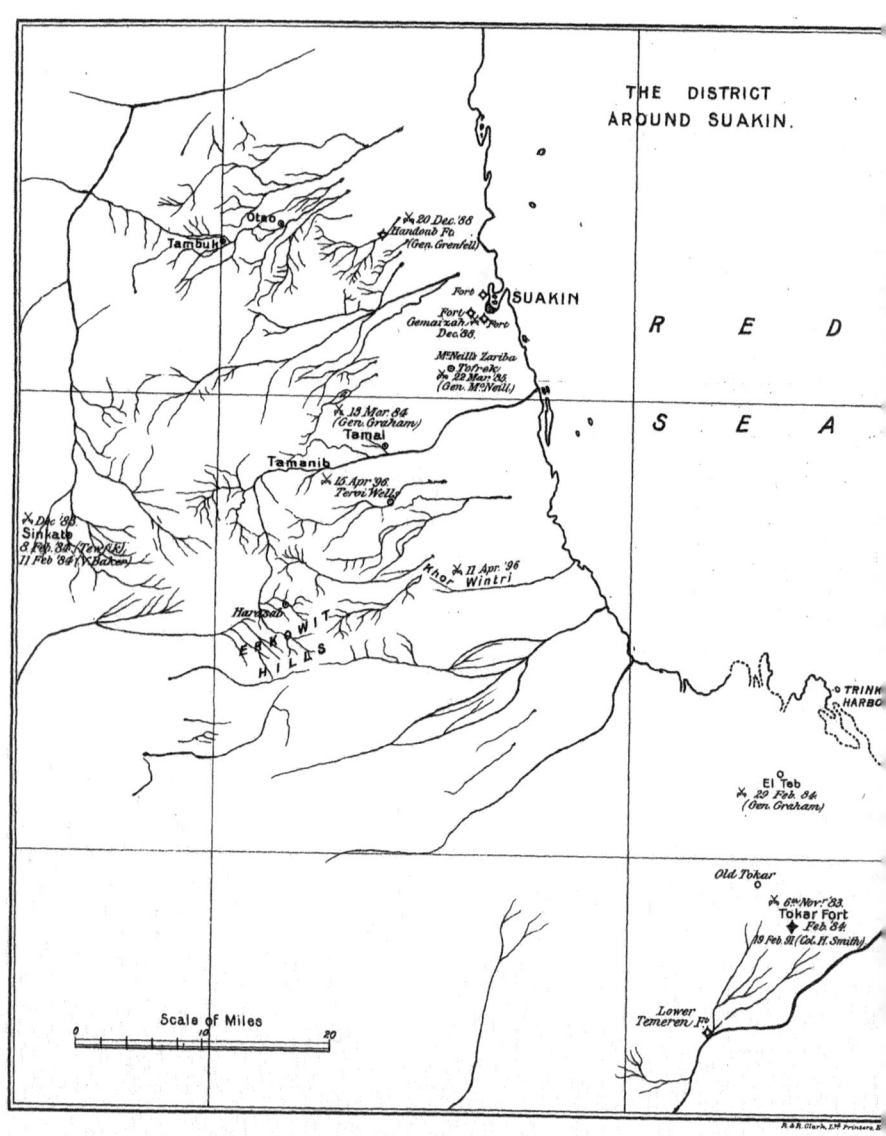

CHAPTER III

AROUND SUAKIN

Description of Suakin—Osman Digna arrives—The fight at Khor Wintri—Captain Fenwick's gallantry—The Indian contingent.

WE will now turn to the Red Sea Littoral, where, the first week in April, Osman Digna had arrived with 300 cavalry, 70 camelry, and 2,500 foot, and was now threatening Suakin and its outlying posts.

Suakin is a barren island which is more picturesque than pretty. Most of the houses are of white coral, and nearly every other building is a *café*. It was strongly fortified, being surrounded by a wall and a ditch, with eleven enfilading forts at its angles, and was well provided with artillery. Tokar was defended by three works, had two Krupps and a Gatling gun, and was well supplied with ammunition and provisions. It was now held by the 10th Soudanese, who were sent there at the end of March. Handoub and Tambuk had supplies sufficient for four months. The latter place was unassailable by any force not supplied with artillery. It is situated on a high rock, and consists of a store and block-house, with a look-out tower which affords a view for many miles around, and commands the road to Berber and the wells at the foot of the rock.

The War Office authorities at home had prolonged consultations relative to the defence of Suakin, and although no decision at the time was arrived at, arrangements were at once made to reinforce the Egyptian forces with British troops if needed. From the former attitude of the Hadendowa and Shukrieh tribe, some reliance was placed on their assistance if necessary. Up to the present the Dervishes had confined themselves to cutting the telegraph wire between Suakin and Tokar.

Osman Digna remained at Harasab, in the Er'-kowit hills, with his cavalry and foot soldiers, where he was held in check from harassing Suakin by Omar Tita, a friendly chief, who repulsed him near the Khor Wintri in an engagement on the 11th of April.

As Osman Digna's force was too strong for Omar to attack, and was daily growing stronger, whilst, on the other hand, through the desertion of avowed "friendlies," Omar's was becoming weaker, the latter's position became untenable. In consequence of this a force started to his assistance, from Suakin, on the 15th of April in co-operation with the detachment stationed at Tokar.

The force was composed as follows:—Commanding: Lieutenant-Colonel Lloyd (South Staffordshire Regiment); Chief Staff Officer: Captain Souter (Black Watch); Brigade Major: Captain Judge

(Shropshire Light Infantry); Staff Officer, Intelligence: Captain Fenwick (Royal Lancashire Regiment); Principal Medical Officer : Captain Dunn (Army Medical Staff.)

The troops consisted of:—8th Squadron Egyptian Cavalry; 2 mountain guns; 1 company Camel Corps; 3 companies 1st Battalion Egyptian Army, under Major Heygate (Border Regiment) and Captain Matchett (Connaught Rangers); 3 companies 5th Battalion Egyptian Army, under Borham Bey; 1 company formed from the depôt of the 9th and 10th Soudanese; 1 company Mule Transport.

The force thus composed was joined subsequently, as we shall see, by 250 men of the 10th Soudanese Battalion from Tokar, under Major Sidney and Captain Fergusson, and by the Tokar Camel Transport.

In order to make the column as mobile as possible, every man was mounted, and every available camel in the district was requisitioned—1,050 camels being obtained. The deficiencies were made up by mules and donkeys, there being 60 of the former and 120 of the latter. Two hundred Arabs accompanied the column to hold the camels when the troops halted or formed square. The mules carried the guns, the artillery ammunition, and the reserve infantry ammunition, while the donkeys carried the stretchers, entrenching implements, and the signalling equipment. The artillery ammunition consisted of 200 rounds shell, and each man was provided with 200 cartridges. Every camel carried six days' forage and rations, one day's reserve of water in skins, and a blanket.

The force paraded outside the walls of Suakin at 5 P.M. on the 14th, and bivouacked there. At daybreak on the 15th it started for the Teroi Wells. The progress at first was slow. Most of the camels never having had a saddle on their backs before, became irritated with them and threw off their burdens. By the exercise of great patience, however, matters righted themselves, and more satisfactory progress was made.

After marching four or five hours the cavalry met a number of Dervish scouts, who retired. The column now marched in square formation, the front face of which consisted of the 9th and 10th Soudanese detachments, with the guns in the centre. The Camel Corps formed the rear and flank guards on the move, and the rear face when halted. The hospital corps and baggage was in the centre of the square.

The country, after a time, became very difficult, being intercepted by a broad watercourse encumbered with loose rocks and thorn bushes, whilst high hills on each side rendered vigilant scouting indispensable, more especially as a large body of Dervishes was known to be in the neighbourhood.

The Teroi Wells were reached in the afternoon, the column having covered a distance of nineteen miles. Here the force bivouacked. The cavalry was now sent to reconnoitre, and to endeavour to establish touch with the Tokar force, and to inform the officer commanding the latter that Colonel Lloyd would remain at the wells for the night. It had previously been arranged with the Sheikh Omar Tita that he should hold the heights and pass of the

Khor Wintri, while the two Egyptian forces concentrated.

The cavalry, numbering thirty-eight officers and men, under Captain Fenwick, set out for the Khor Wintri, but never succeeded in establishing communication with Major Sidney, for soon after they had started they were suddenly attacked by a body of 200 Dervish cavalry, supported by a large body of infantry armed with rifles and spears. Fenwick's party retired at a trot, but it was soon seen that the Dervish horsemen were gaining on them fast, so they galloped towards the open country, where many of them became entangled in the bush, or were tripped up by the uneven ground, and, falling off, were instantly speared by the Dervishes. Fenwick withdrew to the rear flank and ascended a hillock, where he and his men kept the enemy off by firing volleys. About 200 horsemen and 1,000 footmen attacked, and the small handful of Egyptians were threatened throughout the night by masses of Dervish swordsmen and spearmen moving round and round the base of the hill and collecting for a charge. Happily there were very few riflemen among them, and the fire from these was erratic. Captain Fenwick himself fired 120 single shots during the night, and encouraged his men in every way. He was well backed up by two Egyptian officers—lieutenants in the cavalry.

At last the enemy drew off, and Fenwick succeeded in leading his men through the scrub back to the Teroi Wells. This fight was a striking instance of what can be done by a determined and gallant officer against enormous odds.

Colonel Lloyd, on hearing the firing, had immediately despatched two volunteers from the Mounted Police to discover the whereabouts of Captain Fenwick and the Tokar force, but they were both killed.

The next morning, the 16th of April, the column left the Teroi Wells, and moved towards the Khor Wintri, eight miles distant. Owing to the thickness of the bush and the roughness of the country, the troops were obliged to proceed on foot. The camels were not required, and the food and reserve ammunition was sent on towards the hills held by Omar's men.

In the evening, when the Suakin force arrived at the Khor Wintri, they found the Tokar contingent, under Major Sidney, in possession of the place. Sidney had surprised the enemy at the Khor on the previous afternoon, and they had retired up the pass. As soon as he had arrived at the Khor, the Dervishes, about 700 strong, were seen advancing up the pass. The column formed square and opened fire on them. The enemy twice attempted to turn the column's right flank and rear, but in each instance were met by a heavy fire, causing them to eventually retreat up the pass, with a loss of forty killed and many wounded.

Shortly after the junction of the Suakin and Tokar forces, Omar Tita arrived and reported that his tribesmen had abandoned the heights and pass to the enemy; but as the latter had retreated bodily to Harasab, it was decided that the column should return to Suakin the following day.

On the 17th the column bivouacked again at Teroi Wells, and returned next day to Suakin, where it was enthusiastically welcomed by the inhabitants.

Great demoralisation set in after this in Osman Digna's camp at Harasab, and the Arab tribes who had hitherto held aloof from both sides, in readiness to throw in their lot with the likely victors, now joined us. A large number of Dervishes deserted their leader and fled to the hills, and, to add to their general discomfort, the scarcity of food began to make itself keenly felt in Osman's camp.

During May it was decided to send a contingent of Indian troops to Suakin, so as to relieve the Egyptian battalions, which were required on the Nile. On the 30th of May this contingent arrived at Suakin. It was composed as follows:—

26th Bengal Infantry; 35th Sikhs; 1st Bombay Lancers; 5th Bombay Mountain Battery; 2 Maxim guns; section of Royal Engineers; section of field hospital.

The force[1] numbered a little over 4,000, and was commanded by Colonel Egerton, C.B., D.S.O. (Corps of Guides).

The question as to who should pay for the Indian troops—the British or Indian Government—raised a heated discussion, which resulted in India having

[1] For names of officers with Indian troops, see Appendix.

to pay the actual expenses (about £5,000 a month for seven months) and England the "extra" expenses.[1]

After the arrival of the Indian contingent nothing of special interest happened at Suakin during the Dongola expedition. Only two cases of cholera, both fatal, occurred there, but an outbreak of scurvy in August carried off a few men, and a large proportion of the British officers were invalided home with fever.

[1] The "extra" expenses came to £145,000, and were made up as follows: For transporting the troops from India to Suakin and back, £59,000; land transport, £25,000; commissariat, £35,000; and the balance was made up of items for the Pay, Medical and Ordnance Services.

CHAPTER IV

WADY HALFA

Its situation—Raids—Description of the place—Wingate and Slatin—Camel Corps—The black recruits—Daily routine—Our quarters—The war correspondents—Native dance—The end of the day.

WADY HALFA, situated five miles north of the Second Cataract, first came into prominent notice in 1886, when it was selected as the frontier station of Egypt. The reason for this selection was that to the south of Halfa lies a vast stony wilderness, the Batn-el-Hagar, or "Belly of Rocks," which forms an impassable barrier to any invading force of savages; parties of depredators have managed to get through it from time to time, but never in sufficient force to threaten the tranquillity of Egypt.[1]

Halfa was attacked in October, 1887, and in July, 1888, but each time the Dervishes were repulsed with considerable loss. In 1892 Osman Azrak

[1] What General Gordon wrote twenty years ago is equally true to-day: "From Wady Halfa southwards to Hannek, a distance of 180 miles, an utter desert extends, spreading also for miles eastwards and westwards on both sides of the Nile. For the same length the river is also encumbered with ridges of rock. ... It was therefore this boundary that kept the warlike and independent tribes of the Soudan quite apart from the inhabitants of Egypt proper, and has made the Soudanese and Egyptians two distinct people."

raided the villages in the neighbourhood, and several raids were committed subsequently, but seldom with any more serious result than one or two villagers being wounded, and their goats and bullocks driven off. The last raid, prior to the Dongola expedition, was in December, 1895, whilst General Knowles was actually making an inspection of the garrison there.

Wady Halfa comprises the two villages of Tewfikieh and Halfa, and the fortified lines — all on the east bank. The first thing one sees, coming up the river from Assouan, is the white minaret of the mosque of the village Tewfikieh. This village contained the only shops (of European goods) in Upper Nubia; in one street—the Regent Street of Halfa—nearly all the shopkeepers were Greeks. The village of Halfa proper consists of some two dozen mud huts, situated at the foot of the Second Cataract, amongst thick palm groves and many acres of "halfa" grass, from which the district takes its name.

It is the "lines," the combined Aldershot and Woolwich of Nubia, with which we and the general public are chiefly concerned. They lie midway between Halfa and Tewfikieh—from each of which they are about ten minutes' walk. Every building is of mud unadorned, the roadway is the sandy desert soil, and there is no wheeled traffic of any sort, an occasional camel or donkey being the only means of transport. Except the hospital, no building can boast of a first floor, or of glass in

Col. Wingate.   Slatin Pasha.
THE INTELLIGENCE DEPARTMENT, E.A.

LANDING STORES AT WADY HALFA.   [*To face p.* 77.

the windows, but there is a shady verandah round each block of buildings.

The whole place is a fortified camp, entirely built of mud, and surrounded with a wall and parapet, with forts at each end where the latter meets the river. The principal block of buildings, known as the "Commanderia," lies along the river-bank. Here were the offices and quarters of the Sirdar and his staff, and the Intelligence Department, presided over by Major Wingate, R.A., with Slatin Pasha as his chief assistant. We saw a good deal of these two during that wearisome period of waiting, and they frequently dined in our mess. To look at Slatin, with his cheery manner, one could hardly believe that he had gone through such dreadful experiences, and had witnessed the last days of Khartoum, even to gazing upon the severed head of its defender!

Major Wingate was full of anecdotes, and one good story which he told us deserves repetition. It was in the 1885 campaign, and the "Fuzzy-Wuzzys" had for some days been beating their drums, called "nagara," which was a sign that they were making warlike preparations. The chief of the Intelligence Staff—Wingate's predecessor—duly reported this to the General, who sent the news to Cairo. Here things were rather mixed, and the news was sent to the authorities at home that "that *fierce and formidable tribe*, the Nagara, have been continuously beaten during the last few days!"

But to return to Wady Halfa (figuratively). Not

far from the "Commanderia" is the hospital, the best building in Halfa. It was formerly the railway terminus, but it was found more convenient to have the latter nearer the river-bank. Outside the hospital is a tree under which lies buried the head of King John of Abyssinia. The head was sent from Omdurman to Halfa after the battle of Galabat, together with some documents which were forwarded to England. Speaking of this reminds us of the little British cemetery, which lies out in the desert beyond the walls. When we first arrived there were about eighty graves, chiefly of those who had died during the last Nile Expedition; but, alas! by the time we left for Cairo it was crowded to the utmost of its capacity. Here lies young Cameron of the 79th, surrounded by six of his men, who all fell at Ginniss—and many others who are waiting for the "Great Reveillé."

Next to the railway station were the workshops, including the engine "hospital," which was never without one or two inmates. To say that Halfa at this time was like a gigantic beehive is to speak inadequately, as any one will acknowledge who ever stood between the river and the railway and watched the fatigue parties hard at work, all day long, carrying stores from the boats to the trains. Corn and railway material formed the greatest part of the loads, which, when not borne by convicts in chains (under the eyes of armed sentries), were carried by the soldiers. To see those Egyptians working under the broiling sun filled one with admiration.

There was no need for non-commissioned officers to stir them up; they all went at it fully alive to the fact that 10,000 of their comrades at the front were depending on their labours for their daily rations. It was a case of "corn in Egypt," indeed! We have frequently heard it said that the Egyptian soldier is the ideal fatigue man and the Soudanese the ideal fighting man—this is more or less true, but at the same time we must add, the Egyptian soldier is something better than a mere beast of burden, and has been turned into a valuable soldier—a conviction which we feel sure the reader will share before he closes this book.

Halfa was the headquarters of the Camel Corps, and all day long the men were being drilled and young camels were being brought in and trained. The corps was a most important feature of the expedition; it afforded great assistance to the Transport Department, and, in the later stages, was invaluable for reconnoitring work.

Whilst the camels were being exercised in the desert, outside the walls, the barrack squares were resounding with the voice of the drill-sergeant. Here the jet-black recruits were first initiated into the mysteries of the goose-step by very smart English non-commissioned-officers, and very amusing it was to watch them. The average Sambo, on enlistment, had not the faintest idea of how to count, and when these recruits "numbered" and "formed fours," "the result was exasperating to the instructor—at least, we presume so, judging from the language evoked. Again, when they were ordered to "Right-hand—Salute," up would go a number of right hands and just as many left hands, whilst some, to make *quite* sure, would put up both!

We may mention incidentally that flogging is in vogue in the Egyptian army, but is only resorted to in serious breaches of discipline.

When we (Staffords) first arrived at Halfa we were told that the Dervishes had been in the vicinity quite recently, and that we were to be ready for any emergency—in fact, the day following our arrival we were told off to our defence posts on the walls, under the supervision of the Sirdar himself. One night, when we had been there a week, we were disturbed in our sleep by the shouts of one of the sentries, and in almost less time than it takes to narrate every company fell in opposite its barrack-room. But it turned out to be a false alarm, caused by a young over-excited sentry, and we were not troubled by any more scares of that nature.

With the exception of occasional fatigues, there was not much work for us to do. It was a dreadfully slow time, waiting for a chance of doing something, and at times we began to despair of ever going up to the front (Akasheh) at all. What made it a hundred times worse was the way in which utterly groundless rumours were incessantly flying round: first, that we were going back to Cairo at once; then that we would never go south of Kosheh, but would be kept there as a reserve; then that only half the battalion would go up eventually to the front, as there was not room in the gunboats for all, and so on, until we got tired of discussing what was going to happen to us. As it turned out in the end, a certain number of us *were* left behind. It quite took the life out of one, living under such disheartening circumstances in that awful heat, and no wonder that the sick list after a time became abnormally large.

Our daily routine was monotony exemplified. In the morning we went into the desert and practised square formations and the stereotyped attack drill, and some of the companies went through the annual courses of musketry and *field training!* After lunch every one changed into pyjamas and slept, read, or played picquet or whist. The heat from 10 till 5 was more than we can attempt to describe — but the natives have a saying that "the ground is like fire and the wind like flame," which we can vouch for as being literally true, and the place was commonly spoken of as "Wady Hell-fire"!

The afternoon was usually well advanced before we were able to leave our quarters. The latter were like barns when we first went into them. There were two officers in each room. There was no floor but the ground, no paper, but white(*sic*)-washed walls, and, of course, no glass in the window, so that when a dust-storm blew, we had to close the shutters and light a lamp. The only articles of furniture we found on our arrival were native bedsteads, called *angareebs*, made of fibre strung on a rough wooden frame. The rooms swarmed with every species of vermin. In ours, for instance, we counted two birds' nests and two hornets' nest, to say nothing of scorpions, rats, mice, beetles, and noisome insects innumerable. However, by dint of much scrubbing and sweeping we managed at last to make ourselves tolerably comfortable.

There were a few sailing-boats to be had, of a primitive cut and rig, in which we sometimes went for a sail up to the cataract, or explored the ruined temple on the opposite bank. There was a racquet-court, which had been built at a small cost by the English officers of the Egyptian army; though made of mud and rather undersized, it was an immense boon in such a place.

Whatever form of recreation we took, we usually congregated before dinner at the "Club," as the Egyptian mess was called. All its original owners being at the front, this establishment was now used by the waifs and strays in Halfa, chiefly the war correspondents. We saw a good deal of the latter, and very cheery companions they were. Some of them had a mess of their own, near the Sirdar's quarters, and afterwards, when we all moved south, they messed in couples. There was Scudamore (*Daily News*), fresh from Armenia, and full of its atrocities, usually to be found with Knight (*Times*), who had come direct from the Ashanti Expedition. Atteridge (*Daily Chronicle*) shared a mess with Garrett (*New York Herald*), but the latter died of fever later on, and about the time the cholera broke out Atteridge returned to England. The others included Beaman (*Standard*), Dodsworth (*Morning Post*), Bennett Burleigh (*Daily Telegraph*), Pearse (*Graphic*), Seppings Wright (*Illustrated London News*), and Gwynne (Reuter's agent).

We often had smoking-concerts to finish up the day, when we first arrived, but our *répertoire* being necessarily limited, even the most popular songs began to pall after a time. Sometimes we were provided with a unique entertainment in watching the native dances outside the walls. It was a remarkable sight: the women with their long, greasy, woolly curls hanging straight down on each side of the face; the jet-black Sambos waving their long staffs, and gesticulating and shouting; the boy squatting in the middle and hammering away at a drum, gradually getting faster and faster, whilst the dancing became more furious and the dancers more excited.

Glad to get to the end of another day, we always turned in early, and slept undisturbed save by the sentries, who, with their shouts of "No. 1, All's well," "No. 2, All's well," passed along the walls, broke the silence of the surrounding desert every half-hour through the night.

On the Queen's birthday we had a big parade,

the Egyptian artillery firing a royal salute. We wore our red coats for the first (and last) time, which circumstance reached the Khalifa's ears and convinced him that the English were actually taking part in the expedition—a fact which he had hitherto doubted. We heard the result of the Derby two hours after it was run—and there is nothing else to relate of our life at Wady Halfa.

CHAPTER V

THE BATTLE OF FERKET

The preliminary reconnaissance—The fight—The Dervish of 1896—Progress of the railway and telegraph.

IN the first week of June the whole of the Egyptian army, with the exception of a few details scattered along the line of communications, were assembled at Akasheh, and every regiment stood in readiness to move at a moment's notice.

The Sirdar had transferred his headquarters to this place, as we have seen, on the 1st of the month. On the same day Colonel Hunter and his staff reconnoitred the river route to Ferket, getting within sight of the Dervish camp without being seen by the enemy. At the same time the cavalry under Captain Broadwood reconnoitred the desert route to Ferket. Thus every yard of the two routes to Ferket—which is sixteen miles from Akasheh—was well known; whilst the ceaseless vigilance of our mounted troops kept the Dervish scouts at such a distance that they never got a clue as to our intentions. Even the scouts who were late out on the eve of the attack returned to Ferket in ignorance of the fact that a *coup de main*—we had almost called it a *coup de grâce*—was about to take place.

On the other hand, our Intelligence Department knew exactly the position of affairs at Ferket. There were 3,000 troops and no fewer than fifty-seven leading Emirs in the Dervish camp, under the Emir-in-Chief Hamuda. It was the Sirdar's intention to surprise Ferket and capture all these leaders, thereby inflicting a crushing blow on the Khalifa's cause. It was known that the Khalifa had a number of spies in the Egyptian camp, disguised as a camel-drivers, &c., so the coming move was known to the majority of officers only at the last minute.[1]

The following was the Sirdar's plan of attack :—

The main body—the River Column—under the Sirdar was to leave Akasheh on the evening of the 6th of June, follow the river, bivouac near Sarkametto signal station (three miles from Ferket), and at 4.30 A.M. on the 7th, deploy and attack the Dervish position. The River Column was composed as follows: 1 Infantry Division (3 brigades), under Colonel Hunter, with 2 field batteries; 2 Maxim guns; 1 field hospital.

The following was the composition of the Brigades: 1st Brigade,—under Major Lewis—consisted of the 3rd and 4th Battalions (Egyptians) and 10th Soudanese; 2nd Brigade—under Major Mac-

---

[1] It was chiefly for this reason that the North Staffords were not brought up from Halfa.

donald—consisted of the 9th, 11th, and 13th Soudanese Battalions; 3rd Brigade—under Major Maxwell—consisted of 2nd, 7th, and 8th (Egyptian) Battalions. Total strength of the River Column, 7,000.

The remainder—the Desert Column—under Major Burn-Murdoch, were to leave the river at Akasheh, and follow the desert route for some distance, following the old railway formation, and rejoin the Nile valley half a mile south of the Dervish camp, thus turning the enemy's position. This column was to occupy a position on the heights east of Ferket village at 4.30 A.M., and then co-operate with the River Column. Major Burn-Murdoch was to pursue the enemy vigorously and to follow up the victory by occupying Suarda, thirty miles beyond Ferket. The Desert Column was composed as follows: 1 Cavalry Brigade of 7 squadrons, under Major Burn-Murdoch's immediate charge; Camel Corps (670 rifles), under Captain Tudway; 12th Soudanese Battalion (717 all ranks), under Major Townshend; No. 1 Battery, Horse Artillery, under Captain Young; 2 Maxim guns, under Captain Laurie; details of field hospital, etc. Total strength of the Desert Column, 2,100.

Every man in the force carried ninety rounds of ammunition and two days' rations.

The troops moved off from Akasheh, in column of route, on the afternoon of the 6th of June—and we will first follow the doings of the River Column.

Every one was in high spirits, laughing and chatting, but as darkness fell this ceased, for strict orders had been issued that there was to be no talking, smoking, bugling, or firing, except by express command of Colonel Hunter. The way by the river was very rough and broken, there was no moon, and in places the men had to pass in single file, which caused repeated halts and increased the length of the column considerably. Not a sound was to be heard, and any one twenty yards off would have had no idea that a great body of men was on the move, which alone speaks volumes for the general state of discipline. By 9 P.M. the head of the column reached Sarkametto, after a march of twelve miles; and by a quarter past one every one had replenished his water-bottle, the outposts were all posted, and the force was fast asleep—three miles from the enemy.

At 2.15 A.M. the head of the column moved off again, and within twenty minutes the bivouac ground was vacant.

The 1st Brigade led, with the 10th Soudanese in front, and as they drew near to the enemy's position (about 4.30 A.M.) they deployed into firing line.

At 5 A.M. some drums were heard in the Dervish camp, and every one thought that our troops had been discovered—but no, it was only the call to prayer. However, a few minutes afterwards, a puff of smoke came from an outpost on one of the hills, and the enemy sprang to arms.

No sooner had the Dervishes discovered the

The Main Attack on the Dervish Position at the Battle of Firket.
From the "Graphic."

[To face p. 89.

THE BATTLE OF FERKET

presence of the River Column than the Desert Column made its appearance in their rear, and they found themselves caught in a trap. This accurately-timed co-operation of the two columns was one of the most skilful achievements in the whole campaign.

On the right of the plain of Ferket was the Nile, with the huts of the village amongst the palms; our troops were extended across the plain; and 200 yards from their left flank was Ferket Mountain. The latter bears a striking resemblance to Table Mountain, as all of us who had been to the Cape remarked directly we saw it. On the left bank of the Nile were the friendly Kababish Arabs, mounted on camels, who effectually stopped any attempts at retreat on the part of the Dervishes in that direction.

The enemy held three distinct positions [1]—first, the Jaalin camp, then the Jehadia camp, and lastly, where their final stand was made, the Baggara camp.

Our troops advanced across the plain in good order, pouring in steady volleys, and then rushing forward some yards, just as regularly as if "doing the attack" on parade; whilst the Horse Artillery and the Maxims fired away as hard as they could. The officers with the latter under Captain Laurie were especially conspicuous, and Lieutenants Goldfinch (North Staffords) and Blunt (Connaught Rangers) were seen themselves pulling their guns over the rough ground in order to get closer to the enemy.

[1] See Plan, page 94.

The 1st Brigade was told off to attack the Jaalin camp by the river-bank, and it came in for some hot work. The 10th Soudanese circled its left round, so that the enemy were caught on two sides. The 3rd Battalion, led by Captain Sillem, charged a large body of Baggaras in fine style. The 4th Battalion, on the other hand, under Captain Sparkes, were charged by a body of desperate Baggara horsemen, but they repulsed them with steady volleys. There was a lot of hand-to-hand fighting in the huts; no quarter was given and none asked.

The 2nd Brigade was sent against the Jehadia camp, and had very rough, hilly ground to work on. They advanced over it at a sharp pace, stopping repeatedly to pour in volleys, and then charging the enemy along the hill-tops.

The 3rd Brigade came up later and deployed into fighting line to fill the gap between the 1st and 2nd Brigades. They were, through no fault of their own, too late to take much part in the fighting.

The Dervishes fought with their customary bull-dog pluck, but were too greatly outnumbered. Even when compelled to retire, owing to the fire getting too hot for them, they would walk away slowly and calmly, with the rifle sloped carelessly on the shoulder, as if disdaining to recognise our presence, much less our superiority. Here and there they collected in little groups, and died fighting desperately. It is sad to think that men with such innate pluck should be such brutes. At least 75 per cent. of those at Ferket belonged to the tyrannical Baggara tribe; the others being Jaalin and Jehadia, who would willingly have deserted to us, but were forced to fight by their masters, the Baggara, in front of whom they were placed during the battle.

By 7 A.M. the fight was over and the enemy had fled. Some had made for a small island, where they had resolved to make a last stand, but some troops were sent to rout them out, which did not take long.

As a result of the morning's work our losses were 20 killed and 80 wounded, including Captain Legge, who got a cut on the wrist whilst leading a charge. It is hard to ascertain the enemy's losses, but they must have lost quite a thousand, including at least 40 Emirs. Hamuda, the Emir-in-Chief, and Gebir, Yahia, and Wady, his chief assistants, were amongst the slain. Over 500 prisoners were taken, besides a quantity of arms, ammunition, camels, goats and horses. Some of the latter were sent down to Wady Halfa and were put up for auction, but they were such miserable beasts that none fetched more than a few shillings.

This battle was the most decisive fight in the Dongola Expedition. It was certainly not a glorious victory, for our troops were superior in numbers, better armed, and had the advantage of surprise on their side, making the defeat of the Dervishes a foregone conclusion. But the dash and discipline of the Egyptian troops came so prominently to the fore, that the 7th of June will always be a red-letter day in the history of the Egyptian army. The battle was a terrible lesson to the Khalifa, and a grand example of generalship on the part of the Sirdar—and his assistants, Colonels Rundle and Hunter—to whose well-thought-out plans were due our slight loss and the successful issue of the day.

The Dervish was now a very different person in appearance from our antagonists of the Nile Expedition of ten years before. In those days their coats were nothing but a collection of patches, for it was one of their vows not to put on a new garment until they had destroyed the Turk—as all Christian races were called. The Khalifa now clothed his army in a coarse white cotton coat, called a *jibbah*, and substituted for the unsightly patchwork, large square patches, neatly sewed on, of distinctive colours. The colour of the patches varied with each tribe; thus the Baggara were distinguished by red and black patches, the Jaalin by blue, and so on. There were usually three patches in front and behind, and a couple on each sleeve. The *jibbah* itself resembled exactly the coat which the Crusaders used to wear under their armour, and it is very probably the actual origin of it.[1] It had short sleeves and came down only as far as the knees. The Dervishes now wore their hair very short, in fact almost shaved; and wore a little skull cap, round which they wound a

[1] During our entry into Dongola we saw, lying on the ground amongst some dead Dervishes, a magnificent suit of chain-armour of the Crusaders' period.

large white turban. A pair of sandals completed the costume.

Their arms consisted of spears—some being eight feet long—and guns. Most of the latter were those taken from Hicks's ill-starred force.

The Emirs—or commanders—were all mounted, and wore *jibbahs* about a foot longer than the men's, and more adorned with coloured facings, the latter being, in most cases, highly embroidered. Each Emir had, besides his spears, a broad sword with a cross-shaped hilt, like a short claymore.

Exactly a week after Ferket was occupied the railway was begun there in a northern direction. On the 20th of June the first train reached Akasheh from Halfa, and by the end of the month the permanent way to Ferket was completed—wanting only the rails—and the telegraph had been carried as far south as Suarda.[1]

[1] The following is a copy of the first postal time-table in the reconquered) Soudan:—

DONGOLA EXPEDITIONARY FORCE ORDERS.

FERKET, 28*th June*, 1896.

1.—Commencing to-morrow, the 29th inst., the postal service between Akasha and Suarda will be as follows:—

AKASHA	*dep.*	8.— p.m.	SUARDA	*dep.*	1.— p.m.
FERKET	{ *arr.*	5.30 a.m.	AMARA	{ *arr.*	—
	{ *dep.*	3.— p.m.		{ *dep.*	8.30 p.m.
AMARA	{ *arr.*	8.— p.m.	FERKET	{ *arr.*	5.30 a.m.
	{ *dep.*	8.30 „		{ *dep.*	12 noon.
SUARDA	*arr.*	5.30 a.m.	AKASHA	*arr.*	5.— p.m.

By Order
(*Signed*) G. F. GORRINGE,
D.A.A.G. *for* A.A.G.

PLAN OF THE BATTLE OF FERKET.

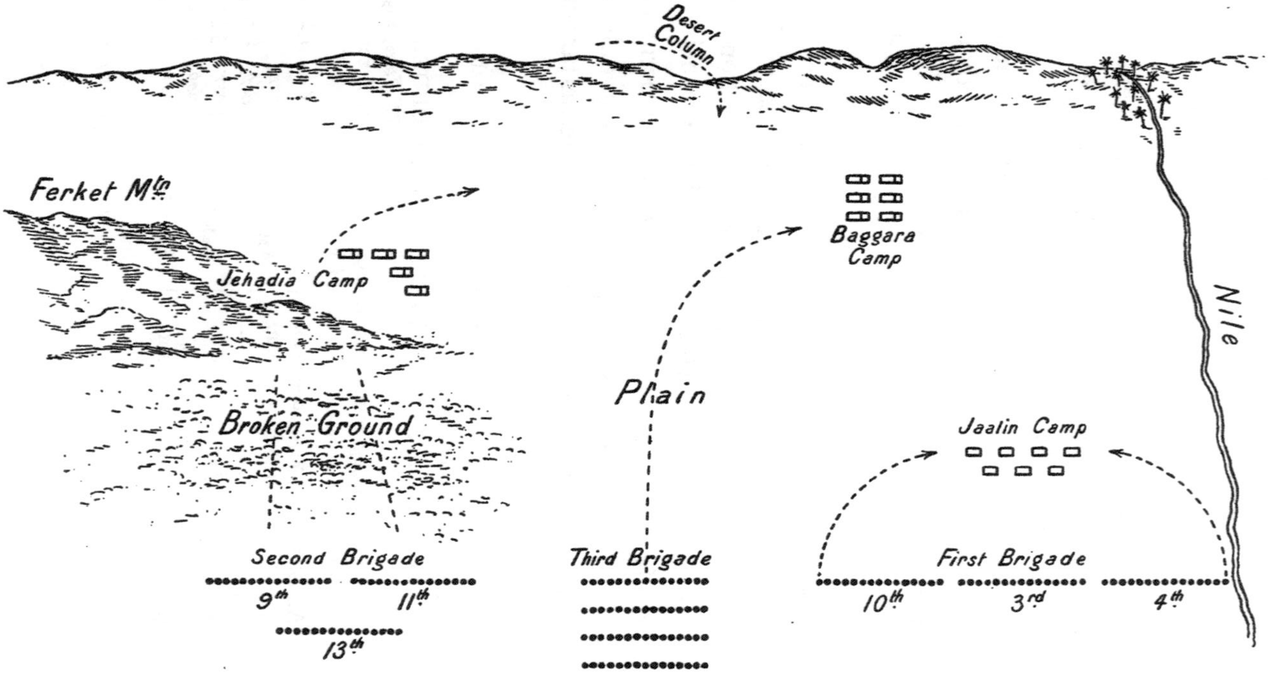

CHAPTER VI

THE CHOLERA

Creeping up the river—Reaches Halfa—The night march to Gemai—The " Belly of Rocks "—Struck off the strength—Deaths of British officers — Headquarters at Kosheh—Reconnaissances — The Staffords' cairn—Daily routine—The railway reaches Kosheh—Getting up stores—An unexpected deluge.

UP to the middle of June the general state of health had been highly satisfactory, but with the rise of the 'Green' Nile (green owing to the quantity of vegetable matter brought down) came a slight spread of fever, and during the last fortnight of June quite a large proportion of officers and men were on the sick-list. Of the Staffords, Colonel Beale, Lieutenant Hutchison, and a number of men were invalided down to Cairo, and Major Currie succeeded to the command of the battalion.

Towards the end of the month there was a rumour that the cholera was creeping up the Nile from Cairo, and, almost before we had time to realise the full significance of this report, the plague was upon us. On the 29th of June there were some cases at Korosko, and on the 30th it appeared in the village of Tewfikieh, outside Halfa.

Orders were issued for us to march away as soon as possible, and pitch our camp at Gemai, about sixteen miles off. At five o'clock in the evening of the 1st of July, we marched out of Wady Halfa, having spent exactly three months there. All night we followed the railway track, and no one who took part in that march is ever likely to forget it. Before we had gone half a mile the band-serjeant fell out sick, and when we reached Gemai next morning we heard he had died of cholera. We were told that after two hours' marching we should be able to replenish our water-bottles, but in the darkness we missed the proposed halting-place near the river. On and on we went, marching in couples, for the railway was not wide enough to allow four abreast, stumbling over the sleepers, and at times slipping down the embankment. At last, about 3 A.M. the "halt" was sounded, and every one started off to find the river the best way he could. No one had any idea where it was, until, after about twenty minutes of aimless wandering, some of us heard the welcome sound of rushing water. Then we filled ourselves and our bottles to the brim, and started back to the bivouac ground, but of course in the dark, this was harder to find than the river had been. However, the buglers were blowing away at the "regimental call," and we got back in time to have half an hour's rest.

Gemai was reached about six in the morning, and we spent the next few hours in pitching the camp, amidst a terrific sandstorm.

We will describe our new surroundings before re-

THE CAMP OF THE NORTH STAFFORD REGIMENT AT GEMAI.
(Sketched by Lieut. Farley, North Stafford Regt.)
From the "Graphic."

lating our experiences there. Gemai is half-way between Halfa and Sarras; apart from our camp it consisted merely of a fort on the top of a hill overlooking the river, and a few mud huts. The railway ran within a hundred yards of the river, through the middle of the camp, and the arrival of two or three trains which passed through on their way to the front with stores, or down to Halfa with invalids, was the only event that broke the monotony of the dreary camp life.

Behind the camp rose the great black hills which extend for eighty miles along the east side of the Nile, and are known as the *Batn-el-Hágar*, or "Belly of Rocks." Black rugged rocks are everywhere heaped together in endless confusion; some are hills of a thousand feet high, some are only a hundred feet. They are separated by "wadies," or valleys, which once or twice a year become raging torrents, but are most of the time as dry as their cindery surroundings. The "abomination of desolation" is here attained, and no sign of life is visible, with the exception of a few small birds—whose black plumage is in harmony with their surroundings—and an occasional jackal or vulture.

During the first three weeks of July, three hundred fatal cases of cholera occurred amongst the natives at Wady Halfa. The cholera tracked us to Gemai. One after another of our men was carried off by it; and for the greater part of July our existence might be summed up in the question "Whose turn next?"

H

Every night without exception a clause appeared to the effect that "The following men having died this day, are struck off the strength of the battalion." Those horrible words ring in our ears even now! How eagerly we all scanned those pages, and with what genuine grief we read the names of our comrades, needs no telling. In times like these the ties that bind officers and men together are drawn closer: in time of peace the British soldier is inclined to think that his officers are put over him solely for the purpose of giving him his pay and "telling him off." This is but the survival of olden times, when the officers themselves looked upon their duties and responsibilities from much the same point of view. That class of officer, however, is happily extinct; and the officer of to-day realises that it is his duty to interest himself in his men's welfare to the best of his ability; and the soldier is beginning to learn that his best friend is his officer. But we are digressing.

On the 11th of July we heard that "Roddy" Owen[1] had fallen a victim to the cholera at Ambigole Wells, where he was in command of the camp, being the only white man there. The news came as a shock to every one, for few men were more popular in or out of the service.

[1] Major Roderick Owen (Lancashire Fusiliers) had seen service in 1892 against the Jebus, in 1894 in Uganda, and in 1895 in the Chitral Expedition. He was a well-known sportsman, and one of the best amateur horsemen of the day. In 1892 he rode Father O'Flynn to victory in the Liverpool Grand National. For photograph see opposite page 166.

A Night Funeral at Gemai. (Sketched by Lieut. Farley, North Staffordshire Regt.) From the "Graphic."

[To face p. 99.

On the 20th of July Lieutenant Farmar[1] died at Suarda, and on the 26th Captain Fenwick[2] and Surgeon-Captain Trask[3] died at Kosheh. Two days afterwards we heard that Lieutenant Polwhele[4] and Garrett, the special correspondent of the *New York Herald* had succumbed to fever at Wady Halfa.

In order to relieve our gloomy surroundings as much as possible we used to have smoking-concerts nearly every night, and (with the same object) the funerals always took place in the evening. A group would silently gather outside the hospital tent, and the mournful little *cortége* would make its way, by the light of a couple of lanterns, to the cemetery, where the chaplain awaited them, his clean, white surplice forming a marked contrast to the rough kharki of the others. The corpse, shrouded in nothing but a blanket, would be placed in its last resting-place—

"By the struggling moon-beam's misty light
And the lantern dimly burning,"

—whilst, from the other end of the camp, the chorus of some popular song would reach our ears. No

[1] Lieutenant Farmar (60th Rifles) was gazetted 1890, and had served in three expeditions: the Miranzai, 1891 (medal and clasp), the Black Mountain, 1892, and the Chitral, 1895 (medal and clasp).
[2] Captain Fenwick (Royal Sussex Regiment) joined the Egyptian army in 1888; was at the battle of Arguin, and severely wounded at Toski, after which he received the Medjidie, 4th class, and Khedive's star. He had greatly distinguished himself at Ferket and Suakin.
[3] Surgeon-Captain Trask, A.M.S., had been conspicuous for his gallantry at Ferket.
[4] Lieutenant Polwhele, R. E., had been employed in the construction of the railway.

volleys were fired nor hymns sung, but those simple funerals were more impressive than the most imposing pageant could ever have been, and we realised the beauty of Wolfe's verses better than we ever had before.

When, in days to come, the tourist passes through Gemai in the train, he will see a strange-looking monument on a hill about 300 yards off, and he will probably find it referred to in his Baedeker as the cairn of the North Staffordshire Regiment, erected near the cemetery as a memorial to the many brave lads that they lost there.

This cairn was built by Captain Rose, who himself fell a victim to fever immediately on his return to Cairo. Poor "Jock"! He had a bad time when we left Halfa for Gemai, for he was at the time laid up with fever, and had to be left behind. The orderly who attended him in hospital was seized with cholera and died; the only other orderly and the doctors were so overworked that Rose saw little or nothing of them—so he literally took up his bed and walked, and got into the first train he could find bound for Gemai. It certainly did not improve his temperature, but it probably saved his life, for the other orderly died from cholera the next day!

The Egyptian regiments were faring no better than the British battalion. The Sirdar had left Ferket at the end of June, and had moved his headquarters and the Egyptian troops to Kosheh, ten miles further south. Here the cholera, ere long, made its appearance with disastrous effect. On the first signs of its presence the regiments moved into the desert and encamped about a mile outside Kosheh, under straw *tokuls*. The battalions were scattered in a manner which had little the appearance of a frontier camp. As an example of how rapidly the change of camp was effected, the 9th Soudanese marched out of Kosheh at 5 A.M., and by 10 A.M. their new quarters had been erected in the desert. These *tokuls* are made of palm branches; the roof is made first and set upon the uprights, and then the walls are built round. The Soudanese are very skilful at making these habitations.

By the middle of August the last traces of cholera had flickered out. The heat at this time was more terrific than ever, and in the straw huts, with thick roofs, it frequently reached 122°, and occasionally rose to 129°. Before five in the afternoon any form of exercise was out of the question: the only recreation was a walk by the river in the cool of the evening. Some of us took to fishing, but the fish were usually too muddy to be palatable.

Whilst we were existing at Gemai in this manner, the primary causes of our inactivity were coming to an end, for the railway was nearing its destination, and the river was rising rapidly.

As soon as the Sirdar had moved into his new quarters at Kosheh (the first week in July), active measures were taken to find out what the enemy were doing. Captain Mahon reconnoitred beyond the Kaibar Cataract, occupied Surda without meeting any resistance, and ascertained that the Dervishes were hard at work reinforcing and fortifying Kerma, whither they had fled after Ferket. A friendly chief, Abdul Azim Bey, succeeded in reaching the Nile, from Murat Wells, at Dar Shagiyeh (near Merawi), and gave the natives a true account of how the Dervishes had been defeated, which news was received with unconcealed delight.

On the 24th of July the first train ran across the battlefield of Ferket, and the first week in August, just as the cholera came to an end, the railway was completed (for the present). The first train entered Kosheh on the 4th of August, and the next ten days were spent in forming a large coal depôt there. The successful completion of the railway was a source of great satisfaction to all concerned. It was 105 miles long; the greatest length laid in a day was a mile and a half, and the work was as arduous as anything of the kind in modern times. Here and there it was not laid quite as carefully as an English mainline, and the curves at some places were very sharp, with the result that a train would occasionally run off the rails. One engine-driver was killed, but the casualties on the railway were wonderfully few, all things considered.

During the construction of the railway, stores had been rapidly collected at the front. The train took them as far as Akasheh (or whatever point the "Railhead" had reached), thence they were taken by boat to the north side of the Dal Cataract, then came a portage of three and a half miles, and finally they were shipped in fifty boats to Kosheh and

Suarda. The work of getting up these stores was under the supervision of Quarter-master Drage, A.S.C., at Kosheh, and Lieutenant Blunt, A.S.C., at Halfa. The native boats which brought them up were known as *nuggars*, or *gyassas*, solid one-masted vessels of from ten to twenty tons burden.

The prevailing wind in these parts is from the north, a providential institution which to some extent counteracts the great natural heat. It was most useful in helping the boats up-stream, and with all sail set a boat used to make as much as twenty miles a day against the current. Unfortunately, just at the time when the wind was most urgently required, it suddenly shifted, and for the greater part of August a horrible southerly wind set in, which made us feel more dead than alive, and was a serious handicap to the transport department, for the reasons explained above.

As if this was not bad enough, the country was suddenly visited by severe thunderstorms, an unusual occurrence in this district, and these were a very serious inconvenience. All the camps were flooded, and the deluge was followed, as a rule, by a violent sandstorm, which blew down any tents that were left standing. This continued off and on for a fortnight; but the worst part of it was yet in store for us.

CHAPTER VII

THE CATARACTS

The " Great Gate "—Getting the boats through—The boats at Kosheh —Absárat occupied—A disastrous storm—The North Staffords move to Sarras—A state of squalor.

ABOUT the middle of August the river had attained a sufficient height to enable us to commence the task of hauling the " boats " (stern-wheelers) over the Second Cataract, at the foot of which seven had been collected. Four of these were gunboats, viz. : the *Tamai, El Teb, Metemmeh,* and *Abu Klea,* and the other three were unarmed post-boats—the *Kaibar, Dal,* and *Akasheh.*

A Nile cataract is caused by ridges of granite crossing the river-bed, and causing the latter to fall in a series of steps. " These obstacles sometimes extend over miles of continuous water, at other places they are short and abrupt, and immediately above and below them the river is smooth and navigable. But however they may differ as to length and nature, the rock that makes them is always granite, sometimes black, as at the Second Cataract, sometimes red, as at the First Cataract, sometimes of green colour. Worn smooth by the action of the water, the sides of these cataract rocks are polished as a marble chimney-piece, and their teeth-like ridges below the water are dangerous to any craft that touches them. When the Nile is in flood it runs with tremendous force, but comparative smoothness, down these rugged stairways, but as the waters subside the rocks begin to show their heads, the angle of descent becomes steeper, and channels of broken water begin to show themselves where before the river from shore to shore had been an unbroken volume. In these lower stages a boat, propelled by oars or poles, or moved by sails, or dragged by tow-ropes, can zigzag from rock to rock, while the force of the current is not so determined and continuous against her; but when the Nile is in full flood, and has submerged almost all the rocks beneath its waves, the descent is easier than the ascent, and the boat, left to the current, is swept along the broad river with great velocity, but with comparative safety."[1]

Occasionally the river is pent to narrow limits between great barriers of rock, and the gorges thus formed, known as "gates," form a very formidable obstacle to navigation. The Second Cataract is about nine miles in length, and has a total descent of about sixty feet in that distance. In the narrowest part of it is a deep gorge known as the Bab-el-Kebir,

[1] "The Nile Cataracts," read by Major-General Sir W. Butler before the Aldershot Military Society, 16th of March, 1897 (Stanford and Co.)

or "Big Gate." It was this gate that had been such an obstacle to the Canadian *voyageurs* in 1884-5, when they had to get their "whalers" over it. An enormous churned-up mass of water rushes through the gate with immense force from a circular pool above, where two arms of the river meet. The gate itself is formed of two precipitous black rocks, about fifteen yards apart, and there is a fall of ten feet in a distance of seventy yards. Below the fall is a long series of pools where the water, though flowing rapidly, appears quite stationary compared with the torrent above.

An Egyptian battalion, sent down from Kosheh, was encamped by the gate, and, with the North Staffords, was waiting in readiness to haul the boats up.

On the 14th of August, a noticeable rise having taken place in the river, the first gunboat—the *Metemmeh*—was hauled through the "gate"; and every morning during the next week we marched from Gemai to the "gate," and back in the evening after a really hard day's work.

The way the boats were pulled over the "gate" was as follows:—five immense cables were attached to the boat, two on each side and one in front, and at each cable 400 men pulled with all their might. At intervals of a quarter of an hour they were relieved by others, one regiment being allotted to each cable. In spite of all this power it took an hour and a half to haul each boat through the "gate," which gives an idea of the force of the current.

HAULING THE FIRST GUNBOAT THROUGH THE "GREAT GATE."
From the "Graphic."

[To face p. 106.

Whilst the boats were being got over the cataract, the new gunboat, the *Zafir* (Conqueror), arrived in sections at Kosheh (16th of August), where it was being put together under the superintendence of Lieutenant Elkington, R.E., and a party of six marines. A branch line of the railway had been brought to the water's edge, and when the sections arrived—each of which weighed ten tons—they were lifted by huge cranes on to the river-bank. The hull was launched four days after the arrival of the sections.[1]

By the 23rd of August all the gunboats had arrived at Kosheh, where the *Zafir* was approaching completion, and a sufficient quantity of stores of all kinds had been collected; and the telegraph line had been carried to Absárat, which had been occupied by some troops from Suarda.

This was the first step of the eagerly awaited forward movement, and on this day (23rd of August) a telegram from the Sirdar was received

---

[1] Besides the *Zafir*, two similar boats, *El Fatteh* (Victorious) and *El Nazir* (Majestic) were ordered, but did not arrive until the Dongola Expedition was over. These boats were flat-bottomed sternwheelers, built entirely of steel, with triple decks, and could accommodate 300 men. Each boat had a protected conning-tower, loopholed shutters round the lower deck for infantry, and was provided with a powerful search-light. The boats were designed by E. B. Thubron, Nile Engine Works, Cairo; the machinery was made by Messrs. Y. Stewart and Son, Blackwall Iron Works; and the hulls by Messrs. Forrest and Son, Wyvenhoe. The whole work was constructed with a view to each boat being transferred complete to its destination in three sections, armament excepted. The latter, on each boat, consisted of one 12-pounder quick-firing (forward), two 6-pounders quick-firing, one howitzer, and twelve Maxims (reduced, in 1898, to four). The dimensions were: length, 135 feet; beam, 24 feet; and, with all its armament on board, each boat drew only 42 inches in the water.

by Colonel Currie, telling him to hold us in readiness to leave Gemai at a moment's notice; when suddenly another check threw us into a state bordering on despair. A fearful storm broke over the whole country on the 25th, and wrecked the railway to such an extent that an immediate advance was out of the question. Between Sarras and Mograkeh seven miles, in one stretch, of the embankment was washed away; sixteen other breaches occurred; and a great number of the railway lines had been twisted and rendered useless along the line. Altogether twenty miles of hard labour had been carried off. The telegraph was destroyed, and all communication was at a standstill for two or three days. All the tents and camp equipment of the railway battalion were washed into the Nile.

When the storm broke on us at Gemai we were quite unprepared for it, in spite of the warnings we had at the beginning of the month. A few heavy drops of rain and the storm was on us. We had been having our meals out in the open by the riverbank, preferring a little roasting to being stifled in a tent. Suddenly down went half the tents, away went our mess table into the Nile, and away went the mess-sergeant—who happened to be standing near—head first after it! It is wonderful what a little excitement will do in a monotonous place like that, and we felt as refreshed (especially the mess-sergeant!) as if we had all been for a change of air.

Next day the regiment moved by train to Sarras

to repair the damaged line there, but a detachment of us was left at Gemai to look after the camp.

On the 27th of August the 1st Brigade, Egyptian army, at Suarda received orders to march to Dulgo, a distance of forty-five miles, half of which was across the desert. Water depots had been established, but the force was overtaken by a terrific duststorm, and the result was disastrous. Out of 3,000 men, 1,700 fell out, and ten died and were buried on the journey, which came to be spoken of as the "Death March."

The Staffords were hard at work at Sarras, rebuilding the embankment. Their camp was pitched on a cemetery, and in one tent half a man's leg was still to be seen above ground! There was only one consolation to make up for their state of squalor at Sarras, and that was that the detachment at Gemai were faring no better.

Those of us left at Gemai were to go up to Kosheh by one of the first trains that could run over the repaired line, so we looked out anxiously for news of our people at Sarras, to hear how they were getting on with the work. At last (8th of September) we heard that they had finished it and that we were to go up by the next train from Halfa. Our limited kit was packed, all the tents were struck and stacked, and at 6 A.M. next morning, when the train steamed in, we thought our release had come. But no—the train was required to take up more stores to Kosheh. All day, and the next, we were in this state of susspense. We found some shade under the mess table, we had a soup-plate to wash our faces in, and a handkerchief for a towel—and what more *could* one want?

On the 10th of September the whole battalion was moved to Kosheh from Sarras and Gemai. The next day was spent in stacking the baggage, which was to be left here, and in issuing orders relative to the coming move. It was then that we heard what we had been so long dreading: that there would not be enough room on the boats for all the regiment—for it had been known all along that we Staffords were to go as far as possible in the boats—and that over a hundred men and a proportion of officers would have to be left at Kosheh. The men left behind were selected from the defaulters, worst shots, and one complete company: and the officers to remain with them were the junior captain, junior lieutenant, and junior second lieutenant.[1]

During the morning of the 11th a loud report was heard all over the camp and we thought that it was some gun being tested on one of the boats. Imagine our dismay when we heard that the boiler of the new gunboat, the *Zafir*—the pride of the fleet—had burst, rendering the boat perfectly useless until a new plate could be sent from Assouan! At first it was thought that all of our men who were to have gone in her would have to remain behind as well, but by means of some overcrowding a good number were stowed away on the other boats, and, in the end, only an additional half company was left.

[1] Captain Astell, Lieutenant Andrus, and 2nd Lieutenant Wyatt.

The *Tamai*.   The *El Teb*.
THE SIRDAR'S FLOTILLA ON THE NILE.
From the "*Graphic.*"

[*To face p.* 111.

CHAPTER VIII

THE ADVANCE TO THE THIRD CATARACT

The Nile flotilla—Kaibar—Bivouacking—A false alarm—Fareig—A preliminary skirmish—Ahead of the army—Preparations for action—The enemy sighted—Arduan Island—A tide in the affairs of man !—Sadek—We leave the boats.

AT half-past eight on the morning of the 12th of September, we steamed away from Kosheh, and the advance (as far as we were concerned) was fairly begun. Our flotilla consisted of the gunboats *Tamai* (Commander the Hon. S. Colville, R.N., who was in charge of the fleet), the *El Teb* (Commander Robertson, R.N.), the *Metemmeh* (Captain Oldfield, R.M. Art.), and the *Abu Klea* (Lieutenant Beatty, R.N., and Captain de Rougemont, R.A.); and the post-boats *Kaibar*, *Dal*, and *Akasheh*.

A few minutes after leaving Kosheh we passed Ginniss, the scene of the battle of 1886.

We stopped the night at Suarda, slept on board, and left next morning at daybreak (13th). About 2 P.M. we passed Absárat, where we saw our regimental horses on their way to the front. Soon afterwards we passed a large mud mosque on the east bank, called Kwyeeka, and later on a large fort on the west bank. About 6 P.M. we passed Dulgo (or Delligo), where the whole of the Egyptian army had arrived in the morning from Absárat, and we now saw them on the march to Kaderma, accompanied by a caravan of camels about two miles long.

The boats were moored up for the night at Kaderma, near Kaibar, and we bivouacked near them, facing the desert and the east, on the right of the Egyptian army. We were now well in the enemy's country, and as every night after this was spent in a similar manner, we may as well give a description of the bivouac here. We all landed in full "marching order," soon after retreat, and slept in our clothes. Each man had a blanket, and no one was allowed to take off his boots or putties. When valises were at hand we used them as pillows, otherwise one's coat folded up was a substitute. The officers slept with their companies, and as a rule had their dinner brought from the boat in a canteen. During the night there was, of course, a chain of outposts round the camp, at a distance of about half a mile. At reveillé the bugle call of the Egyptian army—one of the most musical of any—was sounded at headquarters, and ran down the length of the lines, as one regiment after another took it up. The mounted forces immediately went out to reconnoitre. It was a pretty and impressive sight, in the dim light of the breaking day, to see the cavalry passing at a smart trot down the front of the great line of troops, followed by the rumbling guns of the Field

Artillery and the silent but rapid Camel Corps. As soon as all was reported clear, the staff officers rode off in different directions with their orders, and then the regiments marched off to their different camping grounds next to the boats. The latter were not used when moored up, as the space on board was so limited. As there were no tents with the army, except those belonging to the staff and hospitals, the camping-grounds were invariably situated under groves of palm-trees. Where the latter did not afford sufficient protection from the sun, the men brought their blankets into use, and by the end of the campaign we were all adepts in constructing blanket-tents. A couple of blankets, three sticks, and a piece of string, made a shelter as shady as it was frail.

Whilst bivouacking at Kaderma, we were suddenly aroused from our sleep in the dead of night by a tremendous babel of alarmed cries, shouted orders, and the noise of a regular stampede away on our left; so, thinking the Dervishes were upon us, we stood to arms. It turned out to be a false alarm created by some over-excited Egyptians. We noticed especially the conduct of a Soudanese battalion on our right, which fell in at once without the slightest noise or confusion, in a manner that would have done credit to any regiment in the world, for, in the total darkness, it was a trying moment.

Early on the 14th we steamed off and reached the Kaibar Cataract before breakfast. Along the east bank was regiment after regiment of the

Egyptian army marching cheerfully along, the companies, as a rule, in column formation. As for the cataract, it was not worthy of the name, not at high Nile at any rate. It was very broken water, but a little careful steering soon surmounted the difficulty. As each boat steamed through it became the object of vociferous cheering on the part of the 11th Soudanese, who lined the bank and were filling their water-bottles. The "three cheers" were led by their bugler, who, after sounding the regimental call, followed it up with three "G's"!

We here noticed that the country on both sides showed a marked change: there was more cultivation and many more palms, and we could see that we were well in the province of Dongola. The river at times was quite a mile wide, and very pretty in parts. In fact, the stretch between Kaibar and Hannek has been considered the finest spot on the whole Nile in scenery. Here are some of the wildest spots on the river: enormous rocks, of fantastic shape and marvellously balanced, remain as memorials of the Ice Age; and ruined fortresses, standing close together, remind one of some of the finest reaches on the Rhine.

We reached Fareig (Faredi) at 10 A.M., most of the Egyptian army arriving during the morning. Here we were destined to spend several days, though we did not know this when we arrived. It was the same kind of thing throughout the campaign: from beginning to end, we never knew at one moment where we might be the next. We never saw much of the Sirdar, but this rigid silence which he invariably observed was quite the most noticeable trait in his character.

The enemy had raided Fareig a few days before our arrival, had carried off all the men, and were now reported to be 2,000 strong in the neighbouring hills. There was abundant evidence to show that they had been here quite recently, such as bowls, zeers (earthenware filters), and the remains of fires. Fareig, like all the other villages which appear on the maps, was a collection of some twenty wretched mud hovels, and was situated in a grove of palm-trees which stretched along the river-bank for several miles. During the morning the Sirdar and his staff arrived. The camp stretched for about four miles along the river, and at the north end was the Camel Corps' ground. The camels, with their backs sore from overwork, were sickening to look at, and indeed it was well for the whole force that a prolonged halt was allowed here.

One regiment of blacks was bivouacking opposite the spot where our boats were moored, so that we had ample opportunity of studying them. They were just like children, with their incessant chatter, and in their honest simplicity and love of fun. It was as soldiers, however, that they were most interesting. Never could one wish for a more excellent set of men to lead into action. They love soldiering, and when off parade amuse themselves in drilling each other. In action their eagerness to come to close quarters is almost as much a curse as a blessing, for should they see a stray Dervish anywhere near, they at once forget all about keeping the ranks and vie with each other as to who shall be the first "in at the death." Fenwick, who afterwards fell a victim to cholera, told us at Halfa that he had seen many instances like this around Suakin; but, after all, it is a fault on the right side. We should add that by the end of the campaign they had learnt to keep their ardour under better control, and their state of discipline was as perfect as it could possibly be.

Their average height was six foot, but many were over six foot six inches. They were jet black, and came from all parts of the Soudan; in fact, some were said to be reformed cannibals! Most of them had come originally from the Khartoum district, and were recruited round Suakin. Once a black gets into the clutches of the recruiting sergeant, he does not get away as easily as his comrade the Egyptian; he is much too precious for that. The Egyptian serves for only five years, but a black is usually kept in the army until old age comes to his rescue. There were only five regiments of blacks, and each was distinguished by a different coloured stripe on his *tarboush*.[1] There are six companies to a battalion, and each is distinguished by a different coloured flag. These flags were of the greatest service when the battalion arrived at a

---

[1] The red *tarboushes* were encased in a cover of coarse brown cloth as an additional protection against the sun; and the coloured stripe was worn on the right side. The colours were: 9th Soudanese, green; 10th, black; 11th, red; 12th, yellow; and 13th, blue.

new spot and was taking up fresh quarters there—we were almost saying "pitching tents," but there were none to pitch. We were particularly struck with the rapidity with which they erected shelters on reaching a new camping ground. Within an hour of their arrival anywhere, every one would be comfortably shaded under a hut (*tokul*) of palm-branches. At Fareig the palms were to be counted in hundreds, so that the material was not wanting.

On the 15th a boat was seen about two miles down the river, crowded with Dervishes, so the *Tamai*, with companies of the Staffords and of the 12th Soudanese on board, got up steam and went in chase. The Nordenfelt blazed away at them, but they succeeded in effecting a landing on an island, and disappeared, leaving two boats behind, which were towed triumphantly back, with one Dervish who was taken prisoner. During the afternoon the cavalry pushed south to Barji, and had a slight skirmish in which seven of the enemy were killed.

On the 16th the 4th Brigade arrived, so that the whole army was now concentrated at Fareig. Nothing occurred during the day until about five o'clock, when the alarm sounded through the camp, and we all took up our positions for bivouacking at once. Whenever an alarm sounded, the Brigadier (Colonel Hunter), followed by a trooper carrying the headquarters' flag, would ride to some prominent ground, and the staff would assemble there and decide what was to be done. At the same time the cavalry and camel scouts galloped off to reconnoitre, followed by the artillery.

On the 17th the whole force left Fareig. Reveillé was at 4 A.M., and we in the boats steamed off at 5.30, by which time most of the Egyptian army had started. We soon steamed past them, and found ourselves ahead of the whole army. On the west bank a party of native camel scouts, commonly called "Friendlies," kept up with us most of the time, for we were only going half-speed.

We expected to sight the enemy at any moment, so arrangements were made accordingly. To those who have never gone into action a few details may be of interest. Each man carried eighty rounds of ammunition, and to each officer thirty rounds of revolver cartridges were issued, which, with the field dressing, we carried in our haversacks. The dressing is a neat little packet of bandages, lint, and cotton-wool. Every one was provided with a linen ticket,[1] to sew inside his coat pocket, for the purpose of identification—presumably in case his head was blown off; and a casualty return and ammunition state was issued to officers commanding companies, to be filled in after the action.

As we steamed along the cheering from the natives on the banks became more vociferous than ever. All the way up the Nile the approach of the steamers had been a source of unfeigned delight on

---

[1] Description card for active service. Army form B2067.
    Number and name :   Rank and regiment :
    Nearest of kin :   Residing at :
        Signature of officer commanding company :

the part of these poor creatures: the women uttering the long shrill "trills" peculiar to them—more like the whistle of a steam-engine than a cry of delight—and the men cheering heartily. Now their joy knew no limits, and they leapt and danced on the banks in the unbounded sense of relief from their tyrants. They shouted to us that the Dervishes had raided them only that morning and had carried off all their able-bodied men, but that they had retired hastily on seeing the smoke from our steamers.

About half-past twelve we caught sight of the enemy on ahead, on the right bank, so landed at once at a place called Habberâb, on Arduan Island, and threw out a small line of outposts 500 yards from the boats. To our disgust the Dervishes declined to accept our invitation, and took themselves off. An incident occurred here which shows how marked was the change of *régime* to which the natives were subjected. In the morning the Dervishes had carried off all the property of an old man with the exception of one fowl, which they had failed to catch; immediately on our arrival on the scene this fowl was bagged by one of the officers' servants, so the old man came on board and demanded compensation, which he at once received.

We bivouacked here for the night, whilst the Egyptian army stopped at Barji.

We may here mention that no reliance can be placed on the maps of this part of Africa, for the names, and even the villages, are constantly being changed. When we started on the expedition we procured a map "To illustrate the Dongola Expedition," bristling with names, and we innocently expected to find most of the chief places marked. But no,—Gemai, Kosheh, Suarda, Fareig, not one of them was shown, though there was the Nile with villages shown on each side as thick as flies on a string. It appears that wherever two or three mud huts were gathered together, the name was eagerly put down by the map-maker, without any distinction of size. There are no real villages, in the English acceptance of the term, and the head man of the district calls the latter after himself. When he dies the name is changed by his successor, and frequently the villagers move in a body some way up or down stream, the old village being destroyed, or at any rate deserted; so that the inaccuracy of the maps is scarcely to be wondered at.

Early on the morning of the 18th we left Arduan Island, and reached Sadek at 10 A.M., where we learnt that numbers of the enemy, under Osman Azrak, had been in the neighbourhood during the last few hours. The Egyptian regiments were arriving, after an eight-mile march across the desert.

We disembarked, and the following orders were issued :—

   1. The force will move off at 4 P.M. this afternoon.

   2. The North Staffords will march in front of the guns.

   3. All the gunboats and the post-boats *Dal* and *Akasheh* will proceed (without troops) through the

Third Cataract (Hannek); they will be lightened as much as possible, and the *nuggars* now attached to them will be left at Sadek. One company and a half of the North Staffords will go on board the *Dal* and *Akasheh* above the Cataract.

4. The *Kaibar* will remain behind.
5. Valises will be left on the *nuggars* at Sadek.
6. Blankets, one per man, will be carried on camels with the column.
7. Every man will carry 80 rounds of ammunition, and two days' rations. On the *Dal* and *Akasheh* 100 reserve rounds per man (for the British troops) will be carried.
8. No lights or cooking will be allowed to-night.

The general idea was to march round the Third Cataract and attack the enemy's position at Kerma next morning.

We did not join the boats again. Henceforth we marched in front of the Egyptian army, and, with the exception of a blanket each (carried on the camels), we were dependent on the *nuggars* (or *gyassas*) for our kits and the bare necessities of life. Those of a far-seeing mind had stowed away a few useful things in the aforesaid blanket—such as a canteen, fork, and towel—but most of us had to be content with what we carried in our havresacks. Hitherto it had been ordinary campaigning: now we were about to "rough it" in earnest.

CHAPTER IX

THE BATTLE OF HAFIR

Kabodeh—Kerma evacuated—The fight—Casualties—The passage of the Nile—Our kits at last—The dervish fortifications.

WE left Sadek at 4 P.M., the Staffords being in the 1st Brigade, under Major Lewis. Behind each regiment followed a long camel-train, with the blankets and ammunition. One of us was on the regimental baggage-guard, and rode a camel by virtue of his office, but this privilege was but slight compensation for the task entailed. Every few minutes a load would slip off, or be knocked off by another camel coming too close; then there would be a long argument between all the native drivers as to whose fault it was; when they had quite settled this important question the camel had to be got into a kneeling position with much coaxing and swearing on the part of the drivers, and much "burbling" on the part of the beast. At last the load would be readjusted, but all this time the regiments behind would be closing up, so that it was with a sense of relief that the camel was started again. The baggage-guard would move on once more, the drivers were all peaceful again; and then over would go another load.

After having been confined for nearly a week on the boats, the march was trying in the extreme. The heat was fearful, and by the end of the march several of our men were utterly exhausted, and one dropped dead on the way. Poor lad! He had only joined with a draft of recruits from England just before we started up the Nile. He was carried back to Sadek and buried there.

We passed Kabodeh (spelt also Kabodi or Kabuda) about quarter to seven, and shortly afterwards halted on a vast plain (near Tumbus Island), where regiment after regiment was streaming in. We bivouacked there for the night, within five miles of the enemy.

At three o'clock in the morning of the 19th we were roused individually; the adjutant turned out the officers and the latter woke the men. No bugle was sounded and no lights were allowed. As there was no food to be had, breakfast did not detain us, and we started soon afterwards to attack Kerma. We heard that the enemy had decided to make a stubborn resistance here, and we confidently expected that in a couple of hours we should be fighting a decisive battle. Our expectations were realised, but not quite in the way we had anticipated.

The general orders had laid down, as already shown, that the Staffords were to accompany the guns; but the latter moved off in the darkness, when it came to their turn, leaving us in ignorance as to their whereabouts, and we started in chase two hours afterwards. Nothing came of it, however, beyond affording us another of the lessons that active service teaches; namely that, in the field, there is an absence of that fatherly supervision which characterises peace manœuvres, and that more initiative is looked for on the part of subordinates.

The whole of the Egyptian army, preceded by the cavalry, guns, and the British regiment, marching silently forward over the vast plain—15,000 men, in company after company—with the gunboats on our right steaming slowly up the river, one behind the other, formed a grand and impressive spectacle. Colonel Haggard describes the situation so well that we cannot do better than quote his words:[1] "It is a very solemn and weird sight, this starting of troops in the dark, before proceeding into action. In spite of all attempts at silence, a sort of continued murmur seems to rise into the cold night air; vague forms are seen moving along, which prove perhaps to be the camels; a dull tramping is heard—it is a regiment moving off; a rattling and clanging of chains next attracts your attention—the guns are passing. And no one says a word, no matches are struck, no pipes are lighted; orders are given in a low tone, and passed on quietly from company to company. The dust rises and heavily fills the air, while through that dust is somehow felt to be moving a grim restless force of men, going on to death or to glory, controlled solely

[1] *Under Crescent and Star*, by Lieutenant-Colonel A. Haggard, D.S.O. (Blackwood).

by the love of honour and the iron hand of discipline. . . . The sensation felt upon these occasions was a grim and peculiar sense of subdued excitement—a sensation which completely dies away after the first shots are fired or the first blows struck, but a sensation well worth having lived to have experienced, for it is like nothing else in existence."

We marched on without seeing any sign of the enemy, and before long Captain Adams, who was commanding the cavalry in advance, sent back word to the Sirdar that Kerma was empty! We reached the fort at 6 A.M., and to our unutterable disgust we saw that such was indeed the case. The fort was a large square building constructed entirely of mud, protected by walls five feet high, which could have been levelled in a very short time, and surmounted by a double tier of loopholes. It was ascertained that the enemy had abandoned Kerma during the night, as soon as they heard of our approach, and had crossed over in twenty-seven *gyassas* to Hafir, on the left bank of the river.

The Dervish commander was Wad el Bishara, one of the Khalifa's most prominent Emirs. He was now thirty-two years of age, was a great favourite with the Khalifa, and was given the command of Dongola in 1895. This manœuvre of Bishara's of crossing the river on the eve of being attacked, was one of the most masterly tactics ever practised in Soudan warfare. By abandoning Kerma at the last moment, he, at one stroke, rendered powerless the whole of the Sirdar's force except the artillery and gunboats.

We pushed on past the fort, and about a quarter to seven the field battery, under Captain Young, galloped rapidly into position and opened fire, at 2,500 yards, on the enemy drawn up along the opposite bank. The gunboats arrived shortly afterwards, and the "artillery duel" commenced in earnest, the enemy replying vigorously. When immediately opposite their position, the Infantry Division halted and formed up along the river. Shells and bullets came whizzing towards us, and one shell knocked a hole through a mud hut next to which a group of our men was posted, but no one was hurt.

There were only three gunboats in this action, namely the *Tamai* (Commander Colville),[1] the *Abu Klea* (Lieutenant Beatty), and the *Metemmeh* (Captain Oldfield). Each of these had on board a detachment of thirty infantry, and a company and a half of the Staffords were on board the *Akasheh* and *Dal* post-boats, to try the effect of long range volleys. The two latter boats, being unarmoured, had to keep at a safe distance until the Dervish guns were silenced. During the night the *El Teb* (Captain Robertson, R.N.) had run on a rock at Tumbus Island, near the Hannek Cataract, so was not present.

At first the Dervishes replied feebly, but as soon as they found the range, the shooting became excellent. Their earthworks along the river-bank were

---

[1] Commander the Hon. S. C. J. Colville, R.N., saw service in the Zulu War, 1879, the Egyptian War, 1882, and Nile Expedition, 1884—5; and had served on her Majesty's yacht *Victoria and Albert*.

THE BATTLE OF HAFIR

protected by a ditch and a loopholed wall five feet high and half a mile long. At the south end of the works was a gun-bank with five guns, strengthened by a big ditch.

The gunboats continued pounding away until they reached a narrow channel, 600 yards wide. All at once, just as the *Tamai*, which was leading, reached the narrowest part of the stream, the enemy opened fire with a couple of guns which had hitherto escaped detection. One was posted near a *sakieh* (water-wheel) and the other in a dense group of palms. Between these two a double row of rifle pits had been dug, from which a heavy fusilade was now poured into the boats.

The sight was a remarkable one. The masses of the enemy, conspicuous in their white *jibbas*, amongst the huts and palms, with their banners fluttering gaily in the breeze; the long rows of riflemen, the bursting shells, and the water torn up by hundreds of bullets and occasional heavier shot, formed an animated and exciting picture. Presently their cavalry was seen going at a smart trot across the open, and very pretty they looked with their shining spears and well-kept lines.

About this time Commander Colville was wounded in the wrist, and the boats had to retire. Encouraged by this momentary check, the Dervishes, some of whom had begun to draw off, now returned and opened a heavy fire. With the Field Artillery in support on the bank, the steamers returned to the charge, but again the enemy's fire proved too heavy, and we saw the *Metemmeh*, which was leading, suddenly swing round and go best pace down stream.

The rain of bullets was now extraordinary. Shrapnel was hurtling through the air against the invisible enemy, and rockets were whizzing like fiery serpents amongst the palms. From the top of the latter, a number of Dervish marksmen had been steadily firing on to our decks, but the rockets found them "up a tree" in every sense of the term, and it was laughable to see them come scuttling down again.

At 9 A.M. a passage was found from our bank to a small island, called Antagashi Island, opposite the enemy's lines. The river was here reduced to 600 yards in width, and four batteries, under Colonel Parsons, R.A., and the Maxims, were at once sent across, escorted by two companies of Soudanese, who did good practice with their volleys. It was only with a sense of great admiration that we watched the Dervishes. Shell after shell dropped into their midst, but they never budged an inch, and stuck to their guns splendidly.

About half-past ten, under cover of the field guns and Maxims, the *Tamai* succeeded in forcing a passage, and was followed by the two other boats at distances of 150 yards. The boats approached the spot where the Dervish steamer *El Tahira* and a number of *gyassas* were anchored, and now began a tremendous three-cornered duel—the boats and artillery, the *gyassas*, and the earthworks. The *El*

Tahira was speedily sunk, and the field guns coming up to closer range, the Dervishes found their position getting too warm. They began to withdraw, and many, as they left the cover of their trenches, were knocked over by the Maxims on the gunboats. The Dervish commander, Wad Bishara, was wounded by a shell in two places, and, as he was carried into a place of safety, he exclaimed, "Allah is against me." He had just received a letter from the Khalifa, and had ordered all his attendants out of the tent, except one or two, when the shell burst inside the tent and killed those with him.

The boats now steamed full speed to Dongola, and our artillery soon afterwards silenced the enemy's guns; but rifle fire was going on at intervals throughout the day. Now that the boats were gone, the Dervishes showed themselves more openly, and shouted defiance at us. During the afternoon a mass of fugitives were seen flying south, and a fire was kept on them by the guns. We slept that night on the position we had occupied during the day, with the guns booming and the quick-firers peppering away at intervals until daybreak. The *gyassas*, in which the Dervish army had crossed the river, were laden with all their grain and food, and all night long the enemy made frantic efforts to reach the spot where they were moored by the bank. But unfortunately for them it was a moonlight night, and as soon as they emerged from the shelter of the trees, the Maxims on the opposite bank made it so hot for them that before long they gave up the attempt, and after throwing their dead into the river with stones tied round their necks, they took themselves off. When day broke on the 20th, Hafir was found to be evacuated.

The enemy's loss must have been considerable. As they buried most of their dead in the manner described above, it is hard to form an estimate, but probably 200, at least, were killed. Wad Bishara was severely wounded, as we have seen, and his nephew had his leg blown off. Many prisoners were taken, including an Egyptian gunner who had been in Hicks's force. He said that he and the other gunners at Hafir were amicably inclined towards us, but that the Baggara stood over them as they were working the guns, with drawn swords! There seems to be some truth in their statement, for several shells were sent off without fuses, in fact, one of these was found in the magazine of the *Abu Klea*. What the consequences would have been if it had exploded it is impossible to say; but with one of our remaining steamers rendered *hors de combat*, the day might not have ended quite so successfully. As it was, all three gunboats were considerably knocked about; the *Abu Klea*, for instance, being hit 86 times. Twenty-seven *gyassas*, laden with grain, were captured; 120 boxes of Nordenfelt ammunition, which had been in Hicks's ill-fated expedition, fell into our hands; and the Dervish steamer *El Tahira* was sunk.

The losses on our side were slight. Armourersergeant Richardson was killed whilst working one of the Maxims on board the *Tamai*; Commander Colville was wounded; one Egyptian officer was killed; and one officer (Egyptian army) and eleven men were wounded.

The fight was a decisive one, and a great victory for the Sirdar; for, as will be seen, it settled the fate of Dongola. The Dervishes had chosen their position admirably for contesting the advance of the boats up the river; whether they showed as much judgment in abandoning the position as soon as the boats got past, is open to doubt.

At 6.30 on the morning of the 20th the force began the passage of the river in the captured *gyassas*, which had been emptied of their grain. We left our bivouac at Kerma at 9 A.M., and by 1 P.M. had taken up our quarters at Hafir, across the river. The horses were the greatest difficulty, as there were very few boats which would accommodate them; but they too were all on the other side by sunset. About 5 o'clock we saw the gunboats coming down stream as hard as they could, and they brought news that they had bombarded Dongola, at 300 yards range, and had taken a lot of treasure and a few boats.

We found the *gyassas* waiting for us at Hafir, with our kits on board; they had been brought over the cataract the day before, and it was a great treat to get them again. Since we left the boats at Sadek we had absolutely nothing except the clothes we stood in, so that the opportunity of getting at a pair of socks, razor, and other luxuries was eagerly seized.

We now put no further trust in the transport, and decided to hereafter carry these requisites in our havresacks and blankets as best we could.

The next day (21st) was spent in fatigues, chiefly in landing the commissariat meat and biscuits. The first duty of the day was to bury a sapper (of the Royal Engineers' detachment with us) who had died in the night. During the morning the Sirdar received telegrams from her Majesty the Queen and the Khedive, congratulating him on the result of the fight.

We found time to visit the Dervish fortifications, which had been very much knocked about. The trenches were filled with hundreds of cartridge cases, and bowls, bones, etc.—the remnants of hastily snatched meals. The mud walls were about two feet thick; and we found that the loopholes were so constructed that men could only fire straight in front of them. Here was the *El Tahira*, one of Gordon's steamers, a complete wreck on the bank, with the whole of its starboard side under water. It was a paddle-wheel boat about forty feet long, of an antique type. Along the bank were stored a number of cases of Dervish ammunition, including that above referred to belonging to Hicks.

CHAPTER X

THE CAPTURE OF DONGOLA

The advance resumed—Bivouacks at Beni and Zowerat—The "emergency" *gyassa*—The final move on Dongola—The water difficulty—Pursuit—A cartload of babies—Casualties.

WE left Hafir at five in the afternoon (the 21st), almost directly the fatigues were finished, and started to march south. Before starting there was another medical inspection, and forty more men were weeded out and conveyed the rest of the way to Dongola on *gyassas*. It is interesting to note how our numbers had gradually dwindled down; we left Cairo 914 strong, and of these only 520 marched into Dongola! The 394 are approximately accounted for, thus: Died (up to date), 44; sent down sick to Cairo, 120; left behind at Kosheh, 150; weeded out at Sadek and Hafir, 80; total, 394. These figures should point a moral to those who advocate sending on active service men selected from different corps, instead of sending a complete regiment. Those of us who, after standing so long a test, remained fit to march on Dongola, were probably as physically fit a body of men as was to be found anywhere in the service; and this remnant had the great moral advantage, which would not exist with mixed detachments, of being all one corps. Often we came across men who showed every inclination to "give up," but who nevertheless stuck to it when reminded that they had to keep up the credit of the regiment. This is the spirit, the *esprit de corps*, which demands every endeavour to foster and develop, but which the "composite" battalions, "universal" helmets, and such-like innovations tend to destroy.

We went on until 10 P.M., when the battalion was halted, and we were told to lie down on the ground and go to sleep. This bivouac was at a place called Beni, situated opposite the middle of Argo island. All this we have learnt since, for we saw nothing but a clump of palms; however, one name is as good as another in these parts.

The next morning (the 22nd) we were off again at a quarter to five, and reached Zowerat at 10 A.M. The camels had been left behind at Hafir, and our blankets had been stowed on an "emergency" *gyassa*, which we were told we should meet after a nine-mile march. "Emergency" forsooth!—it was not until we reached Zowerat, having had no food for nearly twenty-two hours, and having covered a distance of twenty-two miles, that we found the *gyassa* waiting for us with our rations. The "mile" Egyptian was always an object of derision, and a distance spoken of in that measurement was greeted by the men with language more descriptive than parliamentary.

THE CAPTURE OF DONGOLA

Zowerat is six miles north of Dongola, and all day we could see the steamers, which had left Hafir with us, throwing shell after shell into the ill-fated town. We spent the night there, and went to sleep again under the belief that we should have our work cut out for us on the morrow.

The 23rd of September was a day of some historical importance. It was memorable to Great Britain as that which made the Queen's reign the longest in English history, and memorable to Egypt as that which saw the Khedive's flag hoisted once again over a long-lost and valuable province.

We began the day in just the same way as we had before marching to attack Kerma. *Reveillé* was at 3.30 A.M.; but no bugle was sounded. It was certainly not required, for owing to the intense cold most of us were already awake, and walking about to get warm. It is extraordinary how different in temperature the nights are from the days in that part of the world. We fell in silently and marched to the rendezvous. At 4.30 A.M. the whole force was assembled, and we moved forward to put the crowning stroke to our labours of the past six months. The ground over which we passed was a great plain, which bore traces of former cultivation, but which the Dervish *régime* had converted into desert, like its surroundings. The troops started in quarter columns, but after marching a couple of hours we neared the enemy's position, and opened out into column of companies. The North Staffords were in the centre of the front line, supporting the guns. On our extreme left was the Nile, with the four gunboats, including the *Zafir*, which had been repaired at Kosheh, and had arrived at 3 A.M. this morning, just in time. Marching by the river, on our left, was the 1st Brigade, and on our right was the 2nd Brigade, each brigade having two Maxims on the inner flank. Next came the 3rd Brigade, and further away to the right, where the vast desert plain rose up into a ridge, were the Cavalry, Horse Artillery, and Camel Corps. Behind us was the 4th Brigade in reserve.

The men of the Maxim battery wore their red coats on this occasion, which lent additional colour to the scene. It was indeed one of the finest sights imaginable; the army of 15,000 whites, Arabs, and blacks, the largest force under an English general since the days of the Crimea; the whole tramping on and on, company after company, and regiment after regiment. We may reasonably conclude that the Dervishes were still more impressed with the sight, and we heartily regretted that our force was of such imposing dimensions, for we were half afraid that at the sight of our numbers the Dervishes would bolt.

The boats went on ahead, and about seven o'clock their guns told us they were engaging the enemy, who were as yet invisible to us. About half past eight we suddenly came in sight of a ridge of hills outside the village of Dame, a suburb of Dongola. This ridge was some way out in the desert, about two miles from the river, and here we saw the

The Final March on Dongola; September 23, 1896.
From the "Graphic."

Dervishes in hundreds, looking very conspicuous against the sky-line. The scouts came galloping in, and we deployed into fighting line and pushed on quicker. As we did so the enemy fell back; plucky and fanatical as they were, they were not disposed to be slaughtered wholesale just yet. It transpired later that they had had a council of war the previous night, in which some were for retiring and some for waiting to see if our strength was as great as it was represented to be. Bishara had gone off on a camel early in the morning, having got more than he bargained for at Hafir.

Meanwhile the gunboats were dropping shell after shell amongst the enemy, and as the latter had thought themselves out of range from the river this disconcerted them considerably. Their retreat became more and more precipitate, and they even threw away their arms and ammunition. The cavalry thereupon pushed forward after them; but the Dervishes only gave one opportunity for a charge, which was led by Captain Adams (Scots Greys). He charged the Dervish leader, they collided, and came to the ground, but neither were injured, and the Emir was taken prisoner. Eighteen Baggara were killed, and on our side one cavalry officer and six men were wounded.

On we went, and as we had to keep up with the Maxims on our flanks it was more a run than a march. Here and there was a Dervish who had fallen dead in his flight. Two we noticed especially, lying doubled up a couple of yards apart, who had been killed by the same shell, and one had all one side of his head shot off. Their white jibbas had made them a conspicuous object from the boats. Every now and then a Dervish would spring up from amongst some bushes where they had been concealed, and the scouts in front disposed of them. But most of the enemy had no fight left in them, in token of which they advanced holding up both hands over the head, and indicating by every means in their power that they were peaceably inclined. It was a ticklish moment for these fugitives, advancing alone towards us, and they probably did not feel at ease until they had finished their examination before the Intelligence Staff. Some of the Baggara who were routed out of the scrub resisted desperately; and as they persisted in assuring us that Allah was on their side, and by way of emphasis, attempted to demonstrate the fact on their hearers, there was no alternative but to put them *hors de combat*.

The mud huts of Dame were the scenes of several exciting incidents. A couple of our scouts, seeing a horse saddled and bridled waiting outside one of them, entered cautiously to see if they could discover the owner, when out darted a gigantic Dervish, sprang on the horse, and was away like the wind, with a defiant yell. He was too sanguine, however, for up went half a dozen rifles—ping, ping, and he was bowled over, falling backwards off his horse, which went careering madly up and down the line until it was eventually secured by one of the specia correspondents. For many of those who were not restrained by the rigid bond of discipline, these huts afforded excellent looting ground, and some valuable articles were picked up here. One man in particular had a narrow escape. He was foraging about on the look out for loot, and entered a hut; his servant remaining outside and holding his horse. Suddenly out of the hut rushed a Dervish, shot the man's servant dead on the spot, and rode off on the horse, leaving its owner flabbergasted.

By 11.30 A.M. the enemy were in full retreat, and we (Staffords) were absolutely done up. For seven hours we had been almost running, without a pause, trying to keep up with the guns. We had long since finished our water bottles, and there was a whole brigade between us and the Nile. At last we reached a pool of sluggish water, and nature could stand no more. The regiment halted and all filled their water bottles, whilst the black regiments marched on, looking as fit as when they started. But then their water bottles were half as large again as ours, and they were marching on their native soil and as much accustomed to desert marches as we were to macadamised roads. Another advantage which the Egyptians possessed was that they were specially trained to do without drink, which can hardly be said of English soldiers. However, British persistence had prevailed, and every man had kept on as long as there was any prospect of being required to fight.

We should be wasting this opportunity if we neglected to emphasise the urgent necessity of supplying our troops, especially those employed in the arduous desert work of such countries as Egypt, with a larger water bottle than that which is now issued to them. Some of the articles in the Press said that some arrangement should have been made for a supply of water to be carried on camels; but it is easy to be wise after the event, and no one knew when we started that we were in for a seven hours' desert march beyond the reach of water.

As we went on, numbers of wounded Dervishes were brought in, carried either by relief parties or on donkeys, and some of their wounds were simply ghastly. One poor fellow had his foot cut clean off by a cavalry sabre—but these are not pleasant details to dwell upon. We saw a number of banner poles lying about; but the banners had, in nearly every case, been stripped off by the enemy. After passing the Dervish quarter of Dongola, and the old European quarter, the whole force halted by the river, with the exception of the mounted troops, who continued the pursuit.

Before noon the Egyptian crescent and star floated on the walls of Dongola, being hoisted on the Mudir's house by Commander Colville, who had landed, unopposed, with a party from the boats. The Sirdar sent a telegram to her Majesty, announcing the capture of Dongola, and at the same time sending her the congratulations of the force on the length of her reign to-day.

THE CAPTURE OF DONGOLA

The pursuit of the flying Dervishes was maintained by the cavalry and camelry till late in the afternoon. They had taken to the desert with their wives and children, but finding the pursuit getting too close they evidently came to the conclusion that children were luxuries that might be dispensed with, so they deposited them on the sand; and these were later on collected and brought into camp in an artillery waggon!

The result of the day's work was, on our side, twenty-eight Egyptians wounded, including one cavalry officer. There were no casualties amongst the British troops. It is practically impossible to determine the number of Dervishes killed, as they carried off as many as they could with them, but the number was probably not very considerable. Eighteen Baggara were killed by Captain Adams' troop, and 900 prisoners were taken, as well as six guns, a large quantity of ammunition and grain, and three immense date "granaries." One of the prisoners was Hassan Nejumi, cousin of the Jaalin leader of that name who was defeated and killed at Toski.

The Staffords bivouacked, not by the river, but by a sluggish piece of backwater, which the principal medical officer, immediately on our arrival, declared to be absolutely poisonous; but the men were quite incapable of marching another yard, so they had to drink it or walk a mile. As it was, a good many drank a quantity of it, with the result that over twenty died of fever shortly afterwards.

Truly the question of water-supply is by far the most important of any in Soudan warfare.

When night came on, the "emergency" *gyassa* was found to have gone astray, so again no blankets were forthcoming. This, however, was a detail to which we were accustomed by this time, and was compensated for by the deep sense of relief which we felt at our labours being practically over.

CHAPTER XI

THE CLOSE OF THE DONGOLA CAMPAIGN

A look round Dongola—The Sirdar's review—Departure of the North Staffords for Cairo—"Where the dying camels lay"—Halfa again—A remarkable funeral—Cairo—British casualties—Subjugation of Dongola—The Sirdar's despatches—Egyptian casualties.

NEXT morning (24th) every one was awake two or three hours before daybreak, and we were all walking about, swinging our arms, to keep ourselves warm. We had no covering of any sort, and nothing between us and the freezing night air but a shirt and a thin Kharki suit. As we took off the coat and folded it over the havresack to form a pillow, we unwound our putties and twisted them round the body to supply its place. Necessity is indeed the mother of invention. It was a bitterly cold morning, and "lying in bed" had no attractions whatever. Never was *reveillé* more welcome than on our first morning in Dongola—and yet four hours later we were perspiring at every pore.

During the morning we made a tour of the place and expected to see a well-built town, but found little more than a heap of ruins. Of course this place, *the* Dongola as far as every one now-a-days is concerned, is *New* Dongola, Old Dongola being a collection of mud huts some sixty or seventy miles up stream, on the other bank.

New Dongola was founded by the Mamelukes, who built their camp here in 1798, after their expulsion from Egypt by the French, and the place is still known locally as "El Ordeh" (the camp). The English were last here on the 5th of July, 1885, and on the 17th of August Abdul Majid el Kalik, acting under Mohamed el Khair, with 3,000 Dervishes, took possession of the place. In a few years the whole province was utterly ruined. In 1889 the terrible famine which raged throughout the Soudan took off numbers of the inhabitants, and Nejumi's army, which passed through about that time, only to be defeated soon afterwards at Korti, entirely desolated the country.

The inhabitants of the province are called Danagla, and speak a dialect of their own; but every one understands Arabic, which is the prevailing language of the Soudan. These Danagla were once notorious slave drivers, but latterly they have experienced all the horrors of slavery themselves at the hands of the Khalifa's Baggara. Poor wretches! No wonder at their paroxysms of joy when they first saw our boats. They deserve a brief description; and we may begin by saying that the average Danagla woman is not a Venus—in fact, she is appallingly hideous. Her woolly hair, all dripping with grease, is parted down the middle, and hangs in straight curls on each side of the face. Her dress consists of a single piece of broadcloth wound round the body. The bigger children wear a *raht*—which is best described as a fringe of boot laces round the middle—and the smaller fry go about *puris naturalibus*. The men are a striking contrast to the women, and very different from the coarse-featured squint-eyed type of Arab so common in Egypt. Their physique is splendid and some of their faces, with their large dark eyes, with a peculiarly wild and mournful expression, were exceptionally handsome.

To return to Dongola; what we now saw was really three villages. Where the North Staffords were bivouacking was the site of the Royal Sussex camp ground in 1884, next to the European quarter, and several very respectable one-storied houses were here, situated in shady grounds. These buildings were once a post-office, barracks, and the residence of the *Mudir* (local governor). To-day they were sheltering some of the Egyptian regiments from the intense heat of the noon day sun. A mile north of this brought us to the quarter of Dongola inhabited by the Arabs in 1884. This was now nothing but a heap of ruins, the Dervishes having destroyed the place from sanitary considerations, for after a time these native huts become too filthy to live in. As we made our way through this once flourishing town, we were, to some extent, reminded of the silent streets of Pompeii. Only one human being did we see, and he was an Arab boy, in the ruined mosque, watching over the tomb of some Danagla notable. He told

L

us he had been put there by Slatin Pasha, who had visited the tomb of his deceased friend as soon as he reached Dongola. Passing northwards through these ruins, we came to the quarter up till now occupied by the Arabs, where certain correspondents and others had gone "a-looting," during our entry into the town. Next to the river was the Bayt-el-Mal, or Dervish treasury, where everything of value had been consigned, and was now being zealously watched by a Soudanese guard. The Sirdar and his staff were in an adjoining building, outside which were the gunboats, moored to the bank. Here, too, was the prison, where all the Dervish prisoners and refugees were brought as soon as they came in; and most of them looked very cheery, in spite of their changed fortune.

On the afternoon of the 24th the Sirdar reviewed the whole of his force, which, after marching past the saluting point, continued southwards for about five miles, and took up a fresh camping ground more desirably situated. The Sirdar addressed the North Staffords in a few words, saying how very satisfied he was with the battalion. Their endurance, he said, had been excellent, and their conduct perfect, and he was proud to have them under his command. His Highness the Khedive had gratefully appreciated their assistance in adding a new province to his country. The Sirdar concluded by saying that he was sorry he could not give them a better fight on the previous day, but he would always speak of the regiment with the highest eulogium. We felt that words like these, coming from such a thorough soldier as Sir Herbert Kitchener, went far to compensate us for our recent experiences.

In our new camping ground we were as much in a state of squalor as ever, except that the *gyassa* with the blankets and kits at last made its appearance, and we were able to eat with a fork off a tin plate, instead of with a pocket-knife out of the tin.

Of course, tents were absolutely unknown, except those of the Headquarters and Hospital, all the others being left at Kosheh, and the only shelter from the sun we ever had was such as we could improvise with blankets, bushes and rifles. The Dervish spears which we got here came in very useful for this purpose. Apropos of this, we read in the papers that "it was a pleasant sight to see the English officers giving up their tents to the wounded Dervishes, and sitting in the sun whilst the latter were having their wounds dressed." It made us angry to read such nonsense, but we were not by any means surprised, after the astounding statements we had already seen in print. Of course, the enemy were attended to in our hospital with as much care as our own wounded received, and the medical staff were always kept pretty busy.

One afternoon there was an auction of Dervish trophies — spears, guns, *jibbahs* (tunics), saddles, *nagara* (war-drums), cartridge-belts, &c. A bugle and drum fetched nearly £2 a-piece, and a much-worn saddle twenty-four shillings. An ordinary *jibbah* fetched a guinea, though the natives were selling them for four shillings. This reminds us of an escapade which occurred to a couple of subalterns in one of the regiments. Like every one else, they were walking about camp on the look-out for Dervish curios of any kind, when they saw a wounded Dervish being carried by his comrades towards the hospital, on an *angareeb* (native bedstead), with some guns lying next to him on the bed. Thinking the guns were Dervish (they were Remingtons, with which many Dervishes were armed) they offered money for them. To their surprise the Dervishes declined to accept payment, but pressed them to take the weapons gratis, which, needless to say, they did. No sooner had they put them away in their tent—or rather blanket-shelter—than up rushed half-a-dozen Egyptian soldiers, who loudly clamoured for their rifles! It turned out that the rifles belonged to a 'Gyppy escort, who had left their charge for a few minutes. Explanations ensued, and the rifles were promptly returned to their rightful owners, when suddenly the acting adjutant appeared on the scene, and—after the manner of the official "jack-in-office"—thought he would gain some "kudos" by bringing the matter to the Colonel's notice. The latter had himself been hard at work all day, getting loot in all directions on his own account, but thought it politic to support his *vade mecum*—and the subalterns came in for an unpleasant interview. The incident of the "wounded Dervish," when we got to hear of it, made us all more circumspect than ever in our "curio-hunting" expeditions.

There being no more work required of them, the Staffords were sent down to Cairo without delay; for, quite apart from the sickness with which the battalion was now imbued, it was highly inadvisable to keep British troops in the Soudan a day longer than was necessary. We left Dongola on the 26th of September in the gunboats, the men being towed in *gyassas*. Whereas our progress up stream had only averaged four miles an hour, we now went at the rate of twelve, which gives an idea of the strength of the current. We stopped at Kerma for a couple of hours to lay a cable across the river to Hafir, thereby putting Dongola in telegraphic communication with the rest of the world. We landed again at Hannek, whilst the two steamers went to see if they could pull the *El Teb* off the rock on which she had stuck before the battle of Hafir; but after trying in vain for several hours they had to abandon the attempt. We watched their efforts from the shore, where we had got under what shelter we could find from the broiling sun. Here we spent most of the day, living in an atmosphere of stench which it is impossible to describe, for the spot where we were halted was a few hundred yards to the leeward side of a large heap of dead camels. It made us feel perfectly sick, and brandy and tobacco were in great request. We marched north about five o'clock, the idea being that the boats should pass through the Third Cataract, lightened of our weight, and that we should join them again three miles down stream. But no touch was kept with the boats, so that at nightfall we had to lie down as we were, and sleep until daylight revealed their whereabouts. This time we had not even our havresacks for pillows, so used our helmets instead. At daybreak we marched another three miles, and then found the boats. This march was the most repulsive one of the whole campaign, for all the way the desert was strewn with the bodies of camels, and in one place alone we saw fourteen carcasses. It brought to our minds one of the songs of our camp-life at Gemai, of which the chorus (with apologies to Kipling) ran :

> "On the road to Dongolay,
> Where the dying camels lay,
> And the sun comes down like hell-fire,
> And grows hotter day by day."

Early on the 29th the boats landed us at Kosheh, and we entrained at once for Wady Halfa. There was not enough room in the guard's van for all the officers, so we subalterns had to sit in the trucks with our companies. The experience of being squashed in a truck with thirty men—with one leg wedged between tents and kit-bags, and the other hanging over the side of the truck—was unique, but certainly not enjoyable! After twelve hours under the blazing sun, we reached Halfa (where the detachment which we had left behind at Kosheh were awaiting our arrival), and never shall we forget the dinner they had ready for us at the "Club"—a separate plate for each course, a clean white tablecloth, and other luxuries of civilisation!

Next morning we were off early in the boats, reached Shellal on the 1st of October, and went round the First Cataract by rail to Assouan in thirty minutes—rather better than our desert march when on the way up the river. We spent four days at Assouan, to allow time for the many sick which we were bringing down with us (including Colville) to be transported round the Cataract without undue haste. We found time to pay a visit to Philae; and left Assouan on the 5th, in Cook's Nile steamers *Nefert-Ari* and *Tewfik*. The latter was almost entirely given over to the hospital patients, who were increasing in number daily. Now that all the excitement was over, a reaction had set in, and the fever, which had hitherto been flickering, broke out with increased vigour.

Soon after leaving Luxor, our Sergeant-major (Cunningham) died of enteric fever contracted at Dongola—after filling his office most capably throughout the campaign—and was buried at Assiut. We will describe the funeral, for it was quite the most remarkable of the many we have seen. Slowly and mournfully the procession started from the boat, until a native told them that the cemetery was five miles out in the desert, whereupon the pace quickened to one of startling rapidity. About halfway, the road became so bad that the hearse (which had been hired in the village) could go no farther, and the coffin had to be carried on the back of a camel! It was the weirdest sight imaginable—the chaplain in front, in his white surplice and scarlet hood, behind him the muffled drums, and then the coffin, covered with the Union Jack, balanced in mid-air.

On the 9th of October we reached Cairo, disembarked at Kasr-el-Nil, and found ourselves again at the Citadel. No less than 76 men were at once admitted to hospital, and of these over 20 (including Captain J. Rose[1]) never came out again alive. Altogether the (64th) North Staffords lost exactly 64 lives (15 at Halfa, 23 at Gemai, 22 at Cairo, and 4 elsewhere); whilst, of the Departmental Corps attached to them (R.E., A.P.D., A.S.C., M.S.C.) 11 lost their lives as the result of the campaign.

* * * * *

As a consequence of the fall of Dongola, every Dervish fled for his life from the province, the mounted natives cutting across the desert direct to Omdurman, *via* Debbeh, and the infantry making for Berber along the Nile—always keeping well out of range of the gunboats, which were prevented by the Fourth Cataract from pursuing them beyond Merawi. They were pursued for a considerable distance by our cavalry and camelry, who killed a good many, and took 900 prisoners. When our troops came up with them the Dervishes always fired at least one volley, which of course had to be returned with interest, so that they brought their heavy losses on themselves.

[1] For photograph see opposite page 166.

Debbeh was seized by Captain Oldfield, in the *Metemmeh*, who held it until relieved on the 3rd of October by the 2nd Brigade (12th and 13th Soudanese) under Major Macdonald. On their way this brigade took 120 prisoners. Korti was occupied by the 11th Battalion (Major Jackson) and a company of Camel Corps (Captain Wilkinson).

On the 7th of October the last of the Dervishes were driven out of the province, and a handful of troops on the *Abu Klea* hoisted the Egyptian flag at Merawi (Merowe), at the foot of the Fourth Cataract. A number of prisoners were taken here, including Osman Azrak's wife and son, and Merawi was soon afterwards occupied by the 2nd Battalion (Captain Shekleton) and 9th Battalion (Major Hackett Pain).

The Sirdar went south from Dongola to inspect the positions, and received the submission of all the principal Sheikhs, and of the Mahdi's relatives, the "Ashraf," whom the Khalifa was only too glad to get rid of, for much jealousy had existed between them ever since the Mahdi's death in 1885. The Khalifa thought an immediate advance on our part would take place, and hastily fortified Omdurman and his advanced posts at Abu Hamed and Abu Klea; but the Sirdar decided to remain at the three strategical points, Debbeh, Korti, and Merawi, for the present, and shortly afterwards nearly all the Egyptian army was in occupation of them. Lieutenant-Colonel Cochrane was appointed Commandant at Halfa, Lieutenant-Colonel Parsons, R.A., took over charge of Suakin, and the Indian contingent were all shipped back to their own country.

The Sirdar left for Cairo soon after the departure of the North Staffords. Before starting, he sent home his despatches on the expedition, in which nearly every officer employed with the Egyptian army was separately mentioned. It caused some comment at the time, these wholesale recommendations, but it was generally understood that these officers were mentioned (and rewarded) not *solely* for their services in the Dongola Expedition, but, in the majority of cases, for the important part they had played in bringing the Egyptian army to its present state of perfection. Of the British troops the Sirdar wrote: "I cannot speak too highly of the excellent conduct of the North Staffordshire battalion throughout the campaign . . . ," and spoke in similar terms of the Maxim battery, R.E., Indian contingent, and other details.

The Egyptian army had, during the six months' campaign, 47 killed and 122 wounded; 235 fell victims to cholera, and 126 died from fever and other causes. Thirty per cent. of its officers either died or were invalided.

PART III
THE OPERATIONS OF 1897

CHAPTER I

THE CAPTURE OF ABU HAMED

Peaceful administration—Revolt of the Jaalins—The new railway—General Hunter's advance—Capture of Abu Hamed—The Fourth and Fifth Cataracts—Occupation of Berber, Ed Damer, and Adarama—The river Atbara—The Suakin-Berber route re opened.

THE province of Dongola having been effectively freed, as we trust for ever, from the Dervish rule, the gentler arts of peace were now proceeded with, and effectual steps were made to morally reclaim the province. The whole country was placed under military law, with Major-General Hunter as Commandant. No man was better qualified for the post than he, and he now proved himself as able an administrator as he is a dashing soldier. In twelve months he brought order out of confusion, and gave to the inhabitants what is essential to the prosperity of every country : an established government ruling through the medium of just and impartial laws.

When the province was occupied, there were no police, there was no civil government, there was not even a house, except the mud huts of the villages. In a word, there was nothing but desolation. One of the first steps was to establish courts of justice, and a system of police. The Egyptian troops were employed in rebuilding the town of Dongola on its old site. The railway, the greatest of the civilising agents in Africa, was at once continued southward towards Kerma, whence steamboats have open water up to the Fourth Cataract (Merawi). The latter place now became the headquarters of the army. By the end of the year (1896) the line reached Kerma, which became the southern terminus.

Although Dongola was by far the most fertile province in Upper Nubia, it had been allowed by its wretched inhabitants to go almost out of cultivation, and to relapse into desert. They had preferred to remain idle rather than sow for the Dervish to reap, and had only cultivated little patches sufficient for their own use. Now, under the new order of things, they not only provide for their own use, but cultivate large areas for export purposes. The province has been opened to commerce, and will, no doubt, ere long regain its former importance as a commercial centre. Before its evacuation in 1885, a large trade was carried on, chiefly in gum, gold-dust, and ivory, which were exchanged for Manchester goods.

It is a remarkable fact that all the trade, which has been revived here by the British and Egyptians, is now exclusively in the hands of Greeks. The troops had scarcely time to encamp anywhere in the reconquered country, before a crowd of

THE CAPTURE OF ABU HAMED

Greeks arrived with their camels and goods, set up their stalls, and established their business. We are surprised that this subject has attracted so little attention. Here are the English and the Egyptians toiling with the sweat of their brows under the desert sun, and bringing hundreds of miles of territory back to civilisation and commerce, and here is England looking out all over the world for new markets where she can send her goods; whilst this excellent opportunity of developing her trade in Africa is allowed to quietly slip away, and the Greek coolly monopolises what the British and Egyptians have acquired!

The Egyptian Under-Secretary for Finance, Mr. Clinton Dawkins, was sent up to Dongola at the end of 1896 to enquire into and report upon the condition of the province. The salient facts of his report are interesting. He says:—

"A comparison of the information now collected with the statistics of 1885, the last year for which there exists statistics more or less trustworthy, illustrates the changes that have taken place in the province during the period of Dervish rule. These changes can be considered under the heads of population, cultivation, cattle, and trade, and it may be convenient to make specific recommendations under these heads as they are discussed in turn. The population in 1885 may be taken to have been 75,000. It now amounts to 56,426, of whom about 47,000 are natives of the province, the rest being Soudanese and Arabs. About 6,000 men are also reported to be absent from the province either in the Soudan or in Egypt, some 3,000 of whom are living in Wady Halfa, and the excess of the female over the male population is striking. The decrease of the population and the general impoverishment of the province date in a large part from 1888, when an unusually low Nile accompanied by cattle disease resulted in actual famine. The expedition of Wad-el-Nejumi in the following year was another calamity. Many of the inhabitants either followed, or were compelled to follow, the Dervish leader in his disastrous undertaking, and the cattle were swept up for his commissariat. The first requisite of the province is population and able-bodied population. The excess of female over male population has already been noticed, and the male population itself largely consists of old men and children. A few of the refugees to Egypt are returning, but the greater number hang back, and there is no rush among the Dongolawis as yet to resume possession of their old homes.

"If the statistics for 1885 are correct, and the 6,451 sakiehs (waterwheels) were in full working order each with a complement of three pairs of animals, there must have been some 36,000 cattle in the province at that time devoted exclusively to irrigation. The number of cattle is now under 12,000."

On the subjects of taxation and proprietary rights, Mr. Dawkins says :—

"The principal taxes under the old *régime* were the saquia tax and the date-palm tax. Minor taxes also existed, such as the pasturage tax, professional tax, Beduin tribute, house duty, and boat tax. The saquia and date tax amounted together to about £E52,000; the remaining taxes brought in about £E2,000. Some of these have been abolished in Egypt, and with a simple administration such as the province can support, it would be well to limit locally-collected taxation to as few articles as possible. The Dervishes took no dues beyond the saquia tax and date tax. It would be wise to follow their example for the present at any rate. . . . The Dervishes to some extent modified the Government system by attempting a rough classification of the areas served by a water-wheel according to their yield, instead of levying an invariable rate. In doing this they followed the general principle of Mohammedan taxation. They calculated the yield of each area, and took nominally a tenth in kind of each crop grown on it. Tax receipts were given, but the tenth was calculated in favour of the Dervish treasury. From inquiries made, it would appear that the money value of the tax they actually collected, not of the nominal tenth, works out at nearly sixty piastres per feddan, (acre) much the same as the former Government rate that existed immediately before the evacuation.

"The cultivators who remained on the arrival of the Dervishes in 1885 were not disturbed in the holdings, and occasional voluntary sales took place under Dervish rule. These sales should be recognised, and the titles of all individuals, or their heirs, now on the land whose names correspond with the entries in the old tax-registers, should be confirmed in possession."

The large decrease of the population since the abandonment of the Soudan, as shown by the above report, speaks volumes for the evil effects of the Khalifa's rule, especially when it is remembered that Dongola was the most remote of his provinces, and furthest removed from the oppression of the Baggara.

Whilst the pacification of Dongola was progressing, the Khalifa was uneasily contemplating the situation in Omdurman, which he took further measures to render in a state of defence. He gathered all his available forces in Omdurman, where they might have remained until the Sirdar's next forward movement, were it not for an unexpected occurrence—the revolt of the Jaalin tribe. This tribe, which had only served the Khalifa under the terrorism of the Baggara, now openly proclaimed their independence. The chief town of their district is Metemmeh, which they placed in a state of defence.

In June, 1897, the Khalifa sent out Mahmud, his nephew and principal general, with a large force, against the Jaalins, and on the 1st of July Mahmud arrived before Metemmeh. Abdulla Wad Saad, the Jaalin leader, had stationed the few men armed with rifles whom he had with him in the forts on the south side of the village, entrusting the defence of the other sides to the rest of his forces, armed only with swords and spears. The Dervishes directed their first attacks against the south front, from which they were, however, repulsed with loss.

M

They then turned their efforts against the north side of the village, where a portion of them eventually succeeded in effecting an entrance. Here Abdulla Wad Saad and his garrison were hemmed in and cut to pieces, the total loss of the Jaalins being estimated at 2,000 killed. The Dervishes, though greatly outnumbering their adversaries, also suffered severe loss. It is a great pity, as far as the unfortunate Jaalins are concerned, that they did not curb their impatience, and hold themselves in readiness until the Sirdar could have joined hands with them. The revolt of the Jaalins was only one of the many signs that the Dervish bubble had burst.

The Sirdar's policy of advancing slowly and deliberately, and at each step consolidating the power of the Egyptian Government, was continued in 1897, and the work of getting up stores to the posts along the Nile, on the Merawi-Debbeh frontier, was proceeded with.

From Abu Fatmeh (and Kerma, the railway terminus), just above the Third Cataract, an unbroken stretch of 220 miles of navigation extends through the entire province of Dongola, as far as its boundary, Debbeh, and on into the next province of Shagiyeh, up to Merawi, at the foot of the Fourth Cataract.

Debbeh formerly marked the boundary between the Dongolawi (or Danagla)—Nubians, the natives of Dongola—and the Shagiyeh Arabs. The latter, who came originally from Arabia, *via* the Red Sea,

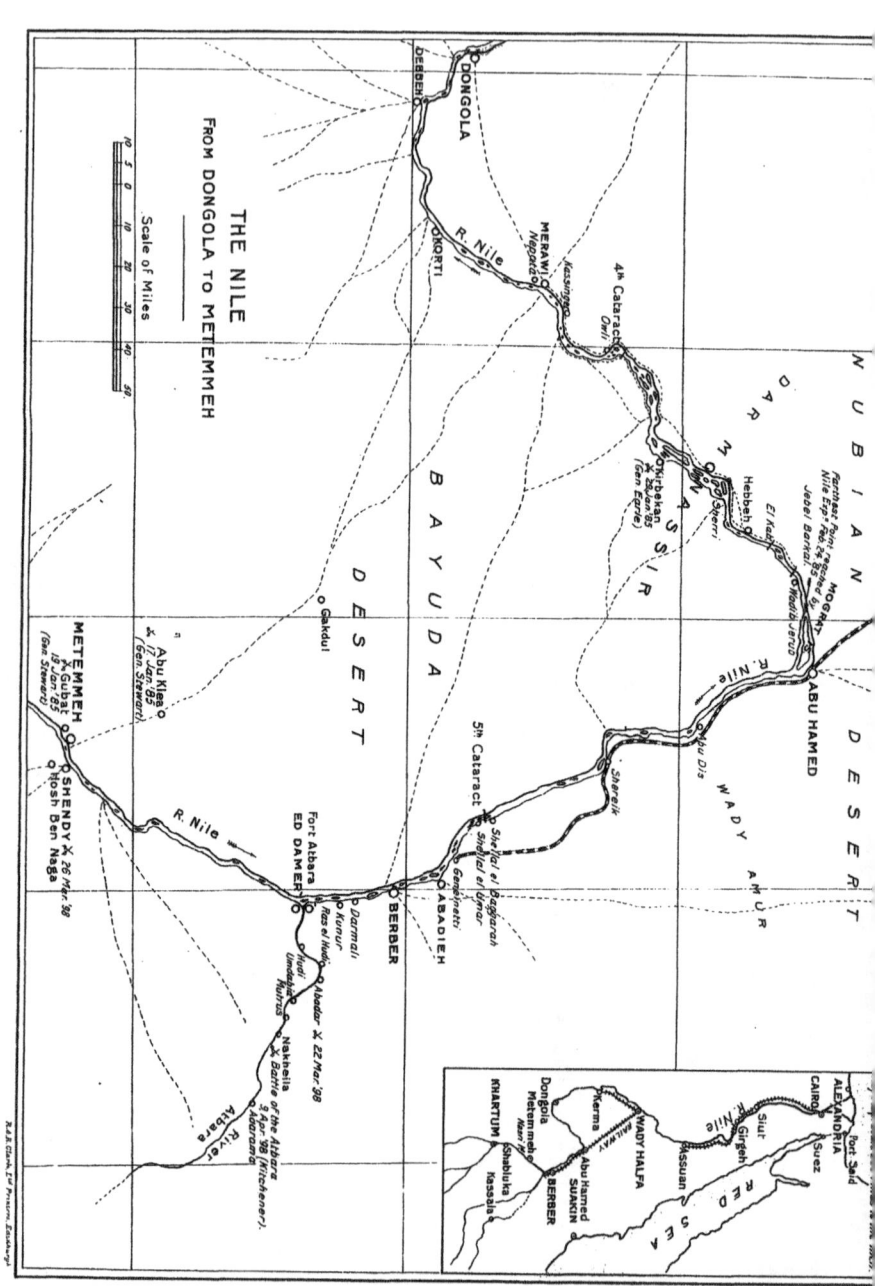

speak good Arabic; whilst the Dongolawi speak a Nubian dialect and indifferent Arabic. At Debbeh the palm-trees—so numerous in Dongola—begin to disappear, and the yellow sands of the desert fringe the water's edge. The islands, however, are numerous and well cultivated.

Ten miles below Merawi is a flat-topped hill, on the right bank, called Jebel Barkal. Here are the remains of the city of Nepata, with the ruins of temples and sphinxes, and a little way off in the desert are several pyramids in excellent preservation. Nepata was the capital of Ethiopia when Candace was Queen, and probably also when the Queen of Sheba ruled that country.

The next few months following the cessation of hostilities in 1896 were utilised by the Sirdar in constructing an entirely new railway, which, branching off across the desert from a point on the Nile near Wady Halfa, and passing rear the Murat Wells, was to terminate at Abu Hamed when that place should fall into our hands. The town at this time was occupied by a small advanced party of the enemy, but the construction of the line was allowed by the Dervishes to go on without let or hindrance. The rate of construction would be considered marvellous by engineers in this country; the line progressed, on an average, a mile a day, and on one record occasion as much as 5,000 yards were laid in twenty-four hours.

By the end of July, 1897, the railway had made such good progress that it was considered unsafe to bring the working parties nearer to Abu Hamed, until that place was in our possession. The time was ripe for another forward movement, but the Sirdar was determined to adhere to his old theory that "surprise is the element of success"; and no special preparations were made which could give the enemy's spies the slightest warning of a coming "rush."

On the 29th of July Major-General Hunter set out from Merawi with the 3rd, 9th, 10th, and 11th Regiments, and a proportion of artillery, to attack Abu Hamed. The route he took was the same as that by which General Brackenbury marched the River Column in 1885. Midway between Merawi and Abu Hamed lies the battlefield of Kirbekan, and the mudhut from which General Earle was shot is still in existence. Fifteen miles further on is Hebbeh, where, in September, 1884, Colonel Stewart and a number of refugees from Khartoum were wrecked in the ill-fated steamer, the *Abbas*, and treacherously murdered by Fakri Wad Oman, the sheikh of Hebbeh, who had offered them assistance. A portion of the hull, the boiler, and other parts were found by Hunter's force on the scene of the tragic occurrence. At El Kab two massive old castles were passed, one on each side of the river, relics of an old-world civilisation.

Hunter proceeded by rapid marches, and the force arrived at Wadib Gerub, within striking distance of the enemy, on the night of the 6th of August. The distance of 132 miles, over a very rough road, being covered in eight days. At dawn on the morning of the 7th, they advanced to attack the enemy's position. The country was very open, and when within a few miles of the town they were sighted by the Dervish sentries in the watch-towers, which gave the enemy time to man their *sangars* (light stone fortifications) and the crests of the small hills in the neighbourhood.

As the force drew nearer—about 5.30 A.M.—it was seen that the enemy occupied a strong entrenched position, in the front of and within the walls of the town; and General Hunter deployed his troops for the attack. The 11th Soudanese were on the right, then the 3rd Regiment, then the 9th Soudanese, and the 10th Soudanese were on the left. The guns accompanied the 11th Regiment. As soon as the deployment was completed, Hunter gave the signal for a general advance.

The column first carried the high ground overlooking the village. The houses were held by a force of 1,000 Dervishes, of which 150 were horsemen and 500 riflemen. An advance was then made on the village, and a stubborn house-to-house fight followed. In several instances the artillery were obliged to advance before it was possible to carry a position. The village of Abu Hamed is a network of houses, crowded together, and separated only by twisting narrow alleys. Most of the fighting was at the point of the bayonet, the Dervishes repeatedly charging in the narrow lanes and streets. When the Dervish horsemen had lost about half their number, the remainder fled, being the first of the enemy to do so. They were followed by about 100 infantry, and these were all of the garrison that escaped.

The Dervish commander, Mahomed Zein, was made prisoner. One well-known Dervish Emir stubbornly defended himself with some followers in a strongly fortified house, and was only killed eventually when the building was destroyed by artillery fire. A large number of prisoners were taken, including a number of Soudanese blacks, who, with Mahomed Zein, were sent to Merawi. A quantity of arms, standards, camels, horses, and property was also captured.

On our side, 2 British officers and 21 men (native) were killed, and 3 Egyptian officers and 61 men wounded. Of these casualties, the 10th Soudanese alone lost 2 British officers and 14 men killed, and 34 men wounded.

Major Sidney[1] fell mortally wounded whilst charging across the open ground, closely followed by his men, and died five minutes later. Lieutenant FitzClarence[2] was also shot at the same time, through the heart, when within forty yards of the

---

[1] Major H. M. Sidney was Brevet-Major in the Cornwall Light Infantry. He had seen considerable service in the Soudan, having served in the Nile Expedition, 1884—5, and had taken part in all the operations in the River Column under General Earle. He was present at the capture of Tokar, in 1890, and received his brevet promotion after the Dongola Expedition.

[2] Lieutenant Edward FitzClarence, Dorsetshire Regiment, served in the Dongola Campaign with the 10th Soudanese. He was a great grandson of William IV.

LIEUT. E. FITZCLARENCE,
Dorsetshire Regiment (E.A.).
Killed at Abu Hamed, Aug. 7th, 1897.
From "Black and White."

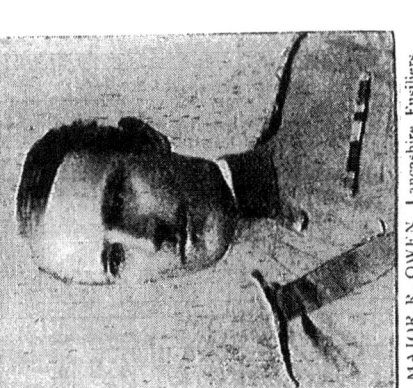

MAJOR R. OWEN, Lancashire Fusiliers.
Died at Ambogol Wells, July, 1896.

CAPTAIN J. ROSE,
North Staffordshire Regiment. Died at Cairo, October, 1896.

BREVET-MAJOR H. M. SIDNEY,
D.C.L.I. (E.A.).
Killed at Abu Hamed, Aug. 7th, 1897.
From "Black and White."

[*To face p.* 166.

enemy's walls. Three Egyptian officers received gunshot wounds of a severe nature. The loss of Sidney and FitzClarence came as a blow to the whole Egyptian army and to all connected with it. Major Sidney was conspicuous for his military ability, and was positively worshipped by his men of the 10th Battalion. Poor FitzClarence was as keen a soldier as ever lived. When, in March, he started for the front (from Cairo, where he had been on leave) he told the writer, who went to wish him good-bye, that he was half afraid he wouldn't come in for the next big fight, as he would probably be stationed at Assouan. But Fate ruled otherwise!

In the assault of the town, the discipline of the troops was especially marked; and the Egyptians and Soudanese seemed to vie with each other as to who could show the greatest steadiness and dash. The march from Merawi to Abu Hamed was through difficult and barren country, and had General Hunter's troops been defeated, there would have been few left to return.

Whilst Hunter was marching on Abu Hamed, a strong patrol of the Camel Corps was sent from Merawi, under Brevet-Major Tudway, to Gakdul, to hold in check the Dervish force at Metemmeh; and at the same time the gunboats were sent across the the Fourth Cataract, or rather the fourth series of cataracts, which extend over sixty miles of river. The Nile is here more obstructed than in any other portion of its course, and the river is filled with masses of rock of every shape and size. Sir William Butler, who in the Nile Expedition of 1885 superintended the boat service over these rapids, thus describes this region :—

"No wilder scene can be imagined than this waste called Dar Monassir. For miles together there is no vestige of vegetation; silence is broken only by the noise of the foaming waters; the rocks left bare by the subsiding current, and black and polished by sand and sun; whenever it is possible to climb one of the rugged hills on either shore, the eye ranges only over a wilder area of desolation, burnt and cindery rocks rise up in every direction, from amid wastes of sand. At times the channels of the river are so sunken beneath the level of the granite wilderness around, that they are perfectly hidden from sight at only a short distance from the shore. At intervals the islands disappear, the river flows gently in a single stream between shores of black granite, as though its waters were resting between the cataract behind and the next in front; but these bits of comparatively smooth water are few, and taking the entire stream from the Fourth Cataract at Owli to the head of the island of Sherri, a distance of about sixty miles of water, there cannot be less than twenty-five miles of actual cataract. Up to a recent period, in fact up to the boat expedition of 1884—5, little or nothing was known about these cataracts of Monassir. This was owing to the fact that they had always been avoided by travellers passing between Egypt and the Soudan; the caravans invariably quitting the Nile at Korti, and striking it again across the Bayouda at Metemmeh or Berber."

Between Abu Hamed and Berber, a distance of 130 miles, there are only two cataracts, the Shellal el Baggarah ("The Rapid of the Cows") and the Shellal el Umar ("The Rapid of the Asses"). The latter is known as the Fifth Cataract.

The passage of the gunboats over the Fourth Cataract was superintended by Captain Colin Keppel, R.N., assisted by Lieutenants Hood and Beatty, R.N., and Captains Fitton, Stanton, and Bainbridge (Egyptian army). With the exception of the *El Teb*, which capsized, all the gunboats

THE CAPTURE OF ABU HAMED

were brought to Abu Hamed by the 29th of August, and by the first week in September all the sailing vessels had been successfully hauled through the rapids, under the superintendence of Major Pink (Egyptian army).

Shortly after the capture of Abu Hamed, the Sirdar heard that Berber was being evacuated by the Dervishes, and a party of Friendlies, under Ahmed Bey Khalifa, who were sent on ahead, succeeded in entering that town unopposed, being followed a few days afterwards (6th of September) by the steamers. On the same day (6th) two gunboats were despatched to Ed Damer, a place of considerable strategical value, a few miles beyond the junction of the Nile and Atbara. Here the Emir Zeki had arrived with a Dervish force, on his retreat from Berber. Some shots were exchanged, and Zeki retired inland, leaving behind fourteen large boats laden with grain, which were captured by the gunboats, and taken to Berber. On the 13th of September General Hunter entered Berber with the greater part of the Egyptian army.

Ed Damer was occupied, a fort was erected at the junction of the two rivers called Fort Atbara, and half a battalion, under Lieutenant Wolseley (Cheshire Regiment, Egyptian army) was sent to hold the place. Until the desert railway could be brought to Abu Hamed, the garrisons holding that place and Berber were dependent entirely for their food supply on the transport from Merawi; and all stores had to be carried on camels from Kassinger, at the foot of the Fourth Cataract, a distance of 270 miles.

The rapid advance of General Hunter's force on Abu Hamed and Berber caused great consternation to Osman Digna, who had taken up a position at Adarama, about ninety miles from Ed Damer, with 5,000 men. Besides the latter there were more than that number of women, double the number of children, and immense drives of cattle, camels, goats and sheep. The approach of the Egyptian army, added to the increasing hostility of the surrounding tribes, made Osman think it was time to retire, and on the 23rd of September he began his departure, crossing the river at Guidi. He had only one large boat and six "dug-outs"—trunks of trees hollowed out—and the passage of the river took him a whole month. His followers and the camels were taken across in the boats and on roughly constructed rafts, and the cattle by means of bladders fastened under the throat. Osman completed his tedious undertaking only two days before General Hunter entered Adarama.

It had been Hunter's desire to push on to Adarama at once with his brigade, and take Osman at a disadvantage, but the transport and supplies had not arrived from Abu Hamed, so the opportunity was lost; and it was not until the 23rd of October that the column left Berber, taking with them twelve days' forage and rations. His force numbered only 400, though it was originally intended to make it 1,000 strong—and consisted of the 11th Soudanese under Major Jackson), two guns (under Captain Peake, R.A.), and detachments of Camel Corps and Transport.

On the 29th of October the column reached Adarama, and found the place deserted, and the surrounding country desolate. All the boats used by Osman Digna had been sunk, and the "dug-outs" smashed. No sign of the recent Dervish occupation, other than the abandoned *angareebs* (bedsteads) was visible. A convoy of stores was captured, which had been smuggled through from Sinkat, and had been intended for the personal use of Osman and his household. This acquisition came in useful for feeding the 5,000 starving women and children of the unfortunate Jaalin tribe, in Berber. When, in the preceding July, the men of this tribe were ruthlessly put to the sword by the Dervishes, at Metemmeh, all the girls were carried off for the Baggaras' harems, and the old women and children—when not thrown into the river—had been left to starve.

The country around the Atbara river was found to be very fertile and capable of growing almost anything, so that with proper husbandry and a peaceful government it might be made a flourishing province. The climate is excellent, though a comparatively heavy rainfall descends in this region. The water of the Atbara is clear and bright, and differs altogether from the muddy, brown waters of the Nile.

Hunter's troops completely scoured the country towards Goz Regeb, cleared it of a few stray Dervishes, burnt Adarama on the 2nd of November, and returned to Berber on the 9th of November, the infantry on the return journey marching 214 miles in eighteen days. The Eastern Soudan was now practically cleared, and the Suakin-Berber route was re-opened for traffic. The Italians still held Kassala, and arrangements were in progress for transferring that place to the Egyptians. An armed party under Major Sparkes (4th Battalion, Egyptian army) crossed the desert from Suakin to Berber, being the first Europeans to cross since the loss of the Soudan. Half a dozen war correspondents also crossed, and, as a result of their journey, seemed convinced that a railway from Suakin to Berber would be impracticable; for in consequence of the very rough and mountainous district which the line would have to traverse, the undertaking, they said, would never pay for the outlay.

CHAPTER II

THE RECONNAISSANCES OF METEMMEH

Distribution of the Dervish force—Mahmud—Dissensions amongst the Emirs—The first reconnaissance—Shendy—Metemmeh—The second reconnaissance—Gunboats reach the Sixth Cataract—Dervish raids near Berber and Ed Damer—The railway completed to Abu Hamed.

IN October the Dervishes were distributed as follows:—Their main body was still concentrated round the Khalifa at Omdurman; 10,000 men were at Metemmeh and Shendy under Mahmud, assisted by Zeki, who had been driven out of Berber and Ed Damer; Ahmed Fedl, from Gedaref, was at Shabluka (Sixth Cataract); and—at the end of the month, after evacuating Adarama—the irrepressible Osman Digna was, with a few hundred men, at Abu Delek, in the desert, midway between Omdurman and Kassala.

As soon as the Sirdar's forward movement was made known to the Khalifa, the latter seems to have concluded that the Egyptians were about to make an immediate advance on Omdurman. He remembered the fate of Wad el Nejumi, and knowing well —no one better—the immense difficulties of transport in moving a large body along the Nile valley, and having, in fact, no food for the purpose, he decided to allow the Egyptian troops to undertake the advance unopposed, except by natural obstacles. He grudged every assistance to Mahmud, being determined to husband his strength for the "Armageddon" at Omdurman. Whether he imagined it good tactics to permit the Sirdar to leisurely complete all his arrangements and to take all the posts he desired, and only to resist him at Metemmeh and Omdurman—or whether he meant to make sure of a large following with which to retire to Kordofan or Darfur— it is impossible to conjecture; but this is certain, that up to this time no really determined effort had been made by the Khalifa to resist the Egyptian advance.

Mahmud was a young man of fine physique; but latterly he had been giving himself up to excesses, and had been drinking heavily. He had recently raided—or had permitted his men to raid—Osman Digna's district, and had carried off a number of women; with the result that a bitter feud now existed between these Dervish Emirs, and Osman refused to have anything to do with Mahmud, and dared not go near Metemmeh. Mahmud, from what can be ascertained, used every artifice to induce the Khalifa to send him supplies to enable him to move forward, but in vain. On the other hand, the Khalifa endeavoured to persuade Mahmud to fall back with his large force to Omdurman, but this did not suit Mahmud's ardent nature, and he decided to remain where he was. Thus it will be seen that a singular lack of cohesion and unanimity had sprung up amongst the Dervish leaders—news of which reached the Sirdar in due course, to the latter's very considerable satisfaction.

Metemmeh was fortified, but it was well-known to Colonel Wingate (Director of Intelligence) that its occupants were not in a position to hold out for any length of time, owing to the scarcity of food. The Khalifa had, up to now (October), sent supplies from Omdurman to Metemmeh by boat, as being the easier and quicker route: but the Sirdar now decided to send up the gunboats and capture the enemy's *nuggars* and *gyassas*.

On the 15th of October the three gunboats *Zafir*, *Fatteh*, and *Nazir* steamed away from Berber to reconnoitre the enemy's position at Metemmeh. We have already described the *Zafir*.[1] The two others arrived from England soon after the capture of Dongola, and were built on exactly the same pattern as the first-named. The *Zafir* was now commanded by Captain Colin Keppel, R.N. (who commanded the flotilla), whilst the *Nazir* and *Fatteh* were under Lieutenants Hood, R.N., and Beatty, R.N., respectively. In addition to its small native crew and a couple of European engineers, each boat on the present occasion carried fifty men of the 9th Soudanese, and a couple of sergeants of the Royal Marine Artillery.

Part II. page 107.

Soon after daybreak, on the 16th, the steamers arrived a few miles north of Shendy without having met with any opposition. They now saw the first signs of the enemy. Two saddled horses were grazing near the water's edge, and their owners were sleeping so soundly on the bank that the boats had quietly steamed up before they woke. That they looked aghast, when, with their waking eyes, they saw the three steamers in front of them, is but natural; but the Maxim quickly brought them to their senses, and killed one, whilst the other escaped into the bush.

Shendy, which lies on the right bank of the Nile, was passed, but was found to be in ruins. A few shots were fired from the boats, but evoked no response. Metemmeh was sighted half an hour afterwards. It is a large mud-built city of the ordinary type, though perhaps not so straggling as the usual Soudanese town. It stands a thousand yards from the river, and the approach to it was guarded by seven substantial mud forts, with immensely thick solid walls, which were situated close to the river's edge, and extended over a couple of miles.

"Approaching the position, but keeping, of necessity, outside the islands and close to the further bank, the flagship gave the signal to form and advance in quarter line, the *Zafir* leading with the *Nazir* following. Several Baggara horsemen could be seen riding furiously from fort to fort, and apparently stimulating and giving final orders to the defenders. The ships from a range of nearly 4,000 yards now opened fire simultaneously on the two nearest works, and soon got the range of these fortifications to a nicety, the Marine Artillery sergeants and the native gunners making splendid practice. A stream of bullets turned on from the Maxim caught two of the Baggara horsemen, who were galloping about the plain, while the rest scampered off to the hills precipitately. These Baggara were the only men to be seen in range, though on the distant ridge a Dervish army had congregated from its camp in the rear to watch the operations. The Dervish gunners replied immediately the ships opened fire, but owing to the inferiority of their old brass weapons their shells fell very short, and, though they burst well enough, the only ones that travelled as far as the ships were practically ricochets or those of a high angle fire, which went over the gunboats without doing much damage. One shell, however, fell on the *Zafir*, and, severing a water-pipe and passing through the deck, mortally wounded a Soudanese. A shrapnel also burst over the *Fatteh*, and a 7 lb. common shell tore through the awning and smashed the pole supporting it. After about an hour's long-range fire the fleet moved up opposite to the position, pouring shell, shrapnel, and double shell into any place in which the enemy was supposed to be. The effect of the double 12-pounder shells bursting in the little forts must have been terrific, and immense damage must have been done to the defenders, whose fire now had slackened off and had become very desultory. As the gunboats passed the forts it was discovered that the embrasures of these erections only commanded the northern approach, and that when once in the rear of a fort the vessels enjoyed an immunity from its fire. This discovery simplified matters considerably. While the gunboats were hugging the east bank a sharp look-out was fortunately kept along it for any traces of the enemy, for when approaching the vicinity of some mimosa scrub and bushes a sharp fire from some twenty or thirty rifles was opened on the vessels from the short range of about 100 yards. No one on board was hit, though the bullets rattled about the ship, and narrow escapes were many. A couple of volleys and a raking Maxim fire from the *Fatteh* at once silenced these sharpshooters, who jumped up and fled into the thick scrub, leaving many of their number dead behind them. The three vessels now steamed slowly past the town, and then, slewing round, retired down stream, still shelling the enemy's position. At about half-past two o'clock fire ceased, and the gunboats were returning down the river, when, rounding a slight bend, they came across a number of Dervishes busily engaged in unloading some half-dozen *nuggars* which contained horses, donkeys, many household effects, grain, and scents. Some of the Dervishes, in their anxiety to save as much of their goods as possible, miscalculated the pace at which gunboats travel and stayed too long, three of them being caught by the Maxim as they galloped off into the desert. The gunboats proceeded with the *nuggars* to an island six miles north of Metemmeh, and there remained for the night.

"On the morning of the 17th of October the gunboats started off again at a little after four o'clock so as to get into position opposite Metemmeh before daylight, and on their arrival at once opened fire on the forts, the Dervish guns, of which there were nine now instead of only seven, replying without a moment's hesitation. It seems that on the previous day Mahmud, fearing a land attack from the direction of the Gakdul Wells, had erected batteries in the desert to protect that flank, and several guns had been withdrawn from these during the night to strengthen the forts along the river. Each of the two advanced forts now carried two guns. The Dervish fire was infinitely more accurate than on the previous day, but the shells still fell short, for the vessels took care to keep out of their range, where they themselves could shell the forts unmercifully. Numbers of those making up the large Dervish gathering, which stretched away for miles, were mounted, and magnificent-looking men they were. A few shrapnel shells fired at a venture from the boats came quite unexpectedly among them, and caused them to retire to the rear of the hills, behind which, in the desert, they had their fighting camp. The same tactics as on the previous day were carried out by the gunboats, and after a few hours' shelling of the position Captain Keppel, considering his reconnaissance complete, gave the signal to withdraw, and retire down the river. The forts, instead of slackening off their fire as on the previous day, now redoubled their energies, and continued firing shell after shell in the most exultant but needless manner long after the vessels had passed beyond their range. Then an extraordinary scene occurred. The whole host—horse, camel, spear, and rifle men—some 10,000 strong, advanced amid a cloud of dust across the ridge of hills, shouting, singing, and waving their banners in exultation over their imagined victory. They were led by a splendidly-built man, attired in a white quilted jibba and mounted on a snow-white Arab, and it was believed at first that he must have been Mahmud himself. However, spies ascertained that it was the Emir Ali Senusi who was in command of the assembled force, and that Mahmud, with another army, was some three miles away in the desert.

"The Egyptian loss was one man wounded, who eventually died. The Dervish loss was never accurately known, but it must have been close on 1,000, counting killed and wounded. Two guns were destroyed, and three dismounted. The gunboats fired some 653 shells and several thousand rounds of Maxim cartridge. The Dervish artillery was commanded by Ahmed Fudel, a celebrated leader who fought in the battle against the Abyssinians when King John met his death, and who had commanded the Khalifa's artillery against the Italians at Kassala."[1]

The gunboats returned at once to Berber, having successfully accomplished their purpose.

The first reconnaissance to Metemmeh had been so satisfactory that the Sirdar determined to follow it up with a second. Accordingly, on the 1st of November, the boats *Zafir* (Keppel), *Nazir* (Hood), and *Metemmeh* (Keith-Falconer), started once more up the river. Each boat carried 50 men of the 3rd battalion, and Major Stuart-Wortley[2] accompanied the Naval Commandant as Staff Officer. The flotilla was reinforced on its way up by the *Fatteh* (Beatty), which had been patrolling the Atbara river. The fleet continued up the Nile until it reached a small island a few miles from its destination, where it lay for the night. Captain Keppel intended to arrive at Metemmeh by daybreak, in order that he might reach the Sixth Cataract, and return, before the night.

When the fleet came within sight of Metemmeh there was great activity and excitement amongst the Dervishes. The hills soon became thronged with infantry, cavalry, and camelry, which was apparently intended as a show of strength, and a warning of what was to be expected if there was any attempt to land.

The gunboats poured a terrific fire into the forts,

[1] We are indebted to the *Morning Post* for the above graphic account.
[2] See page 19.

to which three had been added since the last reconnaissance. The reply, however, was poor and ill-directed, most of the missiles falling into the river. After shelling the place for some time, the gunboats put on extra steam and moved rapidly up the river towards the Sixth Cataract. As they cleared Metemmeh the fleet entirely destroyed a large camp, pitched in a sheltered khor (valley) behind a ridge, which proved to be the camp, or "dem," of Zeki. The fleet reached Shabluka, on the right bank of the Sixth Cataract, and the whole of the country above Metemmeh was observed to be deserted—a certain sign of the Dervishes' presence. There was not a boat or craft of any kind on the river, the Dervishes had moved them for safety above the cataract.

On their return journey the boats came in for a warm reception as they passed the enemy's forts, but, with the exception of three men who were wounded by the bursting of a shrapnel shell, no damage or loss was sustained, and they returned to Berber well satisfied with the result of their mission.

The Khalifa's refusal to send supplies to Metemmeh placed Mahmud's garrison in sore straits. The famishing Dervishes hunted up all the hidden stores of the unfortunate Jaalins, which the latter had left there, and then they turned to their old practice of raiding. A party, numbering about 1,000, set out to raid twenty villages in the vicinity of Berber; a bold enterprise, considering the presence of a strong force of Egyptian troops at Berber and

Ed Damer. These desperados, by means of a night march, succeeded in evading the patrolling gunboats; and not expecting to meet with any serious opposition, and relying on the alarm which their surprise visit would create, they decided to separate into bodies of a couple of hundred and attack five villages simultaneously. But the only alarm created was in their own breasts, for they discovered to their cost that the villagers had been armed with Remingtons, and had been trained to use them with such good effect that the Dervishes were forced to beat a hasty retreat.

One party was observed in the act of raiding on the left bank, by Lieutenant Hood, in the *Nazir*, whilst patrolling south of Ed Damer. Hood immediately landed fourteen men of the 10th Soudanese, three native gunners, and a sergeant of Marine Artillery, who were charged by sixty Dervish horsemen, but the latter were repulsed with the loss of four killed and one wounded. The party then returned to the boat, which pursued the enemy as they rode along the river, and inflicted further loss on them with shrapnel.

On the 31st of October the desert railway from Wady Halfa was opened to Abu Hamed; and the Egyptian Government decided to continue the line to Berber, for which purpose they voted £200,000. The work was continued without delay, for the extension would do much to improve the commissariat arrangements.

CHAPTER III

THE ACQUISITION OF KASSALA

Kassala and the Italians—Arrival of Colonel Parsons and Egyptian troops—Transfer of the native garrison—Aroba seizes El Fasher—Assabala besieges Osobri—Gallantry of the defenders—The formal cession.

THE last important step during the year 1897 was the re-occupation of Kassala by Egypt. This town was constructed by the Egyptian Government in 1840, to protect the province of Taka from the attacks of the Abyssinians, and was held until July, 1885, when, after a siege lasting nearly two years, it succumbed to the attacks of Osman Digna. Nine years afterwards (1894) it was surprised and taken by the unfortunate Italian general, Baratieri, and it had since remained in the possession of Italy. The town is of considerable strategic importance, as being one of the keys to Khartoum,

When, in April, 1891, the Italians obtained consent from Egypt to occupy Kassala, they undertook to deliver the town over to Egypt whenever Egyptian suzerainty should be re-established in the Soudan. Hence the negotiations which now took place between the Egyptian and Italian Governments, which resulted in their mutual agreement that Kassala should be formally handed over to Egypt on the 25th of December, 1897.

On the 29th of November, Colonel Parsons, with Captain Wilkinson and 850 native officers and men of the Egyptian Army arrived at Massowah, the port on the Red Sea, whence, after being reviewed by the Sirdar, they proceeded by easy stages to Kassala.

Kassala was reached on the 18th of December, Colonel Parsons being accompanied during the latter part of the journey by Colonel Count Samincatelli, the Italian Governor of the military zone of Keren, which includes Kassala. The Egyptian troops presented a very smart, soldierly appearance. They had marched from Massowah to Kassala[1] at the rate of fifteen miles a day, which was not a bad performance, by any means, considering the camels and heavy baggage which accompanied them. Only four men out of the whole battalion had "gone sick." The little force marched across the plain playing Italian airs, and were met by Major de Bernardis, the Governor of Kassala, and other officers of the garrison; and a guard of honour composed of native infantry was found drawn up, to receive them. A salute of twenty-one guns was fired, and the Egyptian flag was hoisted on the walls next to the Italian. The Egyptian troops encamped a mile from the fort until the 25th, the date appointed for the formal cession.

The final arrangements were now made for

---

[1] Pronounced Kass'-ala.

taking over the town. It can easily be understood that the transfer of a fortress, and native troops of the garrison, from one Power to another, be they never so friendly, requires considerable tact and delicacy. The native battalion readily consented to transfer their allegiance to the Khedive, but the corps of Arab Irregulars (chiefly of the Hadendowa tribe) were rather reluctant to do so, until they were satisfied that their position under the new *régime* would be in no way inferior, and that they would be permitted to wear the medals which they had earned whilst fighting under the Italian flag. Altogether 700 men were taken over, and added to the Egyptian Army, the corps being known as the "Ortah Wadanieh."

On the 20th of December, Colonel Parsons did a very tactful stroke of business. He paraded these newly-acquired troops, and to their amazement and immense delight, ordered them to make an attack on El Fasher and Osobri, two Dervish posts on the Atbara river, about fifty miles from Kassala. Aroda, a chief of the Beni Amir tribe of Arabs, who had formerly been a cavalry leader under Osman Digna, was to attack El Fasher with 300 regulars and 100 irregulars, whilst Assabala, a chief of the Shukrieh Arabs, was directed to attack Osobri with 120 regulars and 60 irregulars. Colonel Parson's orders occasioned the most tremendous excitement amongst the men concerned, and they rushed off, shouting and gesticulating, to their dusky spouses to tell them of their good fortune.

Later in the day, as the sun was setting, the stalwart and enthusiastic Arabs started on their purpose across the desert. Aroda attacked El Fasher at daybreak on the 22nd, with complete success. Of 200 who composed the Dervish garrison, 19—including three Emirs—were killed, and the rest took to flight. Assabala's task was not disposed of quite so easily. He arrived before Osobri at daybreak on the 22nd, took the occupants completely by surprise, and captured 23 camels and 70 head of cattle; but the 60 Dervish riflemen, forming the garrison, sought refuge in the fortress, and made a most heroic resistance, worthy of a better cause. For six days they held out against thirst and hunger, waiting for help from their comrades at Gedaref—120 miles distant—whilst Assabala invested the fortress as well as could be expected with his 180 men.

Desperate sorties were repeatedly made, but were repulsed by the fierce Arabs forming the investment. The fall of Osobri, on the 27th and 28th of December, has been well described by the war correspondent of the *Times*, and his account shows the reckless bravery of the Dervishes. He says: "The moon had already set, when, at about 10 o'clock, it being very dark, a body of 50 Dervishes, carrying food and water with them, who had come from Safir, made a most gallant effort to relieve the garrison. Assabala's force being insufficient to complete the investing cordon, the fort was surrounded by a ring of isolated companies, with a considerable interval separating the one from the other. Thus, when the Dervishes engaged one of these companies, it was not possible for Assabala to send supports, as by doing so he would have left a broad space open for the escape of the garrison. The men of this particular company exhausted all their ammunition in repelling the enemy, and killed, according to the first accounts that reached us, 20 out of the 50, but these numbers are probably exaggerated. They then fell back on the next company in order to procure ammunition, and the relieving Dervishes, promptly taking advantage of the opportunity, rushed through the gap thus left in the cordon, passed through the gate which was opened to them, and joined their comrades in the fort, when the gate was once more quickly closed. It was certainly a most heroic performance on the part of these 50, for, in view of all the circumstances, they were going to almost certain death.

"At this juncture Aroda arrived from El Fasher with his 200 men, and the cordon was made much closer. The Dervishes from Safir had been so hard pressed that they had failed to carry any water with them into the fort for the succour of the suffering garrison : consequently, about an hour later, 20 mounted men, led by an Emir, made a desperate rush from the fort towards the walls outside. The besiegers were ready for them, and the Dervishes were shot down to a man, the Emir himself falling into the water which he had succeeded in reaching. After this there was a desultory exchange of rifle fire between the besiegers and besieged, until a few hours before dawn, when a small body of Baggara horsemen (from 13 to 15) suddenly appeared. They had come from Gedaref, having made a circuit so as to avoid our post at El Fasher. They attacked a party of our men who were guarding the Safir road; and the besieged, on hearing the firing, began to open a very heavy fire in the direction of the wells which are on the other side of the fort. This was intended as a feint, and it proved wholly successful. Our men closed in round the wells to keep the Dervishes off the water, but the Dervishes suddenly issued from the other side of the fort, where the road was now left open to them, and fled in the direction of Safir, their retreat being covered by the Baggara horsemen."

Most of the wretched garrison that escaped the bullet or spear met with a worse fate. In their hasty flight they had left behind them their baggage, provisions, and water. Between them and the nearest wells was a twelve hours' march over the parched desert. They had suffered dreadfully during the siege from thirst and hunger, and were, at the time of their escape, well nigh physically exhausted.

The siege demonstrated that the Dervish was still capable of great bravery in the face of the enemy; not mere reckless bravery during the heat of battle, but bravery that unflinchingly faces hunger and privation, and that most awful of all agonies, thirst.

The native troops under Aroda and Assabala behaved splendidly throughout. These sons of the desert could be made into a most formidable body of soldiers, equal in physique, stamina, and mobility to any in the world. The Italians had subjected them to a certain kind of discipline; they were not drilled in the rigid manner of the Egyptians, but a happy medium had been found, which though not damping the fierce ardour of these warriors, enabled them to be properly handled and directed in the field. The British have never attempted to bring the Irregulars—the " Friendlies " as they are called— whom they have made use of in the Soudan, under any discipline at all, and in this respect we might certainly do worse than follow the example of the Italians.

Whilst the " Friendlies " were slaughtering their foes, Kassala was handed over to Egypt. The formal ceremony took place at noon on Christmas Day, and, though short, was very impressive. The troops of the garrison, under the command of Colonel Samincatelli, formed in line on the north side of the entrance to the main gate of the fort. The Egyptians, who had marched from their camp, were formed up in line facing the Italian troops. Colonel Parsons, riding down between the lines, asked in Arabic for permission to enter Kassala. Colonel Samincatelli replied in Italian: " Excellency! I am ordered by my Government to cede to you the

INSIDE THE FORT, KASSALA.
From a Photograph by Signor T. A. Evaristi.

[To face p. 190.

fortress and territory of Kassala." The Egyptian relieving guard crossed the drawbridge and took the place of the Italian guard. The Egyptian artillerymen entered the fort, lowered the Italian flag, and fired a salute of twenty-one guns, at intervals of two minutes; whilst the Italian force marched away across the desert to Zabderat, their new frontier.

It was a very melancholy business for our Italian friends, who were giving up what they had gallantly captured and held, at the expense of so many of their comrades, whose graves lie scattered under the ramparts of Kassala; and they were leaving a splendidly disciplined native force, over which they had spent much time and trouble, and to whom they were attached by so many ties of mutual confidence and affection. The only consolation they had was that they were voluntarily giving up all this to friends, and not to foes.

PART IV
THE NILE EXPEDITION, 1898

CHAPTER I

BRITISH REGIMENTS TO THE FRONT

The situation at the beginning of 1898—General Gatacre's British Brigade proceeds up the Nile—Renewed Dervish activity—Mahmud crosses the Nile—The Sirdar concentrates his army at Kunur—Mahmud takes up a position on the Atbara—The Sirdar advances to Ras el Hudi.

AT the beginning of 1898 the position of the opposing forces was as follows. The Egyptian army were in occupation of Berber and Abu Hamed, and the various important posts along the line of communication in rear. Their most advanced position was Ed Damer, at the junction of the Nile with the Atbara. Armed posts had been established at Ombak and other wells in the Suakin—Berber road. Kassala, and several important posts in the vicinity, were held by the Egyptian forces and friendly Arabs, under Colonel Parsons.

An expedition conducted by Mr. Rennell Rodd, who was sent by H.M.'s Government to the King of Abyssinia, had proved an unqualified success; by a treaty drawn up with Menelik, it was agreed that the latter should not assist the Dervishes in any way whatever.

The railway—the most formidable enemy of barbarism—was being pushed with unheard-of rapidity towards Berber, and at the beginning of January it had reached Abu Dis, about thirty miles south of Abu Hamed. The Egyptian railway from Cairo had been prolonged to Assouan. Large quantities of war material were forwarded to the front, and collected at Berber, and everything was steadily developing for a further advance of the Egyptian Army.

The position of the Dervishes was as follows: The main body, of which one-eighth were provided with rifles, was with the Khalifa at Omdurman, about 40,000 strong. At Metemmeh, the Dervish advanced post, was a force numbering 20,000, under Mahmud. Osman Digna had moved from his desert outpost at Abu Delek to Metemmeh, his differences with Mahmud having apparently been settled.

Early in January rumours reached the Sirdar of an intended advance of Mahmud down the Nile for the purpose of attacking the Egyptian line of communications, Berber being the objective. At the first these rumours were not credited, for Mahmud had been reported as being destitute of food, and without camels, transport, and boats. The Sirdar however was determined to be prepared for contingencies, and telegraphed to Cairo for British troops, for the Egyptian Army had never yet met any such force of Dervishes as that under Mahmud, and it was thought prudent not to run any risks.

GENERAL GATACRE.
*Commanding the British Troops.
From " Black and White."*

[*To face p.* 197.

On Sunday, the 2nd of January, orders were issued to the 1st Battalion Royal Warwickshire Regiment (at Alexandria), and the 1st Battalion Lincolnshire Regiment and the 1st Battalion Cameron Highlanders, (both in Cairo) to proceed immediately to Wady Halfa.[1] The detachment of the Camerons at Cyprus rejoined headquarters at once. At the same time, orders were cabled to the 1st Battalion Seaforth Highlanders at Malta, and the (5th) Northumberland Fusiliers at Gibraltar, to move to Egypt without delay. At the end of the third week in January the Lincolns, Warwicks, and Camerons had arrived at Wady Halfa. Their journey up the Nile was conducted in the same way as has been already described.[2] Two sections of Mounted Infantry were despatched to the front, together with four Maxim guns and a detachment of the 16th Company R.A. The Seaforths remained for the present at Assouan.

The command of the British Brigade thus formed was given to Major-General Gatacre,[3] who, at the time of being selected for this enviable appointment, was commanding the 3rd Infantry Brigade at Aldershot.[4]

[1] The North Staffords, Connaught Rangers, and Gloucesters had left Egypt for India.
[2] Part II. Chap. I.
[3] Colonel (temporary Major-General) W. F. Gatacre, C.B., D.S.O., p.s.c., saw service in the Hazara Expedition, 1888 (despatches, D.S.O.), Burma 1889–90, and Chitral 1895 (despatches C.B.).
[4] General Gatacre's staff is given in the Appendix.

The Dervishes were showing signs of activity after the manner peculiar to them. On the 18th of January, a force, 200 strong, under Osman Digna, descended on the village of Gamer, and carried off the women, camels, and cattle; but the Egyptian detachment from Ed Damer pursued them, and recaptured the booty. On the same day, El Sofyieh, about 150 miles east of Khartoum—together with 10 prisoners and 1,300 sheep—fell into the hands of our Friendly Arabs operating round Kassala. The Dervishes also raided the Kababish Arabs, in the Bayuda desert. On the 20th of January, a raid occurred at Kunur, only fifteen miles from Berber, but the Egyptian cavalry attacked and dispersed the Dervishes, killing five of them, and taking two prisoners.

Mahmud made no movement until the 10th of February, when he commenced to convey his troops across the Nile from Metemmeh to Shendy. He raised some boats, which the Dervishes had sunk during the reconnaissances of the gunboats, and, by means of these and other boats and rafts, he commenced his difficult task, which lasted nearly a fortnight. The Sirdar did not attempt to harass the Dervish leader or prevent him crossing, but allowed him every opportunity to carry out his movement, and to march and attack the Anglo-Egyptian Army.

On the 25th of February, Mahmud completed the passage of the Nile, and was ere long afforded an opportunity of proving what a fatal mistake he had made. Had he remained in his strongly entrenched position at Metemmeh, he would have considerably taxed the strength of the Sirdar's force and the gunboats, and would have allowed the Dervishes, even if beaten, an opportunity of falling back on Omdurman, or on Shabluka, above the Sixth Cataract. As it was, Mahmud's army now found itself in the angle formed by the Nile and the Atbara, and it was next to impossible to return without giving battle. This movement had been undertaken at the instigation of the Khalifa, who had ordered Mahmud either to return to Omdurman immediately, or to advance on Berber, break up the railway at Gineinetti, and destroy the Egyptian Army. Had the Khalifa been correctly informed of the strength of the Sirdar's force, he must have known that, no matter how brave his troops, this would be an absolute impossibility—as far as human affairs can be certain. As it was, the intentions of the Dervish leader were known in every detail to his opponent, and nothing could have been more opportune than Mahmud's action of bringing the pick of the Khalifa's forces to be destroyed by the Sirdar.

During Mahmud's move across the river, Captain Keppel, R.N., took the opportunity of making his flotilla's presence felt. Mahmud had entrenched 200 riflemen to cover the crossing; these were driven out by the gunboats, which steamed quite close to the bank, and swept the parapet with Maxim fire. Another gunboat sank a *nuggar* and captured two others. A fourth *nuggar* was in shallow water close to the shore, and 20 yards from the Dervish entrenchment; covered by a sweeping fire of the Maxims, a detachment of the 15th Egyptian battalion landed, and literally hauled the *nuggar* out before Mahmud's eyes.

Meanwhile the British Brigade, after its concentration at Wady Halfa, had been carried across the over-desert railway to Abu Hamed, where it had spent a few weeks, and was now (the middle of February) encamped at Abu Dis. On the 25th of February, Major-General Gatacre received orders to proceed at once with his brigade to Berber. The British troops had been out all day, manœuvring in the desert, and this order was received on their return to camp. Tents were at once struck, and the troops were moved by train as far as Railhead—that ever-changing terminus, which was now near Shereik. The last of the British troops reached Shereik at 8 P.M. on the following day (26th).

Two hours afterwards the whole brigade moved off from Shereik, and, marching all night, arrived at Bash Geredb, early on the morning of the 27th. A desert march of 22 miles was then made, which took but a little over 4 hours, the brigade arriving at Wady Amur on the 28th. Here the troops rested for a few hours, after which they marched to Gineinetti, and then on to Berber. During this march a gunner, and a private of the Lincolns, were temporarily left behind, but were found soon afterwards. On the arrival of the British Brigade at Berber—where Major-General Hunter had his headquarters and two Egyptian Brigades—they were accorded a most enthusiastic reception by the Soudanese, who formed the garrison there. The 9th Soudanese were particularly demonstrative towards the Camerons, with whom they had been brigaded in 1885, and had their teas ready cooked for them on their arrival—an attention which, needless to say, was much appreciated. The brigade ultimately encamped near Kunur, 10 miles north of the Atbara, on the 4th of March, having accomplished a march of 134 miles in $6\frac{1}{2}$ days—98 miles being covered in 4 days—a highly creditable performance. Every effort had been made to get the brigade into condition during its stay at Abu Dis; the use of alcohol had been altogether restricted, and the men had undergone a thorough training by means of route-marches and manœuvres, with the result that this long march had no effect on them, and they were all in excellent health and spirits. Many, however, were nearly rendered invalid, owing to the soles of their boots coming off. This was accounted for in various ways—*e.g.* the rough nature of the country, the heat causing the stitches to give, &c.; but, whatever the excuse, the fact remains that a number of men had to finish the journey bare-footed.

On the 13th of March, the gunboats, which had been carefully watching Mahmud, reported that he had reached El Aliab, on the Nile. A patrolling gunboat had landed a detachment of Egyptian troops, which had encountered a small body of the enemy, killing 38 of them. In this engagement Major Sitwell (Northumberland Fusiliers, 4th Battalion Egyptian Army) was severely wounded in the shoulder.

The Sirdar, on hearing of the approach of the Dervish army, concentrated his force at Kunur, on the 16th of March. His army now numbered upwards of 10,000 men, and was composed as follows :—The British Brigade, under Major-General Gatacre, consisting of the Warwicks, Lincolns, and Camerons; and the Seaforth Highlanders, who had just come up from Wady Halfa. A battery of Egyptian artillery was attached to this brigade. An Infantry Division, Egyptian Army, under Major-General Hunter, consisting of two brigades, under Lieutenant-Colonels Maxwell and Macdonald. Each brigade was composed of four battalions of infantry, a battery of artillery, and some Maxims. Eight squadrons of Egyptian Cavalry, under Brevet-Lieutenant-Colonel Broadwood; three batteries of Artillery, under Lieutenant-Colonel Long; and the Transport Corps, under Brevet-Lieutenant-Colonel Kitchener.

This fine force was paraded in battle array, and inspected by the Sirdar on the 17th of March. Lewis's brigade was on ahead at Atbara Fort; the 1st Battalion Egyptian Army, under Captain Doran, was left to hold the store depot at Berber, and half of the 5th Battalion was at Gineinetti, under Captain

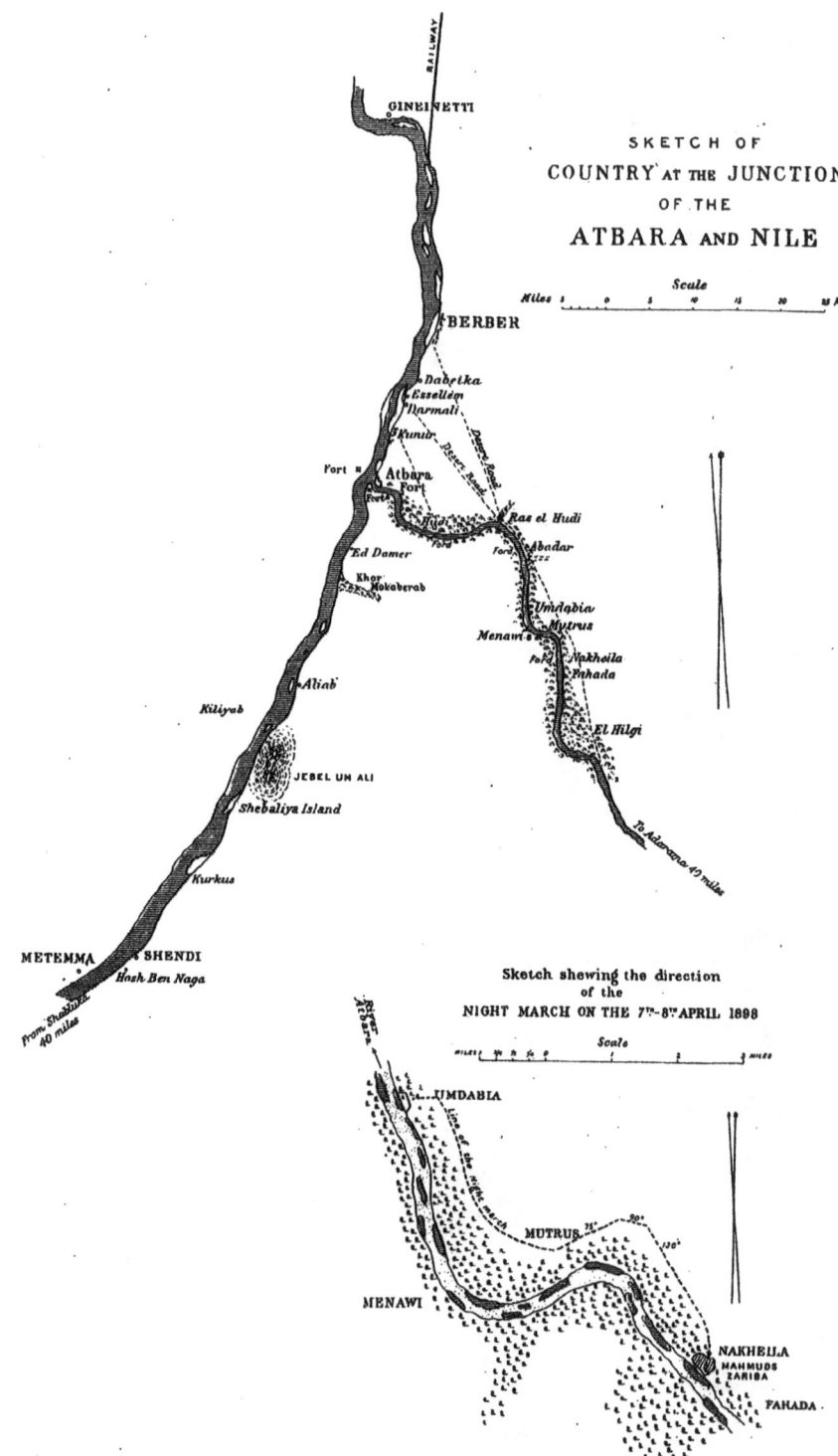

Bainbridge, to watch the railway, which had reached that place.

On the 19th of March the entire Dervish army—18,900 strong—left Aliab, on the Nile, and struck across the desert towards Hudi, on the Atbara; Mahmud's intention being to ford the river at that place, to outflank the Sirdar, and, by taking the desert route, to attack Berber and destroy the railway at Gineinetti.

On the morning of the following day (the 20th) the Sirdar advanced the whole army towards the Atbara, the objective being Hudi, to prevent the Dervishes from availing themselves of the ford. The Cavalry and Horse Artillery formed a screen in front and on the flanks, whilst the main body advanced by echelon of brigades. Gatacre's brigade was in front with the Union Jack[1] and a battery of twelve-pounders and Maxims. Maxwell's and Macdonald's brigades followed behind, on the right and left flanks. The route was shown by a native guide, whilst the direction was checked from time to time by a staff officer with sextant and compass. After a five-hours' march the force reached Hudi, where Lewis's brigade had just arrived from Fort Atbara. A strong zariba was constructed, and the troops settled down for the night.

On the same day (the 20th of March) Mahmud reached the Atbara at a point between Nakheila and Fahada, and there awaited the Sirdar's advance,

---

[1] The colours of the British regiments had been left behind at Cairo.

and reinforcements and supplies from the Khalifa. The Sirdar received news to the effect that a desperate attack had been made on Adarama by Ali Digna—a brother of the notorious Osman—but that after three hours' hard fighting the Dervishes had been repulsed by the friendly Hadendowas, who held the place for us. Fortunately this post was protected, otherwise, as will be seen by a glance at the map, it would have afforded the Dervishes an excellent rallying-point from which they could have threatened the Eastern Soudan.

On the 21st of March, the Anglo-Egyptian force advanced to Ras el Hudi, seven miles further up the Atbara, and here the Sirdar awaited the reports of his cavalry patrols respecting Mahmud's movements.

CHAPTER II

THE ADVANCE TO MUTRUS

Cavalry skirmish at Abadar—Capture of Mahmud's depot at Shendy—General Hunter reconnoitres Mahmud's position—A view of the general situation—The Sirdar moves to Abadar—Another reconnaissance—The Sirdar decides to attack Mahmud—and advances to Umdabia—the bivouac at Mutrus.

ON the 22nd of March, a body of Egyptian cavalry encountered a force of mounted Dervishes at Abadar, who were advancing in considerable numbers down the river, which was thickly wooded. The outposts of Captain Baring's squadron were driven in, and Captain Persse was ordered to clear the bush. Headed by the latter, the Egyptians charged with great gallantry, routed the enemy, and followed them up for over four miles.

Mahmud had taken the precaution to leave a garrison three miles south of Shendy, at Hosh Ben Naga, where he had left a good supply of stores, and also a number of women who had been captured from the Jaalins on the occasion of the massacre at Metemmeh. The Sirdar determined to cut off this, the only means of communication with Omdurman, and, if necessity arose, the Dervish general's only line of retreat. Accordingly, on the 25th of March, the 3rd Battalion Egyptian Army was sent to the Atbara Fort, to take the place of the 15th Battalion, who formed the garrison there; and the 15th were sent up the Nile, together with some friendly Jaalin Arabs. They were conveyed in the three gunboats commanded by Commander Keppel, Lieutenant Beatty, and Lieutenant Hood, the expedition being commanded by Keppel. Every precaution was taken to keep the advance secret. The flotilla arrived at Shendy at 5.30 A.M. on the morning of the 26th, and the force at once landed and attacked the depot. Brevet-Major Hickman commanded the troops, assisted by Major Sitwell, Captain Sloman, and Lieutenant Graham. The place was taken without much trouble, and 160 Baggara were numbered amongst the slain.

The booty which fell into the hands of Commander Keppel on this occasion consisted of a quantity of grain and ammunition, and a large number of cattle, horses, camels, mules, and donkeys; besides which 600 Jaalin slaves were liberated. The forts at Shendy were destroyed, and the place burnt. The gunboats pursued and harassed the flying Dervishes, until their further progress up the river was stopped by the Sixth Cataract.

On the 30th of March, the Sirdar despatched Major-General Hunter to reconnoitre Mahmud's position. Hunter took with him eight squadrons of cavalry, the horse battery, under Brevet-Major Young, and four Maxims under Brevet-Major Laurie and Captain Peake. The force was further increased by two infantry battalions, Egyptian Army, from Abadar. A small Dervish outpost was encountered, and compelled to retire, and Mahmud's entrenchments were thoroughly examined, General Hunter himself getting within 300 yards of the enemy's trenches. The Dervish camp—or "Dem"—was situated on the right bank of the river Atbara, now quite dry, and was found to be surrounded with thick brushwood, and strongly entrenched. The position was slightly commanded on one side, but it appeared to be a very difficult one to take, and certainly did credit to the ingenuity of the Dervish commander. An attempt was made to draw the enemy's fire, but it was unsuccessful, the Dervishes having apparently been instructed to await an attack at close quarters. Not being of sufficient strength to oblige the Dervishes on this point, Hunter returned with his troops to headquarters.

The events of the past month had been somewhat rapid, and were fast approaching a crisis. To sum up the situation: both forces were, at the beginning of April, on the right bank of the Atbara, Mahmud entrenched with 15,000 Dervishes near Nakheila, whilst the Sirdar, with the British Brigade and nearly the whole of the Egyptian Army, was eighteen miles off, at Ras el Hudi, his force numbering about 13,000.

Mahmud's original intention of advancing on Berber, after crossing the Atbara at Hudi, had been frustrated by the Sirdar's rapid move to the latter place; so that he was now, figuratively speaking, "between the devil and the deep sea." He had but three courses open to him: he could return to Omdurman, or attack the Sirdar, or remain where he was. The first course—to retire—would have been morally impossible; the loss of prestige would have had such a demoralising effect upon his forces that he would have lost all control over them. He remembered, moreover, the fate of certain leaders who had returned, unsuccessful, to the Khalifa, and had promptly lost their heads. The second course —to attack the Sirdar—Mahmud considered imprudent, especially when he heard the real strength of his opponent's force. Of the three evils, he chose the least, and elected to remain where he was. His position was desperate, for with his depot at Shendy destroyed, and his line of retreat cut off, he was practically besieged and without hope of supplies. Food was rapidly becoming scarce, and, to make matters worse, a portion of his force (chiefly the Soudanese) was becoming disaffected, and the death penalty for attempted desertion was being inflicted daily. He kept his men hard at work, throwing up entrenchments and making the place as impregnable as possible. He had great confidence in these entrenchments, and seems to have buoyed himself up with some degree of hope that his entrenched and protected riflemen would be able to repulse any attempt the Sirdar's forces might make to carry the position. His half-starved adherents, however, thought otherwise, and were only kept in any form

THE ADVANCE TO MUTRUS

of discipline by the never-tiring energy of their leader. The latter would proclaim, at sunset, that, in obedience to the Prophet's desire, they were to attack and destroy the "Turks" next day, an announcement which was received with plaudits by his hungry followers; but at sunrise next morning he would think better of it, and announce that the Prophet had changed his mind, and considered it better tactics to await the attack of the "Turks," and vanquish them at close quarters.

Looking at the situation from the Sirdar's point of view, the latter was not quite satisfied with the turn affairs had taken. He had devoutly hoped and expected that Mahmud, on finding his retreat cut off, would have advanced to meet him in open battle. In fact it has since been ascertained that the Khalifa had issued distinct orders to that effect though Osman Digna had prudently counselled a retreat in the direction of Adarama.

The Sirdar decided to make another effort to get Mahmud out into the open desert. On the 4th of April, he moved his army five miles on, to Abadar, and on the following morning, at daybreak, he sent Major-General Hunter, with a strong force of all arms, to further reconnoitre the "Dem." On General Hunter's staff were Brevet-Major Kincaid, A.A.G., Captain Sir H. Rawlinson, D.A.A.G., and Lieutenant Smyth. On approaching the position, the enemy came out in considerable numbers, and the Dervish horsemen immediately engaged the Egyptian cavalry in a spirited and plucky manner. A sharp fight followed, in which the enemy were driven back. As they retired, a body of Dervish riflemen, who were in support, opened a heavy fire on the Egyptian troopers, whom they attempted to surround. General Hunter immediately ordered the cavalry to retire, covering their retreat with artillery and Maxim fire; and the Dervish horsemen then engaged them on both flanks, but were driven back by a combined charge, headed by Colonel Broadwood, Major Le Gallais, and Captain Persse; after which both the opposing forces withdrew. Our casualties were six Egyptians killed and ten wounded; Captain Persse received a bullet in the forearm. The Dervishes sustained considerable loss. The Maxims fired over 4,000 rounds during the engagement, which brought into further evidence the great value of this weapon.

Thanks to the reconnaissances, and to the information given by deserters—who were continually coming in—the Sirdar had gained a considerable insight into the condition of his opponent's army, and the position of his "Dem," or zariba; and seeing that Mahmud was intent on holding his ground, the Sirdar decided to settle the matter once and for all, and storm the position.

Needless to say, the news of the Sirdar's intended attack was received with the greatest enthusiasm by the British and native troops, and the prospect of soon meeting the enemy in battle raised their spirits to the highest pitch. Only those who have experienced the hardships and privations of a campaign,

THE ADVANCE TO MUTRUS

can understand the almost electrical effect that an announcement of this description has on the troops. To feel that the campaign is nothing but a dreary course of incessant discomforts, without any apparent compensation, is wearying to body and mind; it is so different from what one had anticipated; but as soon as one is given the assurance that a decisive battle will be the outcome of these pains, the change is magical. For are not the heat, dust, glare, and the hundred and one privations which before seemed almost insupportable, compensated for over and over again by the prospect of a really good fight?

The British Brigade were, as we like to think our soldiers always are, fit to go anywhere and do anything. There were practically no sick, and no general ever took the field with a finer body of men.

Early on Wednesday, the 6th of April, the Sirdar moved his whole force from Abadar to Umdabia, a deserted village on the Atbara, about seven and a half miles from the enemy's position. On their arrival a zariba was constructed out of the thorny mimosa bushes, on the bank of the river, and the troops lay there during Wednesday and Thursday. The men spent their spare time in thoroughly cleaning their rifles, on which they appeared to bestow quite loving care, and nearly every man used his only handkerchief to wrap round the breech and keep the sand out. During these two days the Sirdar was busy with his final preparations. The baggage to be taken was reduced to the barest necessities, and the troops were to move in the lightest possible order. The British Brigade were supplied with 127 rounds of ammunition per man, and the native troops carried from 100 to 150 rounds each.

When the heat of the sun had slackened, a little after five in the afternoon of Thursday (7th), the infantry, Maxims, and two squadrons of cavalry moved out, in battle array, about a mile and a half into the desert. At 6 P.M. the force commenced the march. The remaining six squadrons of cavalry and four batteries of artillery remained for the night in camp and followed in the early morning. Half the 15th Battalion of the Egyptian Army were left behind here in strong zariba, to guard the stores, hospital, and transport. All the camp fires were kept burning, so that should any patrolling Dervishes be in the vicinity, they might continue under the impression that the army was still there.

The route was shown by native guides, as usual, and the direction was checked by Captain Fitton, D.A.A.G. Gatacre was in front with his British Brigade, behind them came Macdonald and his Soudanese, then came Lewis's Brigade and the Camel Corps, and lastly Maxwell's Brigade. Each brigade marched in battalion squares, in echelon, the intervals being about 300 or 400 yards.

The march lay through the desert, at a distance varying from half a mile to a mile from the river, thus avoiding the stiff mimosa shrubs along the bank. When the moon rose, the light was obscured by the sand and dust, carried by a strong wind that was blowing. One could just distinguish the dim outline of the squares; there was no talking and not a sound was heard save the monotonous tramp of thousands of feet, as they struck the desert sand. Frequent halts were rendered necessary, in order to preserve the proper formation, owing to the broken nature of the ground; but after marching for three hours the force arrived at Mutrus, not three miles from the Dervish position. Here they rested, the officers and men throwing themselves on the sand with their arms by their side. One of the correspondents heard a sentimental Highlander remark to a comrade: "Ah! Tam, how many thousands there are at hame across the sea, a-thinkin' o' us the nicht," to which "Tam" replied: "Right! Sandy, and how many millions there are that don't care a d——. Go to sleep, ye fule!"

CHAPTER III

THE BATTLE OF THE ATBARA [1]

It was now Good Friday, the 8th of April. The force was aroused about 1 A.M., and within half an hour the advance was resumed. After a slowly measured march the troops arrived at a quarter to four within a mile and a half of the enemy's position, and another halt was made till daylight. The march from Mutrus had been without incident, but for a mysterious pillar of fire that was seen moving between Mutrus and Nakheila, which must have been either a signal to the Dervishes, or an accidental fire. At 4.30 A.M., the brigades were deployed from square to attack formation: British on the left, Macdonald's in the centre, Maxwell's on the right, and Lewis's Brigade, with the transport and water, in reserve. Every battalion now formed into line, with two companies in support, except that the left battalion of the British and the right of Maxwell's Brigade were in column, to protect the flanks.

The force advanced in this formation over a

---
[1] Pronounced At'-băra.

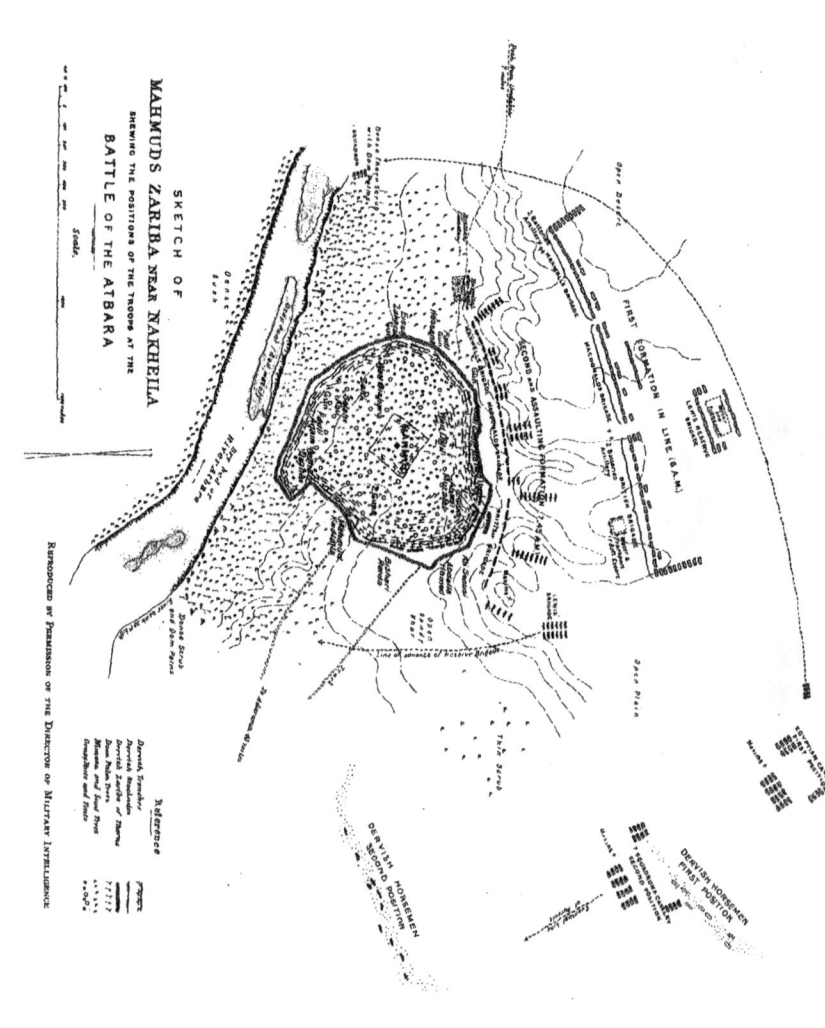

THE BATTLE OF THE ATBARA

gravelly ridge, until at 6 o'clock it halted on a commanding position about 600 yards from the "Dem." The silence during the march was remarkable; scarcely a word was spoken among the 13,000 men, and then only in a whisper—every one seemed too intent thinking of what was about to take place.

The "Dem" was situated on the north bank of the Atbara river, which was now nothing but a dry river-bed, with a few pools of brackish water here and there. The position looked a formidable object to assault; forming the outside barrier was a strong zariba of mimosa bushes, behind which were palisades of strong palm logs, and in the interior of the work were innumerable cross-trenches, casemates, and straw huts. It was evident that the advance was well-known to the enemy, for one could plainly see the Emirs moving about, giving their final orders.

At a quarter past six the guns were run into position and opened fire. Two good artillery positions had been chosen, so as to bring a cross-fire on the enemy's entrenchments, which were now subjected to a raking cannonade. Twelve guns came into action at each of these points, and were assisted by a rocket detachment under Lieutenant Beatty, R.N. The rocket battery was first of all on rising ground on the left, but finding the range too great for effective use, it moved round to the right, and, getting into range at 500 yards, succeeded in setting the "Dem" on fire in several places—the straw *tokuls* (huts) making excellent fuel. Some Baggara horsemen were seen coming out of the bush on the left flank, but the Maxims forced them to beat a hasty retreat—and they moved away to the south. The bombardment lasted an hour and a half, during which time scarcely a sound came from the zariba. About a quarter to seven some impulsive Dervishes fired a few shots at Macdonald's Brigade, but they aimed too high, and the bullets whizzed harmlessly overhead. Considering the destruction that was being dealt out all round them, by this veritable hail of lead and fire, the self-restraint evinced by the Dervishes was truly remarkable.

At a quarter past seven the troops were formed for the assault, as follows : Along the front of the British Brigade were the Cameron Highlanders, extended in line, and following behind them, in column of companies, were the Warwicks (on the left), the Seaforths (centre), and the Lincolns (on the right). Continuing the line to the right was Macdonald's brigade of Soudanese—the 11th, 10th, and 9th Battalions, each with two companies in line, and the remaining four companies behind in column of companies, as a support. The 2nd Battalion (Egyptian Army) followed in reserve, in company column. Continuing the line further to the right was Maxwell's Brigade, the 14th and 12th Soudanese Battalions, each with four companies in line and two in support. On the extreme right were the 15th Soudanese and the 8th Battalion (Egyptian Army), in column of companies; whilst a squadron under Captain Peyton was sent down towards the river-bank, on this flank. On the extreme left (to the left rear of the Warwicks), was Lewis's reserve brigade, consisting of the 3rd and 4th Battalions (Egyptian Army), to keep in check the Dervish cavalry, and to prevent any flank movement.

The Cavalry and Horse Artillery were posted on the left, half a mile away in the desert, to watch the enemy's horsemen. The twenty-four guns, under Colonel Long, were on the right flank, and the twelve Maxims were divided amongst the right and left flanks and the centre.

As soon as the troops had taken up the above positions, they were severally addressed by their commanding officers. General Gatacre, in a stirring speech, told the British Brigade that there was to be no mistake about this, they were to drive the Dervishes right through into the river. Colonel Murray concluded his exhortation to the Seaforths by saying that "The news of victory must be in London to-night." In a novel, or on the stage, these words would doubtless have been hailed with much noise and cheering, but as a matter of fact they were received in grim silence; the men, however, were ready and eager for action, and bent on giving a good account of themselves.

And now the artillery bombardment ceases; the Sirdar and his staff take up a commanding position whence they can best survey the field of action; the other mounted officers, including Generals

Gatacre and Hunter, dismount and place themselves at the head of their men; bayonets are fixed and swords drawn; and the suppressed excitement becomes almost insupportable. At last, at a quarter to eight, the bugles ring out the "Advance," and in an instant the bands of the native regiments, and the buglers of the Warwicks and Lincolns, burst forth into stirring marches, and the pipers of the Highlanders skirl their loudest; whilst the whole force advances in quick time, with colours flying, as steadily as if on parade. A more imposing spectacle it is impossible to imagine, than this array of brave men advancing literally to death or glory. Every few yards the line halts for a moment, and "independent firing" is kept up vigorously. Then the line moves forward again.[1]

Suddenly, as the force arives within 200 yards of the zariba, the Dervishes,—who until now had reserved their defence with remarkable coolness,—open a searching fire. Men begin to drop on all sides, but, steady and irresistible as a great tidal wave, the force sweeps on, still in the same perfect order. Now Maxwell's and Macdonald's troops, in their impetuosity, push slightly ahead. The Camerons at length reach the top of a crest, within a hundred yards of the zariba—whence the ground slopes gently down towards the position—and a bitter and well-sustained fire from the enemy seems to sweep through and through their ranks. One more halt is called, "independent firing" continues

[1] The "volleys and rushes" of the "attack drill" were not attempted.

for two or three minutes, and then the "Advance" is again sounded. With a ringing cheer the Camerons rush forward to the zariba,—which they reach simultaneously with the leading battalions of Macdonald's and Maxwell's brigades,—General Gatacre and his A.D.C., Captain Brooke, being the first of the British Brigade to reach it.

Immediately behind the Camerons are the Seaforths, Lincolns, and Warwicks, still in company column. These battalions have, of course, been obliged to advance in the face of the deadly fusillade, without being able to fire a shot.

Working under a withering fire, the Camerons begin to pull down the zariba, being protected as far as possible by their comrades—alternate companies pulling away the bushes whilst the others keep up a heavy fusillade. In rather less than five minutes gaps have been made at intervals along the line, sufficiently large to admit the troops to pass through.

It was now eight o'clock. Within a quarter of an hour of the general "Advance" being first sounded, the entry into the zariba had been effected. It had been intended that as soon as the Camerons had made sufficiently large gaps in the zariba, the British battalions in rear were to push on, through the ranks of the Camerons, into the "Dem"; and that when the leading company of the Seaforths had advanced fifty yards beyond the zariba, they were to halt and allow the companies behind to deploy on them. The Lincolns and Warwicks were to continue the deployment to the right and left respectively, and a steady advance was to be made by the whole line. A similar plan was to have been adopted in the native brigades. It was found, however, that this scheme was impracticable, for the crowded rifle-pits, with which the interior of the "Dem" was covered, had to be reckoned with. A steady deployment in face of rifle-fire at twenty paces was, of course, out of the question; besides which, it was not likely that the Camerons, after bearing practically the brunt of the fight—we are speaking, of course, only of the British Brigade—up to this point, were going to stand still at the most critical moment, and allow the regiments behind to supersede them. Such a thing would have been morally impossible.

Headed by their officers, the Camerons rush forward through the gaps. Captain Findlay was the first of the British Brigade to cross the zariba, but ere he had gone many yards he was mortally wounded, being shot in the chest and stomach, besides being wounded by a spear. "Go on, my company, and give it them," he called out, and a quarter of an hour afterwards he was dead.[1] The Seaforths rush into the zariba, following closely on the heels of the Camerons, then the Lincolns and the Warwicks get through; and the whole of the British Brigade presses on in line, or rather, in the best attempt at a line that the circumstances permit.

[1] Captain C. Findlay, Cameron Highlanders, served in the Nile Expedition with his regiment in 1885—6, including the battle of Ginniss. He had fourteen years' service and had married only a few months previous to starting up the Nile on this expedition.

MAJOR D. C. URQUHART,
Cameron Highlanders.
From a Photograph by George Milne, Turriff, N.B.

MAJOR R. F. L. NAPIER,
Cameron Highlanders.
From a Photograph by David White, Inverness.

CAPTAIN C. FINDLAY,
Cameron Highlanders.

CAPTAIN A. C. D. BAILLIE,
Seaforth Highlanders.

SECOND-LIEUTENANT P. GORE,
Seaforth Highlanders.

OFFICERS KILLED AT THE BATTLE OF THE ATBARA, April 8th, 1898.
From "Black and White."

The scene inside the "Dem" is indescribable. One sees trench after trench filled with Dervishes, all firing point-blank as fast as they can load; whilst the British and native troops dash forward, clearing the trenches with bullet and bayonet. It is not a question of merely driving the enemy out of the zariba, but rather of despatching every single Dervish separately. The enemy remain at their posts, firing steadily, and officers and men are falling right and left.

Major Urquhart (Camerons) was one of the first to fall, shot through the sporran top by a Dervish who lay hidden amongst his dead comrades in one of the trenches. He managed to call out "Never mind me, lads, go on," and then fell dead.[1] Soon afterwards Major Napier, of the same regiment, was dangerously wounded in the thigh by a large conical bullet from an elephant rifle. The Camerons[2] had sixty men *hors de combat*, after being in action less than that number of minutes. The Seaforths also fared badly : one of the first of that regiment to cross the zariba was young Gore—who had only joined the Service a few months—and he was gallantly pushing on across the trenches when he fell, shot through the heart ; Colonel Murray was shot through the left elbow, went off to have it bandaged up,

---

[1] Major B. C. Urquhart, Cameron Highlanders, joined the service, 1880, served with his regiment at Tel-el-Kebir, and in the Nile Expedition, 1885—6, including the battle of Ginniss.

[2] The number of rank and file who were killed and wounded, and the names of all the killed, are given in the Appendix.

returned at once, and brought his regiment out of action; Captain Baillie had his left leg shattered; Captain Maclachlan was hit by a bullet in the shin, but hobbled on in spite of it; Lieutenant Vandeleur received a dangerous wound in the hip, and Lieutenant Thomson was wounded in the foot The leading company of the Seaforths[1] had eleven men killed and wounded and four men with bullets through their helmets. Of the Warwicks, Lieutenant Greer was slightly wounded, and of the Lincolns Colonel Verner was shot in the face, Lieutenant Boxer in the ankle, and Lieutenant Rennie had one of his little fingers shot off. General Gatacre had a narrow escape; whilst pulling away the zariba, a Dervish sprang at him with a huge spear, the General called to his orderly (Private Cross, of the Camerons), "Give it him, my lad," and Cross rushed forward and bayoneted the Dervish just in time. Poor Cross, who showed great gallantry throughout the fight, died a few weeks afterwards at Darmali.

Meanwhile, on the right, the Egyptians and Soudanese, led by Major-General Hunter waving sword and helmet, had entered the zariba slightly in advance of the British Brigade, and had, with the greatest bravery and tenacity, fought their way over the terrible trenches. Several officers of the Egyptian Army were wounded, including Captain Walter (commanding 9th Soudanese), Captain Walsh and Lieutenant Harley (12th Soudanese),

[1] The number of rank and file who were killed and wounded, and the names of all the killed, are given in the Appendix.

CHAP. III   THE BATTLE OF THE ATBARA   223

and Brevet-Major Shekleton (commanding 14th Battalion, Egyptian Army).

Some of the fiercest fighting took place at a stockade which was built right round the "Dem," about thirty yards from the trenches, and was held by over a thousand of Mahmud's chosen followers. From this stockade issued a most fearful fire, which was received principally by the Camerons, Lincolns, and 11th Soudanese. One company of the latter regiment attempted to enter one of the corners of the zariba, but the fire was galling, and they were all but annihilated. Other companies of these brave Blacks hurried up in support, effected an entrance, and avenged their comrades.

It was here that Piper Stewart, of the Camerons, met his death. He had got on some rising ground, and, nothing daunted by the bullets whizzing round him, was vigorously playing "The March of the Cameron Men," to cheer on his comrades when he was struck by no fewer than five bullets—four in the body and one in the head!

At last the troops succeeded in hewing their way right across the zariba, and it was a case of *sauve qui peut* with the enemy, who now fled helter-skelter through the palm-belt into the broad, dry bed of the Atbara. Many of the Dervishes disdained to run, and walked calmly away, with that dignified air which is one of their chief characteristics. Those who succeeded in escaping from the zariba kept up a sharp fire for a few minutes, but one or two well-directed volleys from the victorious troops—whose orders were not to advance beyond the river-bed—induced them to disappear.

When the "Cease fire" sounded, at a quarter-past nine, the enthusiasm amongst the troops, particularly the natives, was almost frantic; and, needless to say, every individual who found himself unscathed after the ordeal felt a certain sense of relief. The Soudanese danced with delight, and went wildly around shaking hands with every one they came across. As the Sirdar and his staff rode up, they were met with a perfect roar of cheers, and helmets and tarboushes were waved on the ends of the bayonets. The Sirdar was greatly moved by the genuine welcome of his victorious soldiers, and thanked them for the unflinching manner in which they had done their duty. He promoted on the field (provisionally) to the rank of subaltern the sergeant-major of every native regiment that crossed the zariba. Addressing Colonel Money, of the Cameron Highlanders, the Sirdar remarked, "What your battalion has done was one of the finest feats performed for many years. You ought to be proud of such a regiment." He also spoke in highly eulogistic terms of the steadiness with which the other regiments had advanced to the attack, and of the dash with which they entered the zariba.

The troops were then re-formed, in brigade squares, to the right of the ground where the attack had commenced.

CHAPTER IV

AFTER THE BATTLE

The casualties—Mahmud interviewed—The army returns to Umdabia —Congratulatory messages—The Sirdar's formal entry into the Soudan—The troops move into summer quarters—The British Brigade at Darmali—The Sirdar and the War Correspondents.

THE scene in the zariba after the battle was horrifying. The trenches were filled with the slain Dervishes in every position that the agony of death could assume. Many were mangled into mere fragments of humanity far beyond recognition. The artillery fire had played a fearful part in the battle, and the coolness and pluck with which the enemy contained themselves during the bombardment proved that the Dervish was truly brave, not merely when fired by enthusiasm in a fanatical rush, but when face to face with death, without hope of escape or hope of killing his foe. Many unfortunate blacks were found chained by both hands and legs, in the trenches, with a gun in their hands and their faces to the foe—some with forked sticks behind their backs.

Of course the first thing after the battle was over was to collect the wounded, and build shelters for

Q

them from the sun, which began to be very hot, after which the weary troops, not having had a real rest for two or three nights, tried to get a few hours' sleep. A Field Hospital was established outside the zariba, where all the wounded, including the enemy's, had their wounds dressed. In the afternoon all those who had lost their lives in the battle were buried on a gravelly slope near the zariba, and their graves were afterwards covered with a zariba to prevent their desecration. Officers and men were buried in the clothes in which they had fought and fallen, and were wrapped in a regulation blanket. The funeral of the 3 British officers and 18 men was most impressive. It was attended by the Sirdar and his staff, General Hunter and his staff, General Gatacre and his staff, by every officer off duty, and by detachments of all the regiments. As the majority of the killed were Presbyterians, the Rev. Mr. Simms conducted the principal part of the service, but the Rev. Mr. Watson, Anglican Chaplain, and the Rev. Father Brindle, Roman Catholic Chaplain, also took part in the service. No farewell shots were fired, but a firing party presented arms, and the band of the 11th Soudanese and the pipers of the Highlanders played a lament. Three more men of the British Brigade subsequently succumbed to their wounds, two at Umdabia and one at Atbara. Captain Baillie[1] (Seaforths), and Major

---

[1] Captain A. C. D. Baillie, Seaforth Highlanders, joined the service in 1887, and served with his regiment in the Hazara Expeditions of 1888 and 1891.

Napier[1] (Camerons), who were sent down at once to Cairo with the other British wounded, lingered for some time in the Citadel Hospital; but the former died on the 16th of May and the latter on the 23rd of May. We append a summary of the casualties in the British Brigade.

	Killed.		Wounded.		Total Number of Casualties.
	Officers.	R & F.	Officers.	R & F.†	
1st batt. R. Warwickshire Regt.	0	2	1	11	14
1st batt. Lincolnshire Regt.......	0	1	3	13	17
1st batt. Seaforth Highlanders...	1	5	5*	22	33
1st batt. Cameron Highlanders..	2	13	1*	44	60
Army Service Corps...	0	0	0	1	1
Total	3	21	10	91	125

* 1 died subsequently.   † Several died subsequently.

Of the Egyptian army, 57 rank and file were killed; 21 officers (including 5 British), 2 British non-commissioned officers, and 363 native rank and file were wounded. The 11th Soudanese, under Major Jackson, alone lost 100 killed and wounded. Total number of casualties in the Anglo-Egyptian army: 81 killed, and 487 wounded. Grand total, 568.

The Dervish loss amounted to no less than 3,000 killed and wounded, 2,000 dead being found inside the zariba. All the Khalifa's principal Emirs were killed with the exception of Osman Digna, who escaped with the cavalry: the Emirs killed including Wad Bishara, former Emir of Dongola;

---

[1] Major R. F. L. Napier, Cameron Highlanders, joined the service in 1876, and served in the Nile Expedition 1885 and 1886, including the battle of Ginniss.

Mahomed Zeki, former Emir of Berber; Bishara Redy, Emir of the Western Soudan; El Atta Wad Ussul, Emir of the Shagiyeh, and several others.

Two thousand prisoners surrendered, including Mahmud himself. Over 100 banners were taken, and a quantity of ammunition, rifles, grain, war drums, and the usual Dervish loot. Mahmud's 10 guns were captured, only 2 having been fired.

Mahmud was seized by the 10th Soudanese, under Major Nason. He was discovered sitting in a hole in the floor of his *tokul*, under his *angareb* (bed). The interview between him and the Sirdar was dramatic. The Dervish leader, who was a well-built man, not more than 28 years of age, was brought before the Sirdar and General Hunter, and maintained a haughty and sullen demeanour, but was limping from a bayonet thrust in the leg. General Hunter, addressing him in Arabic, said, "This is the Sirdar," which gratuitous piece of information Mahmud appeared to ignore. The Sirdar then asked, "Why have you come into my country to burn and kill?" to which Mahmud sullenly replied, "I have to obey the Khalifa's orders as a soldier without question, as you must the Khedive's." The Sirdar then asked, "Where is Osman Digna?" to which Mahmud replied, "I do not know, he was not in the fight; he went away with the cavalry. All the rest of my Emirs stayed with me. I saw the troops at five in the morning, and afterwards rode round to see that they were all in their places, then I returned to my 'Dem' and

MAHMUD. [*To face p.* 228.
His first Photo, signed by himself for the Artist of "Black and White."

waited. Am I a woman, that I should run away?" He was then marched off under escort, and ultimately taken to Berber.

The troops rested on the gravel ridges, without any shade from the terrible sun, until shortly after four o'clock, when they marched back to Umdabia camp, arriving there before nightfall. One battalion of the Egyptian Army and a squadron were left behind to clear up the Dervish camp. The wounded did not start till half-past eight; they (including the British) being carried on stretchers and *angarebs* by the men of Lewis's Brigade, which also furnished the escort. Though the direct route was but 9 miles, they went 12, in order to obtain a smooth path and avoid jolting the sufferers, and Umdabia was reached at 3 A.M. The services thus rendered by the Egyptians to their British comrades, in carrying the wounded a distance of 36 miles to the Nile, was deeply appreciated and went far to strengthen the good feeling existing between the two forces.

The remnant of Mahmud's army re-formed at Adarama, on the left bank of the Atbara river, at a distance of about sixty miles from Nakheila. It divided, and while one portion went to Gedaref, the remainder, with whom Osman Digna was reported to be, proceeded to Abu Delek. The Dervishes had been beaten, and the consummation of the expedition, so devoutly wished for, had happened. The Sirdar had met a large army of the enemy in a pitched battle and had scattered them. The effect of this victory was more reaching and more important than any event in the Soudan that had happened since the fall of Khartoum. It put an end to the only army in the Soudan intended for aggressive purposes and cleared the whole desert north of the Sixth Cataract of the Dervishes.

After church parade on the 10th of April, the Sirdar read to the British Brigade the message of the Queen, who is ever so thoughtful and solicitous for the wounded, in these words:—"I greatly rejoice at the brilliant victory. I desire to be fully informed as to the state of the wounded." The troops, on the invitation of the Sirdar, gave three hearty cheers for her Majesty. The Khedive's message was read, and others from Mr. Balfour, on behalf of the Government, and from Lord Lansdowne. "Every one, in short," said the Sirdar, "is extremely proud of the conduct of the army in the field." His Majesty the German Emperor, by a timely and cordial cablegram to the Sirdar, made a bold bid to retrieve the mismanagement which had occurred on former occasions in connection with his congratulatory messages to victorious troops.

The reception of the news of the victory by the foreign Powers was very gratifying to us. But nothing succeeds like success, even with the Continent of Europe. The French Press, who, when the Dongola expedition was first proposed, insinuated that there were no Dervishes beyond the creation of "perfidious Albion" for the purpose of prolonging her stay in the valley of the Nile, spoke of the victory in terms of dignity and fairness. The Italian Press were cordial and sincere in congratulations. The German Press were, for the most part, lukewarm, as they usually are when speaking of any foreign successes. The victory was a complete vindication of the policy of the British Government, and it will be long before a possible excuse can be made by the enemies of Great Britain or Egypt to break the inseverable ties which bind these countries together.

The Sirdar made his formal entry into the Soudan (at Berber) on the 14th of April, at the head of Macdonald's Brigade. The route was kept by the troops of the garrison. The town was *en fête* and decorated as well as could be with the appliances and the materials available. Mahmud was given every opportunity of exhibiting himself as the central figure. When the procession had reached the central square in the town, the Sirdar took up his position in a canopied platform, where the whole of the troops marched past in review order. The troops moved into summer quarters, the British Brigade going to Darmali, midway between Berber and the Atbara—and thus ended the second part of the expedition.

* * * *

During the lull in the storm we may conveniently allude to a so-called grievance on the part of the "Specials," which in August, 1897, was taken up with considerable warmth by the papers represented. Briefly, this grievance lay in the fact that the Sirdar had issued an order (August, 1897) by which the correspondents were forbidden to go further south than Railhead (then situated in the Nubian desert, between Murat Wells and Abu Hamed), the reason set forth for this being the difficulties attending the Transport and Commissariat Department. This order the correspondents consented to comply with at the time; but later on—in January, 1898—when another movement was on foot, they raised a veritable whirlwind of indignation against the Sirdar, in their "dailies," at what they were pleased to consider a most uncalled for order. The plea of transport difficulties, put forward by the Sirdar, was only a minor reason for his decision. The truth of the matter was that he, like the majority of the commanders in the field, looked upon the correspondents in the light of a doubtful blessing. The employment of correspondents in war has always been a matter of controversy, and one which on this occasion reached such an acute stage that it deserves more than a passing notice. The war correspondents representing the London daily papers are a class of men upon whose honour and discretion reliance might be placed, and they are furthermore subjected to the censorship of the officers appointed for the purpose; but notwithstanding every precaution being taken, it is quite possible that, unwittingly and by some excess of zeal, information might be published which should have been suppressed. It can be easily imagined that there must be many matters that a leader of an army would not wish to have divulged, even if the information went no further than his own countrymen. Any indiscretion on the part of a correspondent in disclosing some plan of the general's, or causing any sensation or needless alarm, might entail endless trouble—as was shown more than once during the Franco-German war. It was naturally the Sirdar's primary object to prevent the Khalifa obtaining any information as to his movements; and this object was now on a fair way to being thwarted by these energetic gentlemen. Truly "the pen is mightier than the sword." It may be asked, "How could the news in Fleet Street benefit the Khalifa in Omdurman?" The answer is, that there were many individuals outside the Soudan, who, if not actually the Khalifa's agents, were at any rate ready and willing to furnish him with such information as they thought he might be able to turn to good account. Now that the Suakin-Berber route was closed to the Dervishes the transmission of intelligence to Omdurman was rendered far more difficult, but, even now, scraps of intelligence, gathered by the aimless French missionaries wandering in Central Africa, found their way to the Khalifa's ears.

Nor were the Dervishes the only ones to be guarded against in this matter. The campaign in the Soudan was watched, for many different reasons, by a number of more or less interested nations— all eager to take advantage of any information that might prove useful to them. One can have little sympathy, therefore, with those newspapers which attacked the Sirdar so virulently for his action.

There is another side to the question; and we cannot dismiss the subject altogether without acknowledging that war correspondents have, from time to time, yielded great services to the Army. They have brought to light many abuses which would never otherwise have been made public, and it has happened that they have supplied valuable information to the commander, as well as to the country. Again, it must be borne in mind that, in a free constitution such as our own, where the popular will is supreme, it is of the utmost importance that the general public should have the very fullest information of any campaign in which the country may be engaged, in order that they may sympathetically follow it, so that, should they at any time be called upon to decide on the prosecution of the war, they would be in a position to form a sound opinion on the matter, instead of being carried away by false representations. The recent operations on the Indian frontier supply us with a good instance of the danger in obtaining news second-hand and from unreliable quarters. In this case all kinds of false and ridiculous stories were circulated to the discredit of the army and its leaders.

Full information of the doings of our soldiers and sailors encourages a strong national and patriotic feeling, binding the nation closer in a common enthusiasm. What nation is there, ancient or modern, but whose bards have sung the deeds of its defenders? Notwithstanding the nineteen centuries that the gospel of peace has been preached, and the great attempts that have been made by various agencies and societies—to say nothing of the recent well-intended efforts of the Czar—for the abolition of the arbitrament of the sword, the human race is no nearer the Age of Peace than it has ever been. The love of victory and conquest is still strong within us, and the lust for war by the great nations of the world at the present time is only curbed by the fear of the dreadful and lasting consequences that might follow a defeat.

CHAPTER V

THE CONCENTRATION AT WAD HAMED

Fort Atbara—Berber—Abadieh—The new gunboats—Darmali—The additional British force leaves Cairo for the front—Also the Special Correspondents—The first step of the final move—The Sixth Cataract—Jebel Royan—Khartoum in sight—Dervish mishaps—The Anglo-Egyptian army at Wad Hamed.

As soon as the troops were encamped in their summer quarters, preparations were made for the final advance on Omdurman. The Sirdar established the head-quarters of the Expeditionary Force at the confluence of the rivers Nile and Atbara, where a fort, known as Fort Atbara, had been erected, and the place was now an immense depot for supplies. The fort was enclosed on the land side by a deep trench, and a parapet several hundred yards long, and a zariba of mimosa bushes, which, originally intended to prevent a rush of bare-footed Arabs, now served as a laager or fence to shut in the commissariat camels, horses, and other beasts of burden. Inside the compound a series of low, flat, one-storied mud buildings had been erected as barracks, together with other accommodation for officers and men. Outside the fort, the scrub, which had originally encircled the

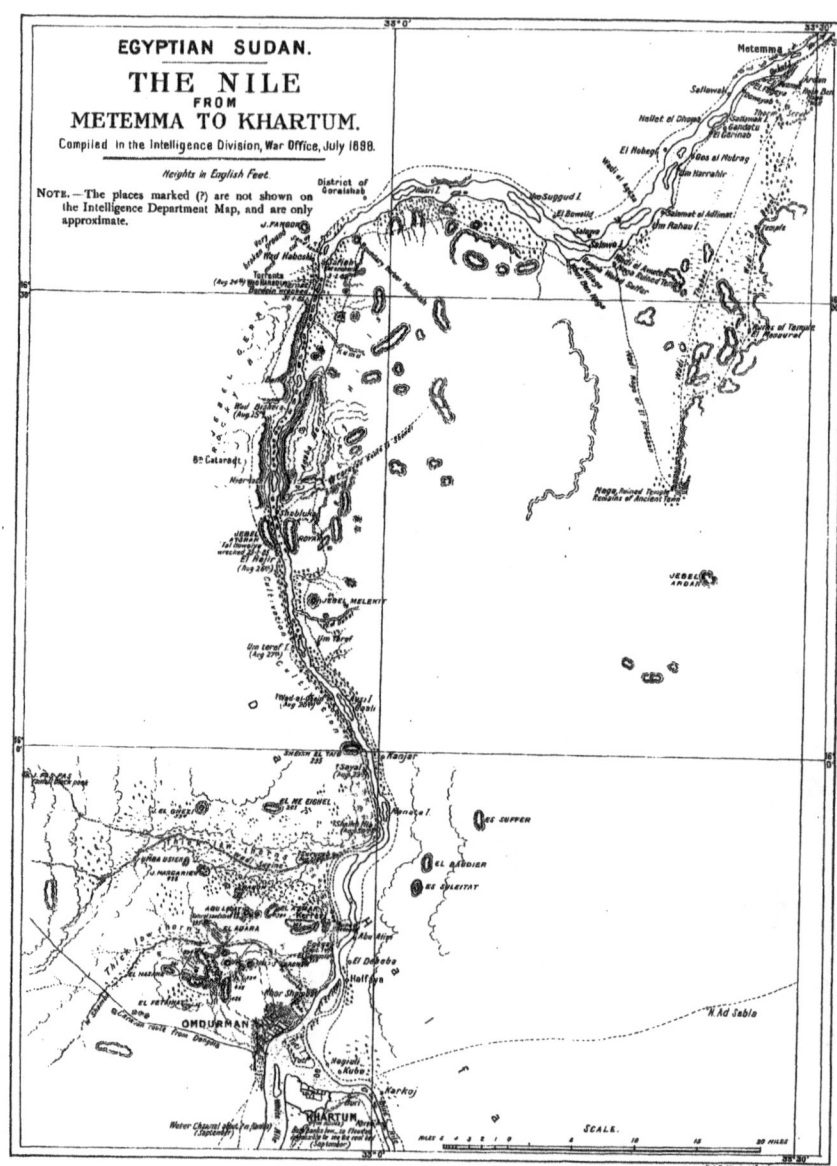

CHAP. V   THE CONCENTRATION AT WAD HAMED

position, had been cleared for several hundred yards, solitary trees having been left here and there to serve as fixed ranges of infantry fire. These preparations had been made in the preceding April, in anticipation of Mahmud's arrival on the scene. On each bank of the Atbara, at its confluence, stood a watch-tower, to enable sentries to give notice of an enemy's approach.

Berber, where the Egyptian army was encamped, had once been an important city, but the old town had been destroyed by the Dervishes, after they had gained possession of the place; and the new town, erected by the Sirdar's troops, was now of but little importance, owing to the two neighbouring military centres, Abadieh and Darmali.

At Abadieh—which the railway reached on April 20th—a large arsenal had been established, and the sections of the three new gunboats, the *Sultan*, *Melik*, and *Sheikh*, which arrived from England in June, were here put together and launched. This work was superintended by Major Staveley Gordon, R.E., and Capt. Hobbs, Royal Marines. These new boats were better armed than the old ones,[1] and drew a foot less of water, but, on the other hand, they could accommodate only 65 men, whereas those of the *Zafir* class (which arrived in 1896), carried 250 comfortably. The most important work of a Nile gunboat was the towing of river boats, and in this respect they were practically useless, for their shallow draught (18 inches) did not permit

[1] For armament, see p. 248.

them to get a sufficient grip of the water, and with a heavy load they could barely steam two miles an hour against the stream.

At Darmali, a pleasant spot on the Nile bank, ten miles south of the Sirdar's head-quarters (Atbara), the British brigade was encamped. The Seaforths and Camerons, with General Gatacre and his staff, were in the town itself, and the Lincolns and Warwicks were a mile off, outside the village of Es Sillem. The brigade was now thoroughly acclimatised, and the general health of the troops was very good. With the exception of an epidemic of enteric fever, in which the Lincolns lost the most men, there was practically no sickness. All ranks were kept in hard condition by route-marching twice a week. Occasionally they were taken, for a change of scene, for a river trip down to Geneinetti: two companies at a time were embarked on barges and towed by steamer, and returned after a visit of a couple of days, the whole trip taking about a week.

Turning for a moment from the affairs in the Nile Valley, we may here mention that during May H.M.'s Diplomatic Agent in Abyssinia, Lieutenant J. L. Harrington, I.S.C., arrived at Menelik's capital.

At the beginning of June a number of the officers at the front, including the Sirdar, went down to Cairo, and some to England, on a few weeks' leave.

In July it was decided to send additional British

troops to reinforce the Sirdar's army at the front, and a second British infantry brigade was despatched from Cairo, together with some cavalry, artillery, and other details. The British Division (two brigades) as now reconstituted, was composed as follows :—

Commanding Division : Major-General W. F. Gatacre, C.B.
Commanding 1st Brigade : Colonel (temporarily Brigadier-General) H. G. Wauchope, C.B., C.M.G.
Commanding 2nd Brigade : Colonel (temporarily Brigadier-General) the Hon. A. G. Lyttelton, C.B.

The 1st Brigade was composed of the British brigade that took part in the Battle of the Atbara, viz. the Warwicks, Lincolns, Seaforths, and Camerons; and the 2nd Brigade, now sent up the Nile, was composed of the 1st Battalion Grenadier Guards, 1st Battalion Northumberland Fusiliers, 2nd Battalion Lancashire Fusiliers, and the 2nd Battalion Rifle Brigade. Besides this infantry brigade, the 21st Lancers; Maxim Battery (detachment Royal Irish Fusiliers); 32nd and 37th Field Batteries, R.A.; and details of the R.E., A.S.C., and R.A.M.C., were sent up.

At the same time two military attachés, Major Calderari and Major von Tiedman—the former representing Italy and the latter Germany—left for the front and joined the Sirdar's staff. A number of special correspondents arrived from England, including the following well-known gentlemen :—
Col. Frank Rhodes (*Times*), the Hon. H. Howard (*New York Herald*), Fred Villiers (*Globe*), Charles Williams (*Daily Chronicle*), Frank Scudamore

(*Daily News*), Hamilton Weldon (*Morning Post*), Bennett Burleigh (*Daily Telegraph*), W. T. Maud (*Graphic*), René Bull (*Black and White*), W. Maxwell (*Standard*), G. W. Steevens (*Daily Mail*), and several others.

The trooping from Cairo of the "additional force" began on July 25th, and by August 10th the last of the troops had started for the front.[1] They were conveyed by rail from Cairo to Shellal, above the First Cataract; a change of carriages being necessary at Luxor, as the narrow gauge line begins here. At Shellal they embarked on steamers for Wady Halfa. By the end of July the Nile had fortunately risen higher than it had done in 1896 (see Part II. Chap. I.), making the passage a comparatively easy matter for the flotilla of stern-

---

[1] Dates of departure from Cairo:—

Monday (July 25th): 32nd Field battery R.A., and staff of 1st British Brigade.

Wednesday (July 27th): Headquarters and four companies 2nd battalion Rifle Brigade.

Thursday (July 28th): Remainder of Rifle Brigade.

Friday (July 29th): Animals and baggage of howitzer battery, R.A., and of Maxim detachment.

Saturday (July 30th): Headquarters and four companies Grenadier Guards.

Sunday (July 31st): Howitzer battery (16th Company, E. Division, R.A.), and Maxim detachment (Royal Irish Fusiliers), Headquarters and four companies 21st Lancers.

Tuesday (August 2nd): Remainder of Grenadier Guards.

Wednesday (August 3rd): Headquarters and four companies 1st battalion Northumberland Fusiliers, and one squadron 21st Lancers.

Saturday (August 6th): Remainder of Northumberland Fusiliers, and one squadron 21st Lancers.

Monday (August 8th): Headquarters and four companies 2nd Lancashire Fusiliers.

Tuesday (August 9th): Remainder of Lancashire Fusiliers.

wheelers, and Wady Halfa was reached within three days of embarkation. From Wady Halfa they were conveyed by rail across the desert to Darmali, in a day and a half.

By the 18th of August the whole of the "additional force" had arrived at Fort Atbara, which place now presented a scene of great activity. It had become a civilised town, and, with its bazaars and cafés, presented a thriving appearance. By the time this force had arrived, 90 days' rations, sufficient for 25,000 men, had been accumulated here. The 3rd Egyptian battalion had arrived here from Suakin; having marched the whole way, via Berber. The 17th and 18th Egyptian battalions had also arrived here, having towed their boats all the way from Merawi, including the passage of the Fourth and Fifth Cataracts.

Meanwhile, during the progress of these reinforcements to the front, the Sirdar had quietly and unostentatiously sent forward the 3rd Egyptian Brigade, under Colonel Lewis, to Wad Habeshi, on the left bank of the Nile, at the foot of the Sixth Cataract, opposite the island of Nasri, under the pretext that the brigade was going to cut firewood for the boats, but in reality this was the first step of the great final move. The regiments forming the brigade were transported from Fort Atbara by the steamers, and the remaining brigades of the Egyptian army followed a few days later. To prevent this movement becoming known, the Sirdar prohibited the war correspondents from cabling

R

home any reference to it, and by the time their letters arrived in England the whole force was within striking distance of Omdurman.

Shabluka, where at one time it was thought the Dervishes might make a stand, was found (Aug. 18th) to be evacuated; and the stores which had been rapidly accumulated at Nasri island were, by the 23rd of August, transported through the Cataract to Jebel Royan—now, at high Nile, an island—where an advanced post, depot, and large bakery was established.

With the exception of a couple of Dervish scouts, who were surprised and shot by an Egyptian picquet at Wad Habeshi, none of the enemy had yet been seen; but from the top of Jebel Royan a view was obtained of Khartoum 34 miles off; the white dome of the Mahdi's tomb in Omdurman was plainly visible; and a number of Dervish scouts were seen reconnoitring the surrounding country. Major Staveley Gordon—General Gordon's nephew—was the first man in the force to sight the goal of the expedition.

The Sirdar made a close inspection of the Sixth Cataract, and found the northern entrance to the gorge at Shabluka defended by four strong forts; three on the left bank and one on the right. These forts came down to the water's edge, and several of the embrasures were under water. They had been constructed by Egyptian gunners (captured by the Mahdi), by whom the Khalifa's artillery was chiefly manned. The gorge, which is very narrow, extends for a distance of about nine miles, and has red granite walls rising almost perpendicularly to a height of 300 feet. Ridges of rocky boulders extend for some miles on each side of this channel, which would have made the turning of the position very difficult if the Dervishes had remained in force to oppose the Sirdar's advance. Under the circumstances, however, the Khalifa made no mistake in abandoning the Sixth Cataract, for to hold it would have required a larger force than he could have afforded to risk; besides which the forts could be turned on the land side, however effectually they might have barred the way to the gunboats.

As an instance of the way in which coming events are wont to cast their shadows before them, the Sirdar, before leaving Fort Atbara, received a deputation of several sheikhs and twelve hundred natives from Kordofan, petitioning him to occupy El Obeid, the capital, near which place it will be remembered that Hicks's army was destroyed by the Mahdists.

The troops of the "additional force" did not remain long at Fort Atbara, and each regiment, within a few days of its arrival, was conveyed in the gunboats a distance of 120 miles, to Wad Hamed (a few miles south of Wad Habeshi), where the whole of the Egyptian Army had concentrated. The 1st British brigade was conveyed to this place direct from its summer camp at Darmali.

The Camel Corps, crossing the desert from Korti to Metemmeh, had passed through the old battlefields of Abu Klea and Abu Kru. At the former place the ground was still white with bones; at Abu Kru little remained except a few mounds, that mark the British graves, which the Dervishes, to their credit, had left untouched. As the troops passed Metemmeh they were forcibly reminded of the recent Dervish occupation. The whole area from the river to the camp was a charnel house of dried carcases of bones. The town was deserted; one saw only dry bones and foul birds; everywhere was stench and desolation. It was a ghastly example of the handiwork of those "brave people struggling to be free," as a very prominent statesman seriously described these diabolical savages.

It was not known, even to the Sirdar, with any degree of certainty, what tactics the Khalifa intended to assume; whether he would sweep down upon his enemy, in keeping with the traditions of Soudan warfare, or would await the attack of his opponent at Omdurman, as Mahmud did at the Atbara. Every precaution was adopted by the Sirdar to prevent being taken by surprise; every step was taken with great caution, leaving nothing to chance; and the camp at Wad Hamed was protected by a strong zariba. This camp was two miles in length, and half a mile wide, and the British division was on the front (south) side.

All kinds of wild rumours were circulated. News was brought of an attempt made by the Khalifa to lay mines in the Nile, to destroy the gunboats. A Tunisian prisoner, who had been employed in

CHAP. V THE CONCENTRATION AT WAD HAMED

making gunpowder, was engaged to construct a box, and fill it with gunpowder; and to tow it out into mid-stream, opposite Kerreri, where he was to fix it in position. But the box exploded, and not only killed the prisoner—who was chained to the boat!—but blew up one of the Khalifa's steamers. Some of the London "dailies" stigmatised the Khalifa's endeavour to destroy the Sirdar's flotilla as "cowardly" and "dastardly"; but this is rather a one-sided view to take, for the construction of submarine mines is perfectly legitimate, and a recognised procedure in civilised warfare. This attempt, however, was the first and last the Khalifa made in that respect.

Another story of an unfortunate occurrence in the Dervish ranks was brought by a fugitive from Omdurman. During a review there of the whole Dervish force, Ali Wad Helu, who was second in command to the Khalifa, was heading a charge which was to be a rehearsal of the final triumphant onslaught on the infidel invaders, when he was thrown heavily; his arm was fractured, and he received other injuries.

On Wednesday, the 24th of August, the Sirdar held a review, at Wad Hamed, of the whole of the Anglo-Egyptian force, in battle array. It seems opportune to give here a list of the troops engaged :—

BRITISH DIVISION (Major-General Gatacre)

1st Brigade (Brigadier-General Wauchope) :—
  1st Battalion Cameron Highlanders.
  1st Battalion Seaforth Highlanders.

BRITISH DIVISION—*continued.*

1st Battalion Lincolnshire Regiment.
1st Battalion Warwickshire Regiment.

2nd Brigade (Brigadier-General Lyttelton) :—
1st Battalion Grenadier Guards.
2nd Battalion Rifle Brigade.
1st Battalion Northumberland Fusiliers.
2nd Battalion Lancashire Fusiliers.

These eight battalions averaged 900 strong, and therefore the British Division numbered approximately 7,500 men.

Besides the foot regiments the following also formed part of the British contingent :—
21st Lancers—about 500 sabres.
32nd Field Battery, R.A., with two 40-pounder Armstrong guns.
37th Field Battery, R.A., with 5-inch Howitzers.[1]
Detachment, 16th Co. (Eastern Division) R.A., with six Maxims.
Detachment of Royal Irish Fusiliers, with four Maxims.
Detachment, Royal Engineers.

EGYPTIAN DIVISION (Major-General Hunter).

1*st Egyptian Brigade* (Lieut-Colonel H. A. MacDonald) :—
2nd (Egyptian) battalion.
9th (Soudanese) ,,
10th ,, ,,
11th ,, ,,

2nd Egyptian Brigade (Lieut.-Colonel J. G. Maxwell) :—
8th (Egyptian) battalion.
12th (Soudanese) ,,
13th ,, ,,
14th ,, ,,

3rd Egyptian Brigade (Lieut.-Colonel D. F. Lewis) :—
3rd (Egyptian) battalion.
4th ,, ,,
7th ,, ,,
15th ,, ,,

---

[1] These Howitzers fired a 50-lb shell filled with the new explosive "Lyddite." The guns were drawn by mule teams led by Egyptians, and the equipment was so arranged that each mule carried four shells into action.

EGYPTIAN DIVISION—*continued.*

4th Egyptian Brigade (Lieut.-Colonel J. Collinson) :—
  1st (Egyptian) battalion.
  5th   ,,   ,,
  17th   ,,   ,,
  18th   ,,   ,,
  Besides the above, the Egyptian Army included :—
  9 Squadrons Egyptian Cavalry.
  8 Companies   ,,   Camel Corps, about 2,500 strong.
  1 Horse Battery[1] ,,   Artillery.
  4 Field Batteries ,,   ,,
  1 Maxim Battery ,,   (ten guns).
  Camel Transport.

The troops were paraded at 6 A.M. The cavalry, the Rifle Brigade, several batteries, and the Maxim detachments, were away at the time, but all came into camp a few hours afterwards. It was truly a magnificent spectacle; the front, when formed into line and advanced in attack formation, extending over two miles. The movements were carried out with a precision and steadiness worthy of an Aldershot review. No such force had ever been seen in the Soudan, and no general had probably ever commanded an army keener on meeting the enemy. The highest praise that could be bestowed upon it was that the Sirdar expressed himself highly satisfied with his inspection.

Throughout the subsequent advance, the troops were supported on the left flank, by the gunboat flotilla, which we may here describe. It now consisted of the following ten steamers [2] :—

---

[1] The Egyptian Horse Artillery battery has Krupp guns of 75-millimetre calibre, and the field batteries have Maxim-Nordenfelts.

[2] For the names of the officers on the gunboats, see Appendix, p. 311.

The *Sultan*, *Melik* and *Sheikh*: screw gunboats, carrying two Nordenfelts, one 12-pounder, one Howitzer, and four Maxims.

The *Fatteh*, *Nazir* and *Zafir*: stern-wheelers, carrying one 12-pounder, two 6-pounders, and four Maxims.

The *Tamai*, *El Teb*, *Abu Klea* and *Metemmeh*: stern-wheelers (old class), carrying one 12-pounder, and two Maxim-Nordenfelts.

The flotilla, under Commander Keppel, R.N., (*Zafir*) scoured the river; whilst the cavalry, under Colonel Broadwood, pushed ahead along the left (west) bank; and the opposite side of the river (right bank) was reconnoitred by the "Friendlies"—including Arabs of the Shagiyeh, Shukrieh, Jaalin, and Bishara tribes—under Major Montagu-Stuart-Wortley (60th Rifles), and Lieutenant C. Wood (Northumberland Fusiliers).

During the day (24th) the mounted troops moved off south; General Hunter started with Macdonald's and Lewis's brigades; and Maxwell's and Collinson's brigades followed at nightfall.

CHAPTER VI

NEARING THE GOAL

Sinking of the *Zafir*—The advance to El Hajir and Um Teref—Skirmishes—Wad el Obeid—Kerreri empty—Sheikh Nib—The Khalifa's army in sight—Sururab—Egega—Reconnaissance of Omdurman.

On Thursday (August 25th) Wad Hamed was evacuated, the British Division marching south. Lyttelton's brigade started at 5 A.M., and Wauchope's brigade left in the afternoon. After an eight hours' march, though the distance was only eleven miles, they reached Wad Bishara. This march was extremely trying, through very heavy sand, under the burning sun, and a number of men fell out on the way; especially in Lyttelton's brigade, who did not get their breakfasts until ten o'clock.

Each day, when the troops halted, they erected blanket shelters, and at night the troops slept in their clothes, with their arms by their side, with only a blanket each. Every man was prepared to fall in at a moment's notice, and the real strain of war now began to be felt. We have described these bivouacs at such length under the Dongola Expedition (Part II.), that it would merely be repetition to give any further description of them here.

The British Division arrived at El Hajir (opposite Jebel Royan) on the 26th inst., where the whole of the Sirdar's force was concentrated. It had been expected all along that the Khalifa would offer resistance at some point between the Sixth Cataract and his capital, and it was thought that the scene of action would probably be in the neighbourhood of Kerreri. There is no doubt that this was the Khalifa's original intention; but, as events showed, he subsequently changed his mind, and the Dervishes fell back before the steady advance of the Sirdar's forces. The Sirdar was kept well informed, by the constant stream of fugitives who came into camp daily, of everything transpiring in Omdurman, and it now appeared certain that the last stand of the enemy would be before the gates of the capital.

On the following day (27th) the army moved to a new camp at Um Teref, a distance of nine miles. The first sign of the enemy's troops was seen to-day. The cavalry, reconnoitring south of Um Teref, caught sight of a few Baggara horsemen, who quickly galloped off to the south. Major Stuart-Wortley's Irregulars to-day had a brush with a body of the Dervishes, who were in the act of raiding a village twelve miles south of Um Teref, on the west bank, and succeeded in capturing five of them.

On Sunday (28th) the Sirdar's forces pushed on to Wad el Obeid, where they encamped in zariba. A miserable night was spent; a violent thunderstorm raged for some hours, and the rain, pouring down in torrents, deluged the camp.

A serious disaster occurred this day. The gunboat *Zafir* suddenly sank near Shendy, at a distance of about sixty yards from the shore, the vessel's funnels remaining visible. All her guns, except a couple of Maxims which were rescued, were placed temporarily out of use, but luckily no lives were lost. There appeared a sort of fatality with this boat to become incapacitated just as she was required for serious business, for it will be remembered that she was rendered useless for the battle of Hafir by her boiler bursting just as the North Staffords were marching on board.

Reveillé was sounded at 4 A.M. on the 29th (Monday), and at five o'clock the advance was resumed. The force marched in double line of brigades, in readiness to meet an immediate attack, in the following order :—

    Wauchope's 1st   Maxwell's   Lewis's
(British) brigade.   (Soudanese) brigade.   (Egyptian) brigade.
    Lyttelton's 2nd   Collinson's   Macdonald's
    (British) brigade.   (Egyptian) brigade.   (Soudanese) brigade.

The Sirdar rode at the head of the infantry columns, the gunboats stealthily gliding up the river, keeping pace with the marching soldiers. The Horse Artillery and the cavalry covered the front, and the camelry the right flank. A battery of artillery was attached to each brigade, with the exception of Collinson's. The baggage column followed in rear, protected by three detached battalions.

The 21st Lancers were very active, and, together with Broadwood's native troopers, never lost touch with the enemy's mounted scouts; but, as the Sirdar's army approached, the Dervishes fell back.

At half-past one P.M. the force reached Sayal, where the infantry halted, and the cavalry pushed on as far as Kerreri, which they found practically deserted. The Lancers, passing through a small village, took prisoner a richly dressed Dervish, who, upon examination, proved to be a messenger from one of the Sirdar's spies in Omdurman.

Starting early on the 30th the force marched a few miles and finally zaribaed at Sheikh Nib, where a quiet uneventful night was spent. Every day, as the troops neared Omdurman, there was keen expectation that they would encounter the enemy, but, so far, they had been disappointed.

On the 31st (Wednesday) the force set out at five in the morning, marching in squares. The army appeared like a vast square, each face about a mile long, and presented a magnificent spectacle. The gunboats proceeded with the troops up the stream, keeping a sharp look-out for the enemy, but everywhere it appeared that they were falling back. In a village through which the troops passed some charred and mutilated bodies were seen, and it was rightly conjectured that these unfortunates had been suspected as spies and burnt in their homes.

The mounted troops made a complete reconnaissance of the city of Omdurman, and saw the Khalifa's army drawn up, in five immense divisions, to the north-west of the town, out in the desert. They reconnoitred five miles to the west of Omdurman, and, as they drew near, the whole Dervish force, numbering between 40,000 and 50,000, moved rapidly over the plain towards them. So swift was their advance that they almost came into action with our reconnoitring force : but the Khalifa evidently considered that the propitious moment had not yet come, and the Dervish army suddenly came to an abrupt halt.

In the afternoon the troops zaribaed on a ridge at Sururab, six miles north of Kerreri, and spent the night there. Another fierce storm broke over the country in the evening, which continued raging all night, and destroyed the telegraph at several points along the line.

On Thursday morning (September 1st), the force

started early, and, marching until about 1 P.M., finally bivouacked at Egega, one and a half miles south of Kerreri—which, as we have already seen, was found to be evacuated—and six miles from Omdurman.

Meanwhile the east side of the river had been cleared by Major Stuart-Wortley's Irregulars, and the gunboats. Stuart-Wortley was ordered by the Sirdar to clear the east bank as far as the Blue Nile, in order to enable the howitzer battery to be landed and placed in position to shell Omdurman. Several villages were found occupied, and these the "Friendlies" cleared, one after the other. One body of Dervishes made an obstinate resistance, in overcoming which the "Friendlies" lost twelve killed and thirty wounded. As soon as all was clear on that side of the river, the howitzers were landed from the barges towed by the steamers, and the bombardment[1] of Omdurman began (Thursday, 1st). The gunboats, at the same time, engaged the Dervish forts of Omdurman, Khartoum, and Tati Island, and heavy firing was maintained for several hours. In the end the whole of the forts were destroyed, several breaches were made in the great wall of Omdurman, and the dome of the Mahdi's tomb—a very conspicuous object—was shattered.

The mounted troops again rode within five miles of the city, and found the Khalifa's army,

---

[1] Before ordering the bombardment, the Sirdar sent a message to the Khalifa, warning him to remove the women and children.

now about 45,000 strong, extending in a long line westwards, on the same ground that they occupied the previous day. It was an extraordinary sight to see these countless jibbah-clad hordes, with their spears glistening in the sun, and banners waving, waiting only for the word to hurl themselves upon the invading force. It appeared certain that the Dervishes would attack, and the Sirdar accordingly advanced his army about a thousand yards into the desert, where he formed up in line of battle, with the cavalry out in front, and the reserves in laager behind. The Lancers had a slight skirmish with the enemy's scouts, but retired after exchanging a few shots; and the whole Dervish army then moved a short distance towards the Sirdar's position, and halted. This was about three o'clock. Nothing further occurred during the afternoon, the scouts of the opposing forces holding each other at a safe distance.

When it grew dark the Sirdar withdrew the troops into the zariba, and the night, which will never be forgotten by those present, was one of strained expectation. The opposing forces were now but five miles apart, and all night long it was momentarily expected that the Dervishes would take advantage of the darkness to hurl themselves upon the camp of the Anglo-Egyptian army. This would undoubtedly have been to the considerable advantage of the Dervishes, inasmuch as the wild rushes—the chief feature of their attack—would have been more telling, and they would have had better chances of getting to close quarters, under the cover of darkness, than in open daylight, when their well-trained opponents could be more easily handled, and their fire discipline could be turned to the best account.

But the Khalifa missed his opportunity.

THE BATTLE OF OMDURMAN.

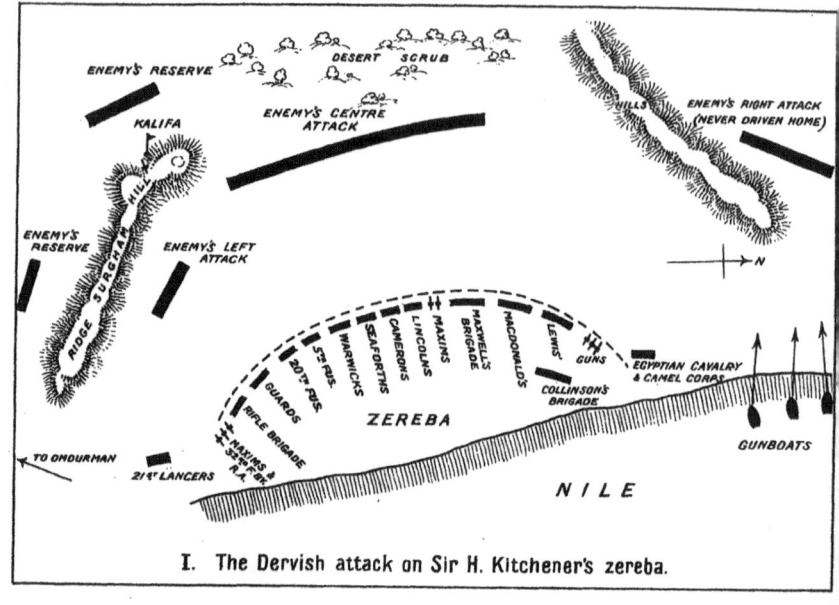

I. The Dervish attack on Sir H. Kitchener's zereba.

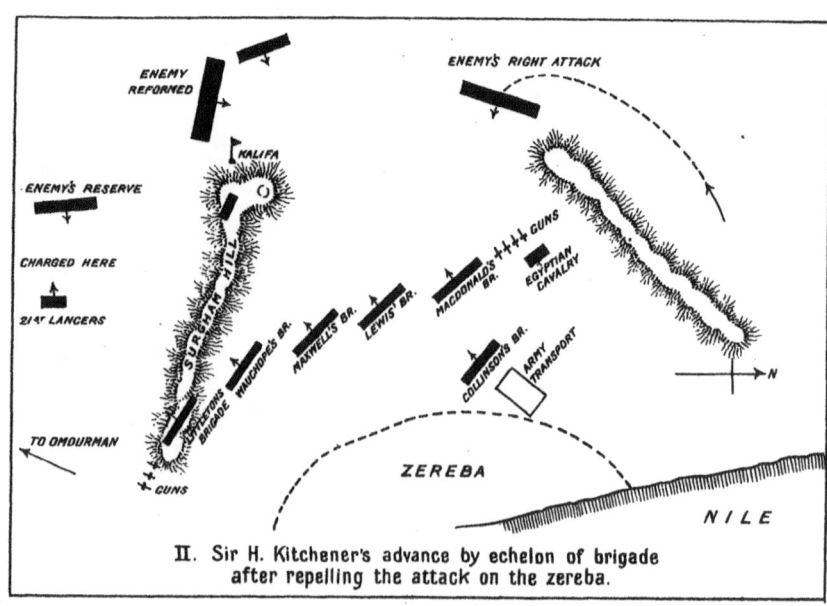

II. Sir H. Kitchener's advance by echelon of brigade after repelling the attack on the zereba.

CHAPTER VII

THE BATTLE OF KHARTOUM [1]

'Like the leaves of the forest when Summer is green,
That host with their banners at sunset were seen;
Like the leaves of the forest when Autumn hath blown,
That host on the morrow lay wither'd and strewn."
—*Byron.*

WHEN morning broke on Friday, September 2nd, it was realised by all that the momentous day had arrived on which the fate of the Egyptian Soudan was to be settled. The men were all in excellent spirits, and determined, as they said, "to avenge Gordon and wipe out Khartoum."

The position occupied by the Sirdar's army was a very good one. In front was an even, sandy plain, forming a glacis for half a mile, beyond which was a vast expanse of coarse grass; but towards the south and west the ground rose into small hills. The camp, which was formed on slightly elevated ground, in the neighbourhood of the village of Egega, was in a horse-shoe shape, both flanks resting on the river, protected by the gunboats. In the centre were a few detached mud buildings, in which the wounded were temporarily attended

[1] We must accept this designation as the one by which the battle will in future be known; although, geographically speaking, the "battle of Omdurman" is more correct.

to; and within the position, on the north, was the little mud village of El Gemuia. The British division had constructed a zariba along their front, and the native troops, having no shrubs nor bushes, had dug a shallow trench. The positions of the different regiments is shown in Plan 1 of the battle.

The whole force stood to arms half an hour before daybreak, ready to march out to attack the Khalifa's force, which, it was thought, would be found drawn up outside Omdurman. At 5.30 A.M. the gunboats and the howitzers—which, as we have seen, had been landed on the opposite (right) bank of the river—began the bombardment of Omdurman, and the booming of the guns could be distinctly heard in the still early morning air. The bombardment had not continued more than a few minutes before the cavalry picquets came galloping into camp with the welcome intelligence that the enemy were advancing in force. The gaps in the zariba were at once filled, the British division formed up in double ranks behind it, and the Khedivial troops lined the trench which they had constructed.

At 6 A.M. the long line of the enemy came into view about 3,000 yards off, advancing in good order, their loud, fierce, fanatical war-cry to Allah being distinctly heard, as they moved rapidly towards the Sirdar's forces. Upon their right, which ultimately bore down upon the British soldiers, was the Khalifa's brother, Yacoub; and upon their left were seen the blue and white banners carried by the troops under the Sheikh El Din, the Khalifa's son.

CAPTAIN G. CALDECOTT.
Royal Warwickshire Regiment.
From the "Graphic."

LIEUT. R. GRENFELL.
12th Lancers.
From the "Graphic."

OFFICERS KILLED AT THE BATTLE OF OMDURMAN, SEPT. 2ND, 1898.

HERR CHARLES NEUFELD.
ONE OF THE KHALIFA'S PRISONERS.
From the "Graphic."

[*To face p.* 259.

CHAP. VII   THE BATTLE OF KHARTOUM   259

At half-past six the batteries under Major Williams opened fire at a range of 2700 yards. The batteries made good practice, the shells bursting right in the enemy's ranks, but without causing the slightest tremor amongst them, the only apparent effect being to make them move faster; and they looked as if they were going to cross the front of the position. Suddenly they wheeled in the direction of the zariba, and bore down towards our south front. The Warwicks, Seaforths, Camerons, and Lincolns set their sights at 1800 yards, and poured in steady volleys; the rattling Maxims joined the musketry chorus, and the enemy pressed on with fanatical courage. About seven o'clock the Rifle Brigade and six companies of the Lancashire Fusiliers moved from the extreme left, and came up, at the double, in support of the 1st Brigade. The Dervishes could make but little headway against the storm of bullets; but they succeeded in getting within 800 yards, when they opened a heavy musketry fire, and casualties began to occur rapidly inside the zariba. Among the first to fall was Captain Caldecott,[1] of the Warwickshire regiment, who was shot through the head, and a few minutes afterwards Mr. Charles Williams (*Daily Chronicle*) was wounded, and Colonel Rhodes, the *Times* correspondent (brother of Mr. Cecil Rhodes), was shot in the shoulder and obliged to leave the field. Captain Clarke (Camerons) received a bullet in

[1] Captain Guy Caldecott joined the service in 1886, became captain in 1892, and was thirty-two years of age.

the groin, and Lieutenant Nicholson of the same regiment, was severely wounded in the elbow. The men were dropping right and left.

Simultaneous with the frontal attack, a formidable attempt was made to force our left flank, and the enemy were seen swarming round Surgham Hill. On they rushed, with their banners aloft, and charge after charge was made; but, though their courage was unsurpassed, their tactics were suicidal, for no troops could live in the face of the awful fire which was poured into them from the zariba, and those who were left alive were forced to withdraw from the field, which had by this time become a veritable shambles.

On the extreme right the Egyptian cavalry, camelry, and horse battery, which, under Colonel Broadwood, were holding Kerreri Hill, had been heavily engaged. A force of 10,000 Dervishes suddenly swept down on them, and before the slow-moving camels could be started, the force was in danger of being surrounded and cut off from the camp, towards which it slowly retreated. The fighting was so severe that the horse battery had two teams killed, and were obliged to dismantle a couple of guns and leave them in the hands of the Dervishes. Elated by this temporary success, the latter pushed forward with renewed energy; but their ardour received a rough check, for they suddenly found themselves under a deadly fire from the gunboats, and were forced to withdraw. The guns were subsequently recovered. In this

THE BATTLE OF OMDURMAN.

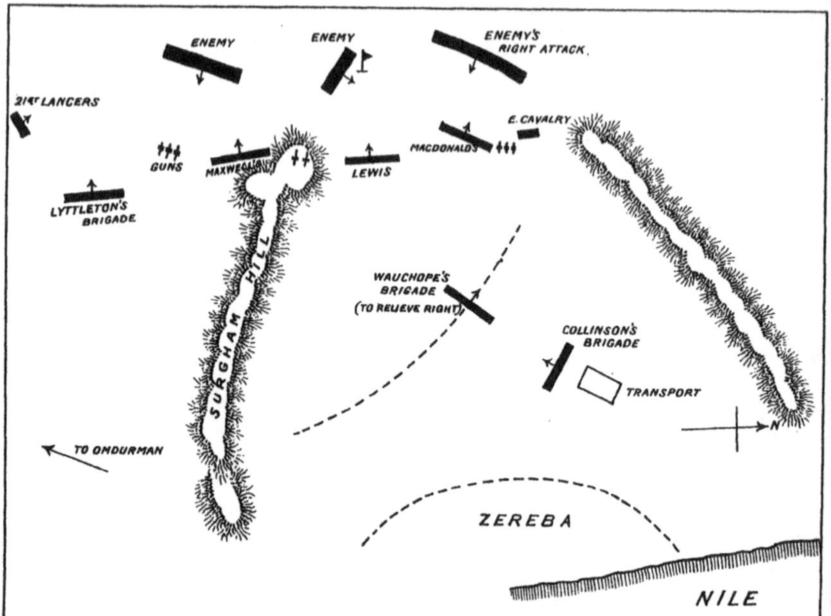

III. Macdonald's predicament on the right.

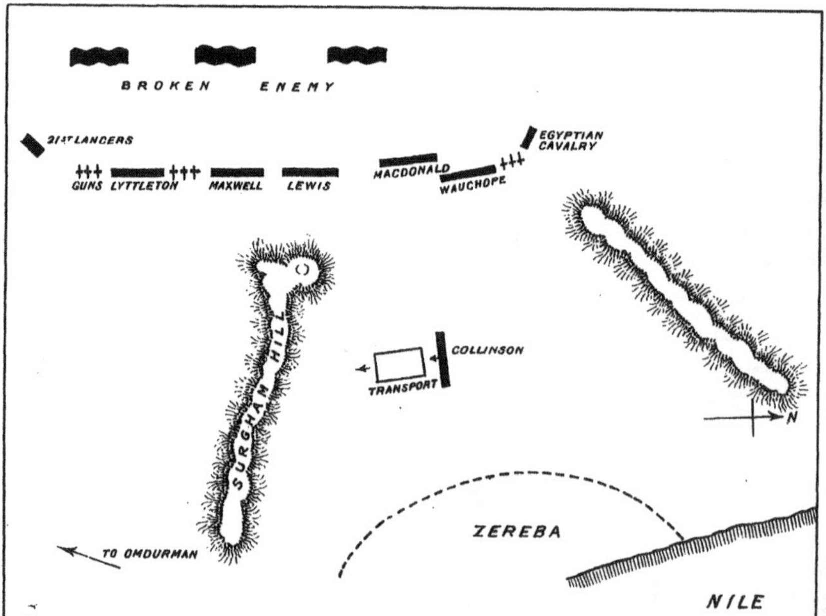

IV. The final advance.

engagement the Camel Corps, under Major Tudway, lost over seventy men, and Lieutenant Hopkinson (Seaforth Highlanders, Egyptian Army) was severely wounded.

The Khalifa retired (shortly after eight o'clock) in order to reorganise his shattered forces, and our cavalry cleared the front up to the neighbouring hills. Thus ended the first phase of the fight; but the battle was not yet over.

About half-past eight the Sirdar decided on making a counter-attack, and ordered a general advance. The force moved towards Omdurman in an échelon of brigades from the left. (See Plan 2.) The ground was of a very broken nature, which considerably retarded the advance.

On nearing Surgham Hill, the Sirdar ordered Maxwell to clear it of a party of the enemy, who were firing at the summit. For this purpose two companies of the 13th (Egyptian) battalion, under Captain Capper (East Lancashire Regiment, E.A.) were detailed, and they gallantly stormed and occupied the position.

No sooner had they done so, than very heavy firing was heard on the right. As Macdonald's Soudanese were moving out to change places with Lewis's brigade—and were at least 1,200 yards from the rest of the army—they were heavily attacked on the right and rear by the Khalifa's re-formed army. Macdonald and Lewis at once formed two sides of a square, Lewis's facing north and Macdonald's facing west, and on the latter brigade—only 3,000 strong—a terrific onslaught was made by 20,000 desperate Arabs, under the Khalifa's banner, followed soon afterwards by a similar attack led by Sheikh ed Din, the Khalifa's son. Thanks to the excellent fire-discipline of the Soudanese, the enemy never succeeded in driving the attack home, though they got within 300 yards of the line.

The Baggara cavalry, on this occasion, showed remarkable and reckless daring. They evidently intended to break through our lines and divert our fire, so as to give the Dervish infantry an opening. To carry this out was hopeless, for it meant riding to certain death,—but they galloped forward in loose open order, their ranks presenting one long ridge of flashing swords. Every soldier in the Sirdar's army watched breathlessly this daring feat. Nearer and nearer they came until the foremost horseman emerged almost within 200 yards of Macdonald's lines. A continuous stream of bullets from our lines was emptying the saddles, but on they came until not a single horseman was left. One Baggara succeeded in getting within 30 yards of the lines before he fell. The whole of the Dervish cavalry had been annihilated. There is no instance in history of a more superb devotion to a cause, or of greater contempt for death, than was shown on this occasion.

This, however, was but a prelude to a display of almost equally reckless courage on the part of the Dervish infantry, in their last despairing effort.

The latter, although they had seen the fate of the cavalry, swept like a great white-crested wave towards our ranks, without the slightest pause or hesitation. Hundreds planted their banners defiantly in the ground, and gathered round them only to drop lifeless at the foot, as the price of their devotion. The carnage was fearful, as the dauntless fanatics hurled themselves to inevitable death. Most noticeable of all was the Emir Yacoub, who bore forward the great black banner of the Khalifa (his brother), surrounded by his relatives and devoted followers. Although decimated by the hail of bullets before and around them, they surged forward, until only a mere handful of men remained around the flag; and these, never faltering, rushed onwards until they dropped dead beneath it.

The whole force of the attack was concentrated against Macdonald's brigade, and but for the consummate generalship of their leader, the Soudanese must have been destroyed. As soon as the Sirdar saw Macdonald's critical position, he ordered Lyttelton's and Maxwell's brigades to form to the right—so that the Dervishes were caught in a deadly cross-fire. At the same time Wauchope's brigade was sent back (the Lincolns moving to the extreme right) to reinforce Macdonald; but, as we have seen, the latter had averted the crisis, practically unaided, before the reinforcements had time to traverse the intervening mile and a half. What at one time had threatened to be a terrible disaster had been averted by the steadiness of the 9th, 10th, and 11th Soudanese battalions, under Majors Walter, Nason, and Jackson; by the admirable management of the batteries under Laurie, Peake, and de Rougemònt; and, above all, by the coolness and skill shown by Macdonald at this critical juncture; and to these are due, in great measure, the honours of the day. The casualties in Macdonald's brigade numbered 168, including Lieutenant Vandeleur (Scots Guards, Egyptian Army).

The appearance of a large force of Dervishes on the new left front of the line formed by Lyttelton's and Maxwell's Brigades, rendered it necessary for them to take ground to the left and cut this force off from Omdurman. After moving half-right for about half an hour, they halted, and the 32nd Field Battery made good practice on this body of the enemy, while the British fired long-range volleys. The Dervishes were checked, and the cavalry went out on the left flank to head them off.

At this point (about 9 o'clock) occurred one of the most brilliant features of the battle. The Sirdar, desiring to cut off the fugitive Dervishes from Omdurman, and to force them into the desert, sent forward the cavalry—the Egyptian troopers to the right, and the 21st Lancers to the left. When the latter, under Colonel Martin, had trotted a short distance, they approached a depression in the ground in which it was thought about 200 Dervishes were concealed. He wheeled the regiment into line, and ordered the "Charge" to be sounded. Suddenly, as if by magic, a body of the enemy, at least 2,000 strong, rose

Second-Lt. C. S. Nesham. Capt.-Cordeaux. Lt. and Adjt. Pirie. Lt. A. H. Taylor. Capt. and Quartermaster Graham.
Lt. Wormald (7th Hussars). Lt. Lewis. Lt. Champion. Capt. & Rdg.-Mstr. King. Lt. Smyth. Surg.-Major Pinches (attached). Lt. Protheroe Smith.
Lt. Conolly Lt. Vaughan Lt. the Hon. R. H. Lt. Brinton Lt. Tabor Vet.-Lt. Dunlop Smith and-Lt. Brinton.
(Scots Greys). (7th Hussars). Montmorency, (2nd Life Guards). (3rd Hussars). (attached)
Maj. Fowle Capt. Doyne Capt. Eadon Col. Martin Maj. Crole Wyndham Major Finn Capt. Dauncey Capt. Kenna
(comndg. B Squadn.). (comndg. C Squadn.). (comndg. 4th Squadn.). (comndg.). (second in command). (comndg. A. Squadn.). (C. Squadn.).

THE TWENTY-FIRST LANCERS—OFFICERS AND ATTACHED OFFICERS.

before them. The Lancers only numbered 320, all told; but there was no time for hesitation—a moment's delay and certain disaster must have followed. Within a minute the Lancers were riding, with lances levelled, full tilt at the human wall in front of them, the Colonel thirty yards ahead of his men. The enemy fired a terrific volley, and then the Lancers were in the khor, cutting and slashing their way through the dense mass of their opponents, right across the ravine, and up the other side.

Captain Eden's squadron was on the right, then Captain Doyne's, then Major Fowle's, and Major Finn's squadron was on the left. The two centre squadrons suffered the most, seven of Captain Doyne's men being killed and eleven wounded, whilst Major Fowle had nine killed and eleven wounded. Fowle himself killed the man he rode at, fired at another and missed him, and, shooting one more, galloped up the bank clear of the Dervishes, the bullets whistling all round him. The right troop of the line was led by Lieutenant Nesham, who got surrounded by the enemy, and was very severely cut across the left arm and right thigh, but fortunately he managed to keep on his horse, and got out of the scrimmage in safety.

Lieutenant Grenfell[1] (12th Lancers) was killed

[1] Lieutenant R. S. Grenfell (a nephew of the distinguished general, Sir Francis Grenfell, G.O.C. in Egypt) had a little less than two years' service, having joined the 12th Lancers in 1896. He was 23 years of age. For photograph see opposite page 259. As will be seen in the Appendix, a number of officers belonging to other regiments were attached to the 21st Lancers for service during the Expedition, the 21st being short of their proper complement of officers.

early in the charge. As soon as he was missed, Lieutenant de Montmorency, Captain Kenna, and Corporal Swarbrick rode back and, after shooting three or four of the enemy, made an extremely plucky but unsuccessful attempt to recover his body.[1]

The Dervishes adopted their old tactics of first ham-stringing the horses, and then cutting their riders to pieces. Every man who was unhorsed—with the single exception of Major Pinches (Royal Army Medical Corps)—was instantly killed. Pinches was saved by the great daring of Sergeant-Major Brennan, who galloped to the rescue, and, after a tough fight, in the course of which Brennan killed several Dervishes, he got the officer on to his own horse and carried him out of danger.

Major Wyndham had his horse shot as he was charging from the khor, and was lying on the ground in a perfectly helpless position, having emptied his revolver, when Captain Kenna galloped back, lifted him up into the saddle, and bore him safely away. Lieutenant Molyneux, of the Blues, came down when a hundred yards beyond the khor, his horse being killed. He ran on and was attacked by a couple of Dervishes, one of whom he shot, but the other inflicted a severe sword-cut on his right arm, forcing him to drop his revolver, and, being thus unarmed, he had to run for his life. Captain the Marquis of Tullibardine (also of the "Blues"), greatly distinguished himself in saving a trooper from the scrimmage. Lieutenant Wormald (7th Hussars)

[1] It was recovered subsequently.

engaged an Emir single-handed, but nearly came to grief. He delivered a terrible blow at the Emir, who was clad in mail, and his sword, on striking the armour, bent up like lead; but quick as lightning, he hit the Emir a stunning blow across the head with the bent sword, before the latter could get his own sword home, and a trooper, opportunely coming on, finished the chieftain. Lieutenant Pirie, adjutant of the Lancers, and Lieutenant Brinton (Life Guards) were both wounded.[1]

The men followed the plucky lead given them by their officers in the most spirited manner, and many were the instances of individual bravery recorded amongst the rank and file. One of the most remarkable was that of Trooper Brown. Seeing one of his comrades, Trooper Varley, dismounted and surrounded by Dervishes, Brown, though badly wounded himself, reined up just beyond the khor, and dragged Varley to a place of safety. He then turned again to rescue Trooper Rowlett, who, wounded in both arms and unhorsed, stood on the edge of the khor with a crowd of swordsmen rushing upon him. Brown galloped up in time, lifted Rowlett on to his horse, carried him into safety, then dressed his comrades' wounds. Many of the non-commissioned officers and men, who were badly wounded, concealed the fact until the fighting was over, in a most courageous manner. Trooper Byrne was wounded first by a Dervish

---

[1] Other officers wounded during the battle were Lieutenant-Colonel Sloggett (Royal Army Medical Corps) and Lieutenant Micklem, R.E.

sword and then by a rifle bullet, but he continued to fight with desperate valour, notwithstanding that his officer had ordered him to leave the *mêlée*; and Sergeant Freeman, although he had been badly slashed across the face with a Dervish sword, which severed his nose, and had received, almost simultaneously, a spear-thrust in his chest, from which blood was streaming, remained mounted until the end of the fight. Sergeant-Major Veysey, though shot through the cheek, continued to rally the men; and Trooper Ayton showed great pluck in rescuing a wounded comrade. These are but a few instances of the gallantry shown by the men of the 21st.

When the Lancers arrived four hundred yards from the other side of the khor, they dismounted, and opened fire on the enemy through whom they had just charged, causing the latter to withdraw westwards—so the Lancers had carried out their orders, to head the enemy off from Omdurman.

The regiment was then formed up, and it was found that, out of the 320 who rode in the charge, no less than 21 were killed (including Lieutenant Grenfell), and four officers and 46 men were wounded. Of their horses, 119 were killed and wounded. This brilliant affair was the more conspicuous inasmuch as it formed no part of the Sirdar's plan of attack. This was the first action in which the 21st Lancers had been engaged, and their maiden charge will for ever hold a prominent position in the annals of the British army.

CHAP. VII THE BATTLE OF KHARTOUM

With the repulse of the Dervish attack on Macdonald's brigade, the battle of Omdurman practically ended; the surviving Dervishes were now in headlong flight, which was hastened by the well-directed shells from the 32nd Field battery, on Surgham hill.

About half-past eleven the whole of the victorious army moved forward in line (Plan 4). Even now, those Arabs who were on the verge of death, endeavoured by every means in their power to kill at least one more "Turk" before entering Paradise; and these fanatics had to be despatched, by an advance party of Soudanese, before the Sirdar's army could advance with any degree of safety across the thickly strewn battle-field.

By noon the battle was practically over, and the force moved south to a muddy creek, called Khor Shambat, to water and feed, having had nothing to eat for over seven hours, whilst the mounted troops continued the pursuit.

Thus was the Khalifa overthrown, and Mahdism crushed for ever. Never had there been a finer force in the Soudan than that under the Sirdar; never a more desperate nor more admirably-trained army of Arabs, than that under the Khalifa; never had there been, in the history of the Soudan, a more bloody battle than that outside the walls of Omdurman.

CHAPTER VIII

THE CAPTURE OF OMDURMAN

AT half-past two in the afternoon, Maxwell was ordered to advance with his Soudanese brigade, and the 32nd Field battery, to occupy Omdurman; it having been previously ascertained that little or no resistance was likely to be offered within the city.

The order of march, (with the battalions in company column) was as follows:

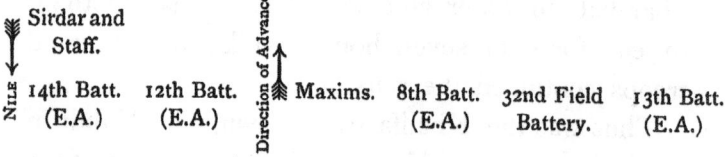

The Khalifa's black flag—which had been captured by the 15th (Egyptian) battalion, under Major Hickman—was carried behind the Sirdar.

The Brigade had not long left Khor-Shambat, before about a dozen sheikhs, bearing a flag of truce, advanced towards them, and told the Sirdar that the populace wished to surrender. The Sirdar replied that the principal Emir must himself come and make his submission, and a few minutes

BIRD'S-EYE VIEW OF OMDURMAN
From the "Graphic."

[To face p. 271.

later that worthy arrived, on a donkey, with his jibbah turned inside out, and, kissing the Sirdar's hand, he asked for pardon. The Sirdar replied that this would be granted on condition that all armed persons at once laid down their arms and surrendered. News of this had no sooner been carried back, than the inhabitants came, in hundreds, out of their houses, and cheered the troops as they marched on. It was evidently a matter of great surprise and relief to them, to find that they were not to share the fate that was usually meted out in the Soudan, to the inhabitants of conquered cities, in the form of wholesale butchery.

When about a mile from the town, a halt was ordered, and the order of march was changed, the Field battery taking the place of the Maxims, which moved to a position between the 14th and 12th battalions, after which, the advance was resumed, and the town was entered.

Omdurman is in the form of a rough isosceles triangle, with sides six miles long, and the base, which is towards the north, three miles in length. The whole surface is covered with buildings, but only the inner portion of it is walled in.

Guided by Slatin Pasha, with the Sirdar at their head, the troops advanced down the principal street, past hundreds of miserable mud hovels, until the great Wall was reached, and as the latter was not provided with banquette or loop-holes, they were enabled to advance right up to it.

We must describe the Wall before going any further, and the reader is referred to the accompanying map. Along the river-bank it is eighteen feet high, and is fronted with mud forts of considerable size. In most of its length it is four feet thick, but, for a mile, opposite Tuti Island, it is ten feet in breadth. Inside the enclosure which it forms, only the Khalifa's body-guard (*Mulazemin*), and the members of his family were permitted to live; outside is a maze of narrow filthy streets. The enclosure is divided, by a straight stone wall, into two parts, which, for convenience, we shall speak of as the "northern" and "southern" enclosures. The southern part, which was by far the most important, contained the Mosque, the Mahdi's tomb, the Khalifa's residence, and the Bayt-el-Amana (arsenal).

On reaching the Wall the following dispositions were made; the 8th and 12th battalions halted at "a" (see map), except one company of the 12th, which was posted with a couple of Maxims at "b" and the 14th remained at "c"; whilst the 13th (Soudanese) with the 32nd Field battery, moved down the road "d" towards the river, headed by Brigadier Maxwell. The Maxims commanded the main road, which was, from time to time, crossed by Baggara, who, as soon as they showed themselves, were shot down. The party on road "d" reached the forts by the river, opposite the grain-store ("12," in map) and found them deserted. On their left they passed the Khalifa's treasury—

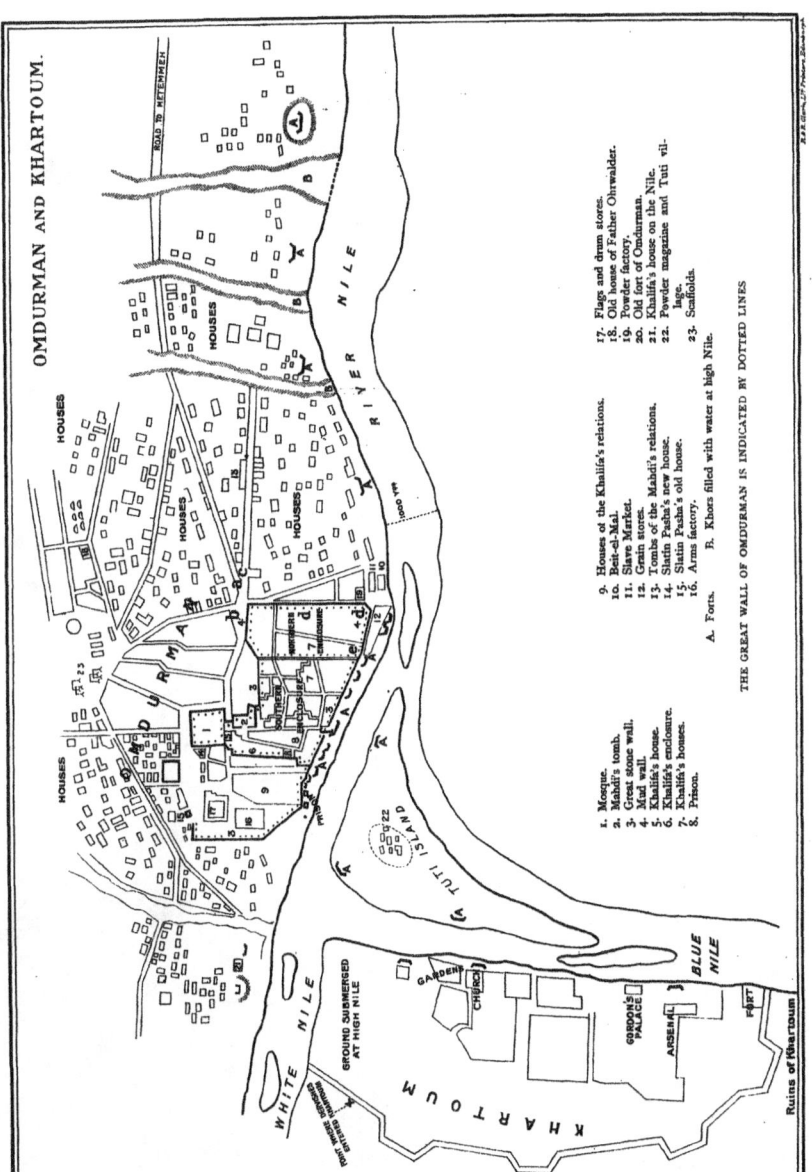

the Bayt-el-Mal—which the populace had already begun to loot. A few prisoners were taken, and then they worked round to the right, until the gate "e" was reached, which the gunboats had by this time demolished. The enclosure was entered and occupied, with very slight opposition, only a few Baggara having to be dealt with.

The northern enclosure being thus captured (about half-past four), the southern one, where it was believed the Khalifa was, with some of his body-guard, had now to be dealt with. Three companies of the 13th Soudanese, under Lieut.-Col. Smith-Dorrien, pushed on until they came to a great wooden gate ("f") which was found to be locked, and had to be forced. Whilst this was being done, they were fired on, from the south end of the river-road, by some Baggara, but the latter were soon scattered by a handful of Soudanese. General Hunter and his Staff now joined the party, and the enclosure was entered. A broad road led straight to the Mosque and the Khalifa's house, but, with this exception, the southern enclosure—like the northern one—consisted of narrow, crooked lanes, down which a few Baggara were seen bolting for their lives into the filthy, evil-smelling mud hovels. A number of Jehadia were met, and were promptly disarmed.

The troops made direct for the Khalifa's house. which was found barred. The gunboats thereupon directed their fire against the building, and, in so doing, very nearly caused the death of the Sirdar, who had taken up a position close by. The latter

T

had a narrow escape ; but one of the correspondents was not so fortunate, and, being hit by one of the shells, was instantly killed. This was the Hon. Hubert Howard,[1] (representing the *New York Herald,*) who had ridden unhurt through the charge with the 21st Lancers, and was killed by almost the last shot fired in Omdurman. An entry into the house was soon effected, but, with the exception of a few Baggara who resisted desperately, and had to be despatched, the place was deserted. The house was of two storeys, with a high verandah, supported by carved pillars, and the rooms were large and lofty.

A move was then made to the Mosque, on entering which a couple of Dervishes rushed out, and charged the Soudanese, killing one and wounding another, but both of these fanatics were instantly bayoneted. It was now nearly dark, but there was sufficient light to see that the Mosque was empty. The Mahdi's mausoleum was quite the finest building in the city. The Mosque measured thirty-six feet square, and was surmounted by a dome forty feet high. In the centre was the wooden sarcophagus, covered with a pall of banners, and enclosed by iron railings brought from the old mission church at Khartoum.[2]

It was now evident, to the intense chagrin of all,

[1] The Hon. Hubert Howard, second son of the Earl of Carlisle, was born 1871 went to Oxford (Balliol) in 1890, saw active service as a volunteer in Matabeleland (wounded) in 1896, and was called to the Bar in 1897.

[2] The building was blown up by Gordon's nephew a few days afterwards, and the Mahdi's remains were scattered to the four winds of Heaven.

CHAP. VIII THE CAPTURE OF OMDURMAN 275

that the Khalifa had succeeded in effecting his escape. The gunboats and Egyptian cavalry and camelry (including the "friendlies") were sent off in hot haste to overtake him, if possible,[1] but, after going thirty miles up the White Nile, the cavalry were compelled to return, owing to the exhausted condition of their horses. The Lancers' horses were almost too tired to move, and had had only one drink (at half-past three) all day.

The Sirdar next went to the Prison, and released the European prisoners, whom the Khalifa had confined there for many years They included the Austrian, Charles Neufeld,[2] Joseph Ragnotti, Sister Teresa Grigolini, and some thirty Greeks, who were all well. Neufeld had been in captivity since 1885, when he started from Assouan, for the quixotic purpose of trading at Khartoum. He was now found dressed in a *jibbah*, and manacled. On the Sirdar opening the prison gate, Neufeld said, in good English: "Thirteen years we have been longing and waiting for this day." He was taken to Colonel Wingate's quarters, where his chains were filed off.

The Sirdar then proceeded to visit the Khalifa's Arsenal, where he found, drawn up outside, about a hundred of the principal Sheikhs of the city, who

[1] Up to the time of going to press, the Khalifa had not been captured, and it is probable that he has escaped altogether into Kordofan.

[2] Neufeld's wife, whom he married in 1880, is an Englishwoman, daughter of a Northwich tailor, and, at the time of her husband's release, was in charge of a hospital, at Marbury. For photograph of Herr Neufeld see opposite page 259.

came to tender their allegiance and submission. Among them were many of the old rulers of the Soudan Departments—Turks and Egyptians, and officers of Hicks Pasha's defeated army. There were present, besides the Governor of Senaar, the builder of the Khalifa's forts, the Chief Ordnance Officer of Hick's Pasha's Force, and Gordon's native doctor.

The arsenal contained hundreds of stands of obsolete weapons of every age, and in every stage of the evolution of arms of precision; basket shields from Equatoria, Nagara drums from Bahr-el-Gazal, transport equipment for hundreds of camels, Hicks's sword-bayonets, flint-locks, barrels of saltpetre, many boxes of gunpowder, artillery charges sewn up in cloth packets, and one old Crusader pikeman's helmet. In the corner of the building was a tower from which the war drum of the Khalifa was beaten when he called his forces to arms.

By sunset, the whole of the enclosure within the wall of Omdurman had been thoroughly searched and cleared of the enemy; and the Khalifa's capital was in the hands of the Sirdar.

Whilst Maxwell's brigade was occupied as described above, the British Division and the remainder of the Egyptian Army had also moved from Khor-Skambat. After a scanty feed (from the rations carried by the camels) the force had fallen in at 4.30 P.M., and had followed in the tracks of Maxwell's brigade, until they arrived at the wall. Then, finding that there was no real opposition, they had made

CHAP. VIII   THE CAPTURE OF OMDURMAN

their way through the narrow, silent, deserted streets, through a sickening stench, until they reached the open, on the west side of the town, where they bivouacked with picquets posted all round. Here they were joined by Maxwell's Soudanese, with the exception of a detachment left to hold the enclosures.

By the time the regiments had severally taken up the positions allotted to them, it was ten o'clock; the men had no water and the baggage camels had not arrived. Shortly after eleven, however, the camels reached the bivouac, and a little rum and water was served out; after which every one lay down for a night's rest, which had never been better earned.[1]

Except between the hours of 2 and 4.30, the troops had been marching, manœuvring, and fighting, on hardly any food, and under the blazing sun, since 3.45 A.M.; yet all were as willing and cheerful now, as they had been at the start. The men of the British Division naturally felt the intense physical strain—to say nothing of the awful thirst—more than their native comrades; but they had shown

---

[1] In the evening the following "General Order" was issued:—

"The Sirdar congratulates all the troops upon their excellent behaviour during the general action to-day, resulting in the total defeat of the Khalifa's forces and worthily avenging Gordon. The Sirdar regrets the loss that has occurred, and, while warmly thanking the troops, wishes to place on record his admiration for their courage, discipline, and endurance.

"(Signed)   H. M. L. RUNDLE.
"*Chief Staff Officer.*"

marvellous pluck and endurance, and had proved that the young Briton is all that can possibly be desired in the shape of fighting material, thereby absolutely giving the lie direct to those who, sitting at home at their ease, seem to take a pleasure in animadverting on the inferiority of our "boy soldiers."

The wounded had all been placed on the hospital barges ("convoy boats") before nightfall. Considering the nature of the battle, our losses were remarkably slight. The following is a summary of the casualties in the British Division:—

	Killed.		Wounded.		Total number of Casualties.
	Officers.	R. & F.	Officers.	R. & F.	
21st Lancers	1[1]	20	4[2]	46	71
1st Batt. Grenadier Guards	—	—	1	4	5
1st Batt. Northumberland Fusiliers	—	—	—	2	2
1st Batt. R. Warwick Regiment	1	—	1	6	8
1st Batt. Lincolnshire Regiment	—	1	—	17	18
2nd Batt. Lancashire Fusiliers	—	—	—	6	6
1st Batt. Seaforth Highlanders	—	1	—	17	18
1st Batt. Cameron Highlanders	—	2	2	27	31
2nd Batt. Rifle Brigade	—	1	—	8	9
Detachment, A.S.C.	—	—	—	1	1
Detachment R. Army Medical C.	—	—	1	2	3
Correspondents	1	—	2	—	3
Total	3	25	11	136	175

[1] "Attached." [2] Including two "attached." [3] One died subsequently.

The Royal Artillery and Engineer detachments had no casualties. Of the Egyptian Army, one officer (Egyptian) and 20 rank and file (natives) were killed; 13 officers (including 5 British), 1 British non-commissioned officer, and 221 native rank and file were wounded. Total number of casualties in the Anglo-Egyptian Army: 49 killed and 382 wounded. Grand total, 431.

The Dervish loss was immense. No less than 10,800 bodies were counted on the field of battle, besides an additional number of 350 in the town of Omdurman. The number of wounded was estimated at 16,000, making the total number of casualties, on the Khalifa's side, amount to at least 27,000. Thousands of prisoners were taken, and three of Gordon's old steamers, the *Bordein, Khasm-el-Mus*, and the *Talahawia*,—the two former still fit for use—were captured.

It had been a glorious day. A most decisive battle had been fought and won, and every man in the force felt that he had done his duty, and had assisted in crushing the power of the greatest scourge that the Soudan—and perhaps the world—had ever seen. Gordon had been avenged, and the exhortation left to the British Government, almost as a legacy, to "smash" the Mahdi, had been fulfilled.

CHAPTER IX

KHARTOUM—AND AFTER

The ceremony at Gordon's palace—British troops return to Cairo—Major Marchand's expedition—The Sirdar occupies Fashoda and Sobat—Capture of Gedaref—A review of the Campaigns.

SHORTLY after 4 o'clock on the morning of the 3rd (Saturday), the Anglo-Egyptain army fell in, and, after marching four miles south, bivouacked just on the outskirts of the town, next to the river. No sooner were the men dismissed, than a rush was made to the muddy water, to get the first good drink they had had for over 24 hours.

The first duty of the day was to bury those who had lost their lives in the battle. During the morning some thousands of Dervish prisoners were medically examined, and those who were found sound—rather less than half—were immediately enlisted in the service of the Khedive. This was a striking instance of the thoroughness with which we follow up our victories.

On Sunday morning (4th) the Sirdar visited Khartoum, being conveyed across the river in the *Melik*, and at the same time representative

MEMORIAL SERVICE, GORDON'S PALACE.
Khartoum, Sept. 4, 1898.
From "Black and White."

detachments from all the regiments crossed over in the stern-wheelers *Dal* and *Akasheh*.

Khartoum, as seen from the river, was a pretty-looking place, with gardens by the water's edge, which, however, had long fallen into neglect. The Government House—or Palace—where Gordon lived, was found in ruins, like all the surrounding buildings. It was about 80 yards long, built of mud bricks, and covered with yellow plaster. The broad veranda staircase, on which Gordon was killed, in front of the house, had disappeared, together with the whole of the upper storey.

As soon as the steamers had moored up, the troops paraded opposite the Palace, in three sides of a square—British on the right (facing the building), Egyptians on the left. The 11th Soudanese formed a guard of honour. At a signal from the Sirdar, who had taken up a position in the centre, the Union Jack was hoisted by Captain Watson (A.D.C.) and Lieutenant Staveley, R.N. on the roof of the Palace, whilst Major Mitford and Major Badri Effendi (A.D.C.), ran up the Khedivial flag; the bands played "God Save the Queen" and the Khedivial Anthem, and the guns of the *Melik* boomed forth a royal salute. The Sirdar then called for three cheers for the Queen, and then three for the Khedive, which were given with enthusiasm. The rejoicings were followed by a brief service in memory of the hero of Khartoum whose shadow still seemed to hover over the desolate city. The British bandsmen played the Dead March in "Saul," whilst the Egyptians followed with another funeral march, and the pipers of the Highland Regiments wailed a lament. The three chaplains then offered prayers, invoking divine mercy and blessing on the Soudan; and the Soudanese bands concluded the ceremony with Gordon's favourite hymn "Abide with Me." The memory of those present went back to the pathetic picture of the lonely man who was locked in the confines of the desert surrounded by bloodthirsty and ferocious enemies, and who, watching hourly for the help that came too late, fell a martyr to his country and his duty.

At the conclusion of the ceremony the Sirdar and troops returned to Omdurman, a detachment of the 11th Soudanese being left to guard the flags and to hold Khartoum.

During the next two or three days the Sirdar received congratulatory telegrams from all parts of the world, including one from H. M. the Queen, H. H. the Khedive, Lord Lansdowne, Lord Wolseley, and a host of others.[1]

The British regiments left the front, for Cairo, as fast as the steamers could take them, and by the middle of the month most of them had again returned to civilisation.

On the 7th of September the telegraph was brought to Omdurman, and, on the same day,

---

[1] News of the victory reached London on Saturday afternoon. No information had been vouchsafed from the Soudan since the previous Tuesday, owing to the telegraph line having broken down, and the anxiety which had been produced served only to increase the enthusiasm with which the joyful intelligence was received.

the astounding news was received to the effect that Fashoda was occupied by the French!

Fashoda, the capital of the Shilluk country, is 918 miles, by river, from Khartoum. In 1865 the Khedive, Ismail Pasha, sent a force to that place, and established a military camp of a thousand men there. In 1882, shortly after the commencement of the great rebellion, Ussuf Pasha, who was then Governor of Fashoda, marched against the Mahdi, but his army was unfortunately destroyed. This important Nile post is, of course, part of the Khedive's dominions; and the fact that his troops had not been in the place for a lapse of years, in no way justified its occupation by another power.

The news of this latest development on the Upper Nile was brought by the captain of the Dervish steamer, *Tewfikieh*, who had been sent up the Blue Nile by the Khalifa, and now returned to find Omdurman in other hands. He at once surrendered to the Sirdar, and stated that, on reaching Fashoda, he had been fired on by a force of natives, under white officers, and, after losing a number of men, had been compelled to beat a retreat.

On receipt of the above information, the Sirdar —seeing possible diplomatic difficulties looming ahead—ordered all the special correspondents to return at once to Cairo. At 6 A.M. on the morning, of the 10th he steamed full speed to Fashoda, taking with him a company of the Cameron Highlanders, under Captain the Hon. Andrew Murray, and the 10th, 11th, and 13th Soudanese battalions. These troops were conveyed in the gunboats *Sultan* (Keppel), *Fatteh*, and *Nazir;* the Sirdar, with Colonel Wingate and Slatin Pasha, going on the *Dal* (post-boat). The party was joined, on the 17th, by the *Abu Klea*.

On Sunday, the 18th, the Dervish steamer *Safia* was captured. On arriving at Fashoda (21st), the information received by the Sirdar proved to be correct, and it was found that Major Marchand, with a small armed force of eight officers and 120 Senegalese soldiers, were in occupation of the place, where they had arrived on the tenth of July and had hoisted the French flag. The Major came on board the *Dal*, and had a private interview, lasting about half an hour, with the Sirdar; in which the latter pointed out to him that he was occupying Egyptian territory, and requested him to haul down his flag and to withdraw. This Major Marchand courteously but firmly refused to do, until so ordered by the French Government; whereupon the Sirdar landed his troops, posted them behind the French encampment, and hoisted the British and Egyptian flags with all due ceremony. This done, he left the 11th Soudanese, under Major Jackson (Gordon Highlanders, Egyptian Army), to hold the place, and proceeded south with the rest of the little force to Sobat, where he arrived on the 22nd, and established a second post —three companies of the 13th Soudanese being landed here. The return journey was commenced on the 23rd, Fashoda being reached the same day. Here the *Sultan* and *Nazir* were left behind, and the Sirdar went on with the Camerons and 10th Battalion to Omdurman, which was reached on the 24th of September. The Sirdar at once cabled to the Foreign Office the result of his mission. The case was now outside the scope of his duties or powers, and had become a matter which diplomacy alone could deal with.

The same day as the Sirdar's return to Omdurman, (Sept. 24th) Major-General Sir Francis Grenfell, commanding the British troops in Egypt, arrived there from Cairo ; and on Monday he reviewed the whole of the Egyptian force, outside the town. Meanwhile, during the Sirdar's journey up the White Nile, Major-General Hunter had proceeded up the Blue Nile with a small force, and, meeting with hardly any opposition, had effectually subdued and pacified that region. Captain Murray's company of Camerons went on to Cairo, where the Sirdar himself arrived on the 6th of October.

The final act for the clearance of the Soudan from the Dervish was the occupation of Gedaref by Colonel Parsons, Commandant at Kassala. As soon as Omdurman had fallen, news was brought to the Sirdar that a band of Dervishes were pillaging villages along the banks of the Nile, whereupon a gunboat was immediately sent up the river to find them. A short engagement ensued, in which the enemy lost 1,000 killed and wounded, and the remainder of them retreated to [1] Gedaref. Colonel Parsons set out from Kassala with the 16th (Egyptian) Battalion and the Arab "Irregulars," his whole force numbering barely 1,300, and, on the 22nd of September, he arrived before Gedaref. The place was surrounded by a wall, and defended by a mud fort; and the Dervish garrison, who numbered about 3,000 men, were armed chiefly with rifles captured by the Abyssinians from the Italians at Adowa. After a fierce fight, which lasted three hours, the place was captured and the enemy were utterly routed. On the Egyptian side the casualties were:—16th Battalion: 3 officers (native) wounded; 20 men killed, and 30 wounded; Arab "Irregulars," Camel Corps, &c.: 1 officer (native) wounded; 17 men killed, and 23 wounded. So that the total number of casualties on our side was under a hundred, whilst the enemy were estimated to have lost 700. On the 28th of September a strong force of Dervishes, under Ahmed Fedl, made a desperate effort to regain possession of Gedaref, but were repulsed by Colonel Parsons's troops, with heavy loss; many of the Arabs surrendered, and the remainder dispersed.

This was the last stand made by the Dervishes, and, after fourteen years of anarchy and bloodshed, peace reigned once more throughout the Egyptian Soudan.

* * * *

In concluding the story of the re-conquest of the

[1] The telegraph from Suakin—which had been constructed by Corporal Lewis, R.E., under the superintendence of Lieutenant Manifold, R.E.—reached Kassala on the 24th of September.

Soudan, we may call attention to some of the salient points of the three years' campaign which mark it out as unique in history. In the first place, the strategy throughout was totally different to that adopted in expeditions of a like nature. It is usual, when once the invading force has started, to push it forward with the least possible delay, until the goal has been reached; in these expeditions, however, all forward movement was entirely subordinate to two important considerations, namely, the construction of the railway and the rise of the Nile. Until the railway was completed to a given point, and stores had been accumulated at the front, no attempt was made to push on further.

In the Dongola Expedition, Akasheh was seized at the outset, and then there was a long pause, to allow time for the railway to be pushed forward. Then came the sudden swoop on Ferket, followed by another stationary period, whilst the stern-wheelers were being hauled through the Second Cataract, the sections of the new gunboats were being put together at Kosheh, and vast quantities of commissariat stores were being conveyed by rail to the front. No sooner were these preparations completed, than the Sirdar, with lightning rapidity, made another swoop on the Dervishes, routed them at Hafir, and struck the final blow at Dongola.

The difficulties which the Sirdar had to surmount in the campaign of 1896, were as great as they were unforeseen. The outbreak of cholera, the exceptionally late rise of the Nile, the prolonged spell of southerly winds (which delayed the storeladen *gyassas*), the phenomenal storms (which destroyed the railway), the untimely explosion on the *Zafir*, the running aground of the *El Teb*,—these are only a few of the many instances that might be cited to prove how the Sirdar was hampered from beginning to end by natural, rather than by strategical obstacles.

The campaign of 1897 presented much the same difficulties as that of the previous year, and the lessons to be gathered from it are in matters of commissariat and transport, rather than strategy. The same policy was pursued by the Sirdar. The railway was pushed forward across the desert as near to Abu Hamed as was compatible with safety, and then a sudden and brilliant move was made by General Hunter upon this point, from Merawi; after which the railway was continued as far as the river Atbara.

The Nile Expedition of 1898 was marked by two striking features. One was the extraordinary manner in which the Khalifa, and his subordinate Mahmud, played into the Sirdar's hands; the other was the admirable administration of the Anglo-Egyptian force. The advance of Mahmud from Metemmeh to the Atbara, was as unexpected as it was fortunate, for it was never for a moment anticipated that he would leave his admirable strategical position on the Nile, and advance to do battle with the Sirdar. It was thought, rather, that he would await the arrival of the invading force in some well-fortified position commanding the passage of the river, when the rise of the Nile should render another advance expedient on the part of the Sirdar's force. The delay in Mahmud's advance afforded the Sirdar time to obtain the assistance of the British brigade; and, with his force thus strengthened, he was enabled to advance, with admirable promptitude, and annihilate Mahmud's army. The total rout of the latter at the battle of the Atbara cleared the way for the final advance, by accounting effectively for the only large Dervish force outside the walls of Omdurman.

A noticeable feature of the final advance was the precision and foresight with which it was carried out, without a single hitch. Comparisons, we know, are odious; but the manner in which the transport and commissariat arrangements of this force—the largest ever sent into the Soudan under civilised conditions—were carried out, will bear favourable comparison with *any* campaign, not only British, of modern times.

The flotilla of gunboats was indispensable to the successful issue of the campaign; and, but for the bombardment of Omdurman—which undoubtedly determined the Khalifa to leave the city and fight in the open—the Sirdar might have found the capture of Omdurman a far more hazardous and formidable undertaking than it proved to be.

We have not yet alluded to what was perhaps the greatest difficulty in the Sirdar's path, namely, the lack of funds. From beginning to end the strictest economy had to be observed; and never, in modern times, has so much country been conquered at such little expense. The actual cost of the Dongola Expedition was £733,000, but this sum included £185,000 for the extension of the railway and telegraph from Wady Halfa to Sarras, and the purchase of the gunboats. Nearly 600 miles of railway were constructed for this sum under the most trying conditions. The record for military railway construction (hitherto held by the Russians over their Trans-Siberian railway) was beaten by the Sirdar's railway staff; although the line lay through a waterless desert necessitating 2,500 workmen being provided with their daily food and drink. The total length of railway constructed during the three years (1896—1898) was 500 miles at a cost of one million pounds; and the total cost of the military operations during that period came to £2,600,000.

Nor was a record attained only in the matter of expenditure; never has so much country been conquered with so little loss of life. Approximately the casualties of the Anglo-Egyptian Forces (1896—1898) numbered 2,300; of whom 1,200 (400 British) were killed or died from sickness; whilst the number of Dervishes killed and wounded during that period cannot have been less than 36,000.

From first to last the three years' campaign was a complete success; was a source of gratification to those who took part in it; and reflected the highest credit upon those who were responsible for planning it out and bringing it to its successful issue.

The masterly grasp of detail and faculty of organisation possessed by the Sirdar, Sir Herbert Kitchener, showed itself clearly from the day he took command of the Nile Expeditionary Force, in 1896, to the day he finally destroyed the Khalifa's army. With machine-like precision he carried out his plans; never in a hurry, but never wasting a moment. Slow and cautious to prepare, and neglecting nothing that might assist his purpose, he was swift and sure to strike. The clash of battle is appreciated by every soldier more than the drudgery of railway construction and the transport of stores; but the Sirdar showed himself a man of iron, endowed with extreme patience. He never gave battle until absolutely certain of victory; ensured the success, beforehand, of whatever he attempted; and no general was ever better trusted by his troops than was "Gordon's Avenger."

The recapture of the Soudan will be followed by the occupation of those Equatorial provinces, which, until the rising of the Mahdi were held by the Egyptian Government, and this will bring into possibility the great Imperial aspiration of opening up the vast area of Central Africa. A British railway running from Cairo to the Cape will be an achievement of the near future: a colony under the British flag, stretching from end to end of the African continent is now more than a mere dream; it is within the range of practical politics, and Great Britain will allow nothing to stand in the way of the realisation of this project.

APPENDIX I

ORGANISATION OF THE FORCES
OF THE
DONGOLA EXPEDITION, 1896
AND THE
NILE EXPEDITIONS, 1897—8
WITH A COMPLETE ROLL OF ALL THE OFFICERS

EGYPTIAN ARMY

Officers only temporarily attached to Egyptian Army, on "Special Service," are shown in italics.

Egyptian Army.	DONGOLA EXPEDITION, 1896.			NILE EXPEDITION, 1897–8.		
	Name.	British Regt.	Remarks, Honours after Dongola Expedition.†	Name.	British Regt.	Remarks, Honours, &c.‡
HEADQUARTER STAFF.* Sirdar; Commanding Expeditionary Force	Brev.-Col. (temp. Maj.-Gen.) Sir H. H. Kitchener, C.B., K.C.M.G.	R.E.	Promoted Maj.-Gen., K.C.B., Grand Cordon Osmanieh.	Major-General Sir Herbert H. Kitchener, K.C.B., K.C.M.G.	R.E.	Raised to Peerage, Sept. '98.
A.D.C.	Capt. J. K. Watson	K.R.R.C.	D.S.O.	Capt. J. K. Watson, D.S.O.	K.R.R.C.	Desp. May 24, (4th Medjidie),Sept. 30, '98.
,,	*Lieut. Lord E. H. Cecil*	Gren.Gds.	4th Medjidie; promised Brev.-Majority	*Brev.-Maj. Lord E. H. Cecil*	Gren. Gds.	Desp. May 24, Sept. 30, '98.
,,				*Lieut. Hon. F. H. S. Roberts*	K.R.R.C.	Joined Aug. '98. Desp. Sept. 30, '98.
Asst. Mily. Secretary				[Bt.-Lt.-Col. J.G. Maxwell, D.S.O.]		Commanding 2nd Brigade E.A., q.v.
Financial ,,				Capt. W. E. O'Leary, p.s.c.	R. Ir. Rif.	From "Suakin District," q.v.
Staff Officer				and Lt. W. E. Bailey	E Lan R.	Promoted from ranks, after Dongola.
Adjutant-General (C.S.O.)	Brev.-Col.H.M.L.Rundle, C.M.G., D.S.O.	R.A.	Promoted Maj.-Gen.	Maj.-Gen. H. M. L. Rundle, C.M.G., D.S.O.	R.A.	Dec. '97, Commandant at Merawi. Desp. Jan.25, May 24, Sept. 30, '98.
Asst. Adj.-Gen.	*Maj. C. G. Martyr*	D.C.L.I.	D.S.O.	Brev.-Lt.-Col. G. W. Hackett Pain	Worc. R.	*From 9th Bn. E.A.* q.v.
,, ,,				Maj. A. E. Sandbach	R.E.	Jan. '98, Commandant Wady Halfa. Desp. Sept. 30, '98.
Dep.-Asst.-Adj.-Gen. (A)	Lieut. G. F. Gorringe	R.E.	D.S.O.	Lieut. G. F. Gorringe, D.S.O.	R.E.	Desp. Sept. 30, '98.
,, ,, (B)	(Hon. Capt.) Qr.-Mr. W. H. Drage	A.S.C.	Promoted Hon. Maj.	Capt. C. E. G. Blunt	A.S.C.	*From Commissariat Department," see "Departments." Desp.May 24,Sept.*

APPENDIX I

Role	Name	Regt.	Notes	Remarks
Dep.-Asst.-Adj.-Gen. (B) Director of Mil. Intelligence	Brev.-Maj. F. R. Wingate, C.B., D.S.O.	R.A.	Brev.-Lieut.-Col.	(Hon. Maj.) Qr.-Mr. W. H. Drage, A.S.C. — Desp. Sept. 30, '98. Brev.-Lt.-Col. F. R. Wingate, C.B., D.S.O. — R.A. — Brev.-Col.; A.D.C.; Dec. '97, Desp. May 24, Sept. 30, '98. 3rd Osmanieh. Desp. Sept. 30, '98.
Asst. ,, ,, ,,	Col. Slatin, Pasha		C.B.	Col. Slatin, Pasha, C.B.
Intelligence Staff	Capt. N. M. Smyth	2 D.G.	4th Medjidie	Maj. Hon. M. G. Talbot, p.s.c. — R.E. — Desp. Sept. 30, '98.
,, ,,	Lieut. Lord Fincastle	16th L.ncrs.	Invalided home, June '96.	Capt. N. M. Smyth — 2 D.G — Wounded at Omdurman, Desp. Sept. 30, '98.
Commandg. Lines of Communications	Lt.-Col. W. F. D. Cochrane	h.p.	C.B. Commandant Dongola District until June '98, when he left the E.A.	[Maj.-Gen. H. M. L. Rundle, C.M.G., D.S.O.] — R.A. — See Adjutant-Gen. above.
Director of Supplies Stores	Lt.-Col. J. Rogers Capt. W. Staveley Gordon	A.S.C. R.E.	C.B. Brev.-Major.	Lt.-Col. J. Rogers, C.B. [Brev.-Maj. W. S. Gordon] — A.S.C. R.E. — Desp. Sept. 30, '98. June '98, superintending gunboats at Abadieh. Aug., on the gunboats, q.v.
Transport	Maj. F. W. Kitchener, p.s.c.	W. Yorks. R.	Brev.-Lt.-Col.; 4th Osmanieh.	Brev.-Lt.-Col. F. W. Kitchener, p.s.c. — W. Yorks. R. — Desp. May 24, '98. (3rd Medjidie.) Sept. 30, '98.
Principal Medical Officer (P.M.O.)	Surg.-Lieut.-Col. T. J. Gallwey, M.D.	A.M.S.		Lt.-Col. T. J. Gallwey, M.D., C.B. — R.A.M.C. — Desp. May 24, Sept. 30, '98.
Principal Vety.-Surgeon	Vet.-Capt. G. R. Griffith	A.V.D.	D.S.O.	Vet.-Capt. G. R. Griffith, D.S.O. — A.V.D. — Desp. Sept. 30, '98.
DIVISIONAL STAFF.				
Commanding Infantry Division, and Commandant Frontier Field Force	Brev.-Col. A. Hunter, D.S.O.	R. Lanc. Regt.	Promoted Maj.-Gen.	Major-Gen. A. Hunter, D.S.O. — Commanded Troops at *Abu Hamed,* Desp. Jan. 25, May 24, Sept. 30, '98.

* For Officers of the *British* Division, attached to Headquarter Staff, see p. 308, 309.
† The British officers serving with the E.A. were, with very few exceptions, all "mentioned" individually by the Sirdar in his despatches of November 3rd, 1896—both those belonging to the E.A. and those temporarily attached to it, and, except those invalided, etc., all received the Khedive's medal and clasps for Ferket and Hafir. In order to avoid repetition, " the mention " is omitted in this column. In the case of those officers who joined the E.A. subsequent to the battle of the Atbara, the date of joining is given.
‡ Those present at the action of Abu Hamed are severally indicated. The others, as far as the authors have been able to ascertain, were present at the battles of the Atbara and Omdurman.

EGYPTIAN ARMY—continued

Egyptian Army.	DONGOLA EXPEDITION, 1896.			NILE EXPEDITION, 1897—8.		
	Name.	British Regt.	Remarks, Honours after Dongola Expedition.†	Name.	British Regt.	Remarks, Honours, &c.‡
DIVISIONAL STAFF—*continued.*						
A.A.G.	Capt. T. E. Hickman, D.S.O.	Worc. R.	Invalided to England. Brev.-Maj.	Brev.-Major W. F. H. S. Kincaid (*and Commanding Engineer*)	R.E.	*From C.R.E. Dionl. Staff, q.v. Abu Hamed,* Desp. Jan. 25, (4th Osmanieh.) Sept. 30, '98.
D.A.A.G.	Capt. H. G. Fitton, p.s.c.	R. Berks. R.	Wounded at Ferket, D.S.O.	Captain H. G. Fitton, D.S.O., p.s.c.	R. Berks.	Aug., 1897, employed with gunboats. Desp. Jan. 25, (4thMedjidie.)Sept. 30, '98.
Staff Officer	Lt. Lord J. H. G. Athlumney	Cold. Gds.	4th Osmanieh.	Brev.-Major B. R. Mitford	E. Surrey R.	*From Brig. Maj. 2nd Brig. E.A. q.v.* Rejoined Nile Force Aug., '98, and appointed Commandant Athara. Desp. Sept. 30, '98. 4th Medjidie. Wounded at Omdurman. Desp. Sept. 30, '98.
,,				Lieut. H. A. Micklem	R. E.	
O.C.; R.E.	Capt. W. F. Kincaid	R.E.	Brev.-Major.			
SUAKIN DISTRICT.						
Governor Red Sea Littoral, and Commandant at Suakin	Maj. (temp. Lt.-Col.) G. E. Lloyd, D.S.O.	S. Staff. R.	Brev. Lt.-Col.	Brev.-Lt.-Col. C. S. B. Parsons	R.A.	*From O.C.; R.A. q.v.* Dec. '97, Commandant at Kassala (4thOsmanieh.Desp. Sept. 30, '98.
2nd Commandant				Maj. B. T. Mahon, D.S.O.	8 Hrs.	*From Cavalry, q.v.*
Staff Officer	Capt. W. E. O'Leary, p.s.c.	R. Ir. Rif.	4th Osmanieh.	Capt. F. G. Anley	Essex R.	*From 2nd Bn. E.A. q.v.*

APPENDIX I

	Name	Regiment	Notes
Staff Officer	Capt. T. Souter	Blk. Watch	4th Osmanieh.
Senr. Med. Officer	Surg.-Capt. P. H. Whiston	A.M.S.	
BRIGADE STAFF.			
Commanding 1st Brigade	Maj. D. F. Lewis	Ches. R.	Brev. Lieut.-Col.	Capt. C. C. Fleming	R.A.M.C.	
,, 2nd ,,	Maj. H. A. Macdonald	R. Fus.	Brev. Lieut.-Col.	Brev.-Lt.-Col. H. A. Macdonald, C.B., D.S.O.	R. Fus.	*From O.C. 2nd Brig. g.v. Abu Hamed.* Desp. Jan. 25, May 24, Sept. 30, '98.
,, 3rd ,,	Brev.-Maj. J. G. Maxwell, D.S.O.	Blk. Watch	Brev. Lieut.-Col.	Brev.-Lt.-Col. J. G. Maxwell, D.S.O.		*From O.C. 3rd Brig. g.v.* Asst. Mil. Sec. at Hd. Qrs. Commanded Nubia District in '97, Desp. Jan. 25, May 24, Sept. 30, '98.
,, 4th ,,	Brev.-Major. E. F. David	R.M.L.I.	Promoted Lieut.-Col.	Brev.-Lt.-Col. D. F. Lewis	Ches. R.	*From O.C. 1st Brig. g.v.* Commandant Dongola, 1897. Desp. May 24, Sept. 30, '98.
				Brev.-Lt.-Col. J. Collinson	Northn. R.	Commanded 13th bn. E.A. (q.v.) at Atbara. Desp. May 24, 3rd Medjidie, Sept. 30, '98.
Brigade Major, 1st ,,	Capt. F. G. Nason	Scot. Rif.		Brev.-Maj. C. E. Keith-Falconer	Nrth. Fus.	*From 13th bn. E.A. g.v. Abu Hamed.* Desp. Jan. 25, May 24, Sept. 30, '98.
,, 2nd ,,	*Capt. B. R. Mitford*	E. Surrey R.	Brev.-Major.	Maj. F. I. Maxse	Cold. Gds.	On 13th bn. E.A.] On Gen. Hunter's Staff at *Abu Hamed.* Desp. Jan. 25, May 24, Sept. 30, '98.
,, 3rd ,,	Capt. H. T. Godden	Bedf. R.		Capt. J. J. Asser	Dorset R.	Desp. Jan. 25, May 24, Sept. 30, '98.
,, 4th ,,	Capt. S. F. Judge, D.S.O.	Shrop. L.I.		Capt. O. H. Pedley, p.s.c.	Conn. Rgs.	June, '98, Commandant Assouan. 4th Medijie. Desp. Sept. 30, '98.
Orderly Officer (4th Brig.)				Capt. Sir H. B. Hill, Bart.	R. Ir. Fus.	June, '98, Asst. Commandant Assouan.

† See footnote, p. 295.   ‡ See footnote, p. 295.

EGYPTIAN ARMY—continued

Egyptian Army.	DONGOLA EXPEDITION, 1896.			NILE EXPEDITION, 1897-8.		
	Name.	British Regt.	Remarks, Honours after Dongola Expedition.†	Name.	British Regt.	Remarks, Honours, &c.‡
CAVALRY.						
Commanding Wing, or Squadron Commander	Maj. B. F. Burn-Murdoch	1st Drs.	Brev.-Lieut.-Col.	Brev.-Lt.-Col.R.G.Broadwood,p.s.c	12th Lrs.	Desp. 4th Osmanieh. Desp. Sept. 30, '98.
"	Brev.-Maj. G. E. Benson	R.A.	Invalided home.	Maj. P. W. J. Le Gallais	8th Hrs.	4th Osmanieh. Desp. Sept. 30, '98.
"	Capt. R. G. Broadwood	12th Lrs.	Promised Brev.-Lt.-Colonelcy.	[Capt. B. T. Mahon, D.S.O.]	8th Hrs.	See "Suakin District."
"	Capt. E. V. McMahon	1st Drs.	Wounded at Ferket, D.S.O.	Capt. Hon. E. Baring	10th Hrs.	Desp. Sept. 30, '98.
"	Capt. N. Legge	20th Hrs.		Capt. D. Haig, p.s.c.	7th Hrs.	Desp. Sept. 30, '98.
"	Capt. R. H. Adams	2nd Drs.	4th Medjidie.	Capt. H. S. H. Prince Francis, J.L.F. of Teck	1st Drs.	Desp. May 24, Sept. 30, '98.
"	Capt. B. T. Mahon	8th Hrs.	D.S.O.	Capt. W. H. Perse	2nd D.G.	Wounded at reconnaissance of Mahmud's zariba. Desp. Sept. 30, '98.
"	Capt. V. G. Whitla	2nd D. G.		Capt. W. E. Peyton	15th Hrs.	Desp. Sept. 30, '98.
"	Capt. W. H. Perse	2nd D. G.	4th Medjidie.	[Capt. N. M. Smyth]	2nd D.G.	On Intelligence Staff, see above.
"	Capt. W. E. Peyton	15th Hrs.		Capt. N. Legge, D.S.O.	20th Hrs.	Re-joined, Nile Force Aug., '98. Desp. Sept. 30, '98.
				Lieut. J. G., Marquis of Tullibardine	R.H.G.	Desp. May 24, Sept. 30, '98.
CAMEL CORPS.						
Commanding	Capt. (temp. Maj.) R. J. Tudway	Essex R.	Brev.-Major.	Brev.-Maj. R. J. Tudway	Essex R.	Desp. Jan. 25, Sept. 30, '98.
General duty	Capt. St. G. C. Henry	North. F. R. Lanc. Regt.		Capt. St. G. C. Henry	North. F.	Desp. Sept. 30, '98.
"	Capt. A. J. King		4th Medjidie.	Capt. A. J. King	R. Lan. R.	Desp. May 24, Sept. 30, '98.
"	Capt. L. F. Green-Wilkinson	Rif. Brig.	4th Medjidie.	Capt. L. F. Green-Wilkinson	Rif. Brig.	Desp. Sept. 30, '98.
"				Lieut. H. C. B. Hopkinson	Sea. High.	From 12th Bn. E.A. q.v. Wounded at Omdurman. Desp. Sept. 30, '98.

APPENDIX I

IRREGULARS, "FRIENDLIES."				*Maj. E. J. Montagu-Stuart-Wortley, C.M.G.*	60th Rif.	Joined, Aug., '98. Desp. Sept. 30, '98.
Commanding	*Brev.-Maj. E. R. Owen, D.S.O.*	Lan. Fus.	Died at Ambigol July 11th, 96.			
General duty	*Brev.-Maj. A. B. Thruston*	Ox. L.I.	4thOsmanieh. [Killed in Uganda, 97.]	2nd Lieut. C. M. A. Wood	North. F.	Joined, Aug., '98. Desp. Sept. 30, '98.
ARTILLERY.						
Commanding	Maj. (temp. Lt.-Col.) C. S. B. Parsons		[Brev. Lt.-Col. Parsons]		R.A.	Commandant Suakin, see above.
O. C. Horse Battery	Capt. N. E. Young	R.A.	Brev.-Major.	Lieut.-Col. C. J. Long	R.A.	Desp. Sept. 30, '98.
				Brev. Maj. N. E. Young	R.A.	*Abu Hamed*. Desp. Jan. 25, (4th Osmanieh. Sept. 30, '98.
" Maxim "	Capt. C. E. Lawrie	R.A.	Brev.-Major.	Brev. Maj. C. E. Lawrie	R.A.	4th Osmanieh. Desp. Sept. 30, '98.
" Field "	Capt. M. Peake	R.A.	4th Medjidie.	Capt. M. Peake	R.A.	Desp. Jan. 25, Sept. 30, '98
General duty	*Capt. C. H. de Rougemont*	R.A.	On the "Abu Klea." 4th Medjidie.	Capt. C. H. de Rougemont	R.A.	On gunboats. Desp. May 24, '98. Wounded at Omdurman. Desp. Sept. 30, '98.
	Capt. H. Oldfield	R.M.A.	On the *Metemmeh*.	Capt. H. Oldfield	R.M.A.	On gunboats.
" "				*Capt. J. W. G. Dawkins, p.s.c.*	R.A.	Desp. Sept. 30, '98.
" "				[Capt. H. Slessor]	R.M.A.	See 1st Bn. E.A.
" "				Capt. G. Mc K. Franks	R.A.	Desp. Sept. 30, '98.
Attached to Maxim Battery				Lieut. C. G. Stewart, D.S.O.	R.A.	Desp. Sept. 30, '98.
"	*Lieut. R. S. Hutchison*	N.Staff.R.	Invalided to England June, 96			
"	Lieut. T. H. Falkiner	Con. Ran.	Invalided to England Aug., 96.			
"	Lieut. W. H. Goldfinch	N.Staff.R.	4th Medjidie. Promoted into Manchester Regiment as Capt. and Brev.-Maj. Oct. 4, '98.			
"	Lieut. O. D. Blunt	Con. Ran.	4th Medjidie			
ENGINEERS.						
Director of Railways	Lieut. E. P. C. Girouard	R.E.	D.S.O.	Lieut. E. P. C. Girouard, D.S.O.	R.E.	Desp. Jan. 25, 1898. Returned to Cairo, Aug. 1898, as President, Board of Egyptian Railways. 4thMedjidie.Aug.'98. Director of Railways,viceGironard. Desp. Sept. 30, '98.
Railway Staff	Lieut. A. G. Stevenson	R.E.	4th Medjidie	Lieut. G. B. Macauley	R.E.	

See footnote, p. 295.   ‡ See footnote, p. 295.

EGYPTIAN ARMY—continued

Egyptian Army.	DONGOLA EXPEDITION, 1896.			NILE EXPEDITION, 1897–8.		
	Name.	British Regt.	Remarks, Honours, after Dongola Expedition.†	Name.	British Regt.	Remarks, Honours, &c.‡
ENGINEERS—*cont.*						
Railway Staff	Lieut. R. Polwhele	R.E.	Died at Halfa, July, '96	[Lieut. A. G. Stevenson]	R.E.	Aug, 1898, on gunboats, q.v.
,,	Lieut. E. H. S. Cator	R.E.	Died at Halfa, Feb. 97.	Lieut. H. L. Pritchard	R.E.	Desp. Sept. 30, '98.
,,				Lieut. G. C. M. Hall	R.E.	4th Medjidie.
,,				Lieut. E. C. Midwinter	R.E.	4th Medjidie. Desp. Sept. 30, '98.
,,				Lieut. E. O. A. Newcombe	R.E.	4th Medjidie. Aug. '98, on gunboats.
"General" Duty	*Brev.-Maj. A. G. Hunter-Weston*	R.E.	4th Medjidie.	Lieut. W. R. G. Wollen	R.E.	Desp. Sept. 30, '98.
				Maj. H. M. Lawson	R.E.	Joined May, '98. Wounded near Kassala, Jan., '98.
,,	*Lieut. H. L. Pritchard*	R.E.	4th Medjidie.	*Lieut. R. B. D. Blakeney*	R.E.	Desp. Sept. 30, '98.
,,	*Lieut. R. B. D. Blakeney*	R.E.	4th Medjidie.			
Director of Telegraphs	*Lieut. M. G. E, Manifold*	R.E.	4th Medjidie.	Lieut. M. G. E. Manifold	R.E.	Desp. May 24, '98.
INFANTRY.						
1st Battalion	Capt. (temp. Maj.) R. H. G. Heygate	Border R.	D.S.O.	Maj. R. H. G. Heygate, D.S.O.	Border R.	July '98, Commandant Debbeh. Aug. '98 with Camel Corps.
	Lieut. E. G. T. Bainbridge	Buffs		Capt. H. Slessor	R.M.A.	
				Capt. W. R. B. Doran, p.s.c.	R. Ir. R.	Desp. Jan., '98. Remained at Berber, Apr., '98.
				Capt. H. C. Smith	R. Dub. Fus.	
2nd Battalion	Capt. (temp. Maj.) H. P. Shekleton	S. Lanc. Regt.	Brevet-Major.	Maj. F. J. Pink, D.S.O.	R.W. Surrey R.	
	Capt. F. G. Anley	Essex R.		Lieut. E. P. Strickland	Norf. R.	From 3rd bn. E. A., q.v. Desp. Jan. 25, May 24, Sept. 30, '98.
	Lieut. E. P. Strickland	Norf. R.		Lieut. F. F. Ready	R. Berks. R.	Desp. Sept. 30, '98.

APPENDIX I

3rd Battalion	Capt. (temp. Maj.) J. Sillem	Welsh R.	Promised Brev.-Lt.-Colonelcy.	Brev.-Lieut.-Col. J. Sillem	Welsh R.	*Abu Hamed*, Desp. Jan. 25, May 24, Sept. 30, '98.
"	Capt. F. J. Pink, D.S.O.	R. W. Surrey R.		Capt. A. Blewitt	60th Rifles	*Abu Hamed*. Desp. Jan. 25, May 24, Sept. 30, '98.
"	Capt. J. R. O'Connell	Shrop. L.I.	4th Medjidie.		60th Rifles Ches. R.	Desp. Sept. 30, '98. Oct., '97, Commandant at Ed Damer. Desp. Jan. 25, Sept. 30, '98.
4th Battalion	Capt. (temp. Maj.) W. S. Sparkes	Welsh R.	Brev.-Maj.	Brev.-Maj. W. S. Sparkes	Welsh R.	Desp. May 24, (4th Osmanieh). Sept. 30, '98.
"	Capt. St. C. Nicholson	Liv. R.		Maj. W. H. Sitwell, p.s.c.	North F.	Wounded at El Aliab, March, '98. Desp. Sept. 30, '98.
5th Battalion	Lieut. F. M. Carleton	R. Lanc. R.		Capt. Hon. W. Lambton.	Cold. Gds.	Desp. Sept. 30, '98.
6th "	Native Officers			Capt. H. G. Majendie	Rif. Brig.	Desp. Sept. 30, '98.
7th "	Native Officers			Native Officers		On Line of Communications.
8th "	Native Officers			Native Officers		
9th " (Soudanese)	Maj. G. W. Hackett Pain	Worc. R.	Brev.-Lieut.-Col.	Capt. (temp. Maj.) W. F. Walter, p.s.c.	Lan. Fus.	Wounded at Atbara. Desp. May 24, Sept. 30, '98.
" "	Capt. W. F. Walter	Lanc. Fus.	4th Osmanieh.	Capt. H. V. Ravenscroft	Manch. R.	*Abu Hamed*. Desp. Jan. 25, May 24, '98.
" "	Lieut. H. V. Ravenscroft	Manch. R.		Lieut. C. F. S. Vandeleur, D.S.O.	Scots Gds.	Wounded at Omdurman. Desp. Sept. 30, '98.
" "	Lieut. A. R. Hoskins	N. Staff. R.		Lieut. A. Blair, p.s.c.	K.O.S.B.	*Abu Hamed*. Desp. Jan. 25, Sept. 30, '98.
" "				Lieut. A. R. Hoskins	N. Staff. R.	Killed at *Abu Hamed*, Aug. 1, '97.
10th Battalion (Soudanese)	Capt. (temp. Maj.) H. M. Sidney	D.C.L.I.	Brev.-Major.	Brev.-Maj. H. M. Sidney	D.C.L.I.	From Brig.-Maj.; 1st Brig. E.A.; 9.v Desp. Sept. 30, '98.
" "	Capt. D. G. Prendergast	S. Lanc. R.		Maj. F. G. Nason	Sco. Rifles	
" "	Capt. C. Fergusson	Gren. Gds.		Capt. C. Fergusson	Gren. Gds.	*Abu Hamed*. Desp. Jan. 25, 1898. Brev.-Major. Desp. May 24, Sept. 30 '98.
" "	Capt. M. A. C. B. Fenwick	R. Suss. R.	Died at Kosheh, July 26, '96.			
" "	Lieut. E. FitzClarence	Dorset R.		Capt. J. A. E. MacBean, p.s.c.	R. Dub. F.	Aug., '97, on Line of Communications. Desp. Jan. 25, May 24, Sept. 30, '98.

† See footnote, p. 295. ‡ See footnote, p. 295.

EGYPTIAN ARMY—continued

DONGOLA EXPEDITION, 1896. — NILE EXPEDITION, 1897—8.

Egyptian Army.	Name.	British Regt.	Remarks, Honours, after Dongola Expedition.†	Name.	British Regt.	Remark, Honours, &c.‡
INFANTRY—*continued*.						
10th Battalion (Soudanese)	....	....	....	Capt. C. S. Cottingham	Manch. R.	Killed at *Abu Hamed*, Aug. 7, 97.
,, ,,	....	....	....	Lieut. E. FitzClarence	Dorset R.	Desp. Jan. 25, May 24, Sept. 30, 98.
11th Battalion (Soudanese)	Capt. (temp. Maj.) H. W. Jackson	Gord. Hig.	Brev.-Major.	Brev.-Maj. H. W. Jackson	Gor. Hdrs.	Aug. 1897, on the gunboats. Desp. Jan. 25, May 24, Sept. 30, 98.
,, ,,	Capt. E. A. Stanton	Oxf. L.I.	....	Capt. E. A. Stanton	Oxf. L.I.	
,, ,,	*Capt. E. M. Jackson*	I.S.C.	....	Lieut. W. E. J. Bradshaw	York and Lanc. R.	Desp. Sept. 30, '98.
,, ,,	Lieut. G. de H. Smith	I.S.C.	....	Lieut. G. de H. Smith	I.S.C.	*Abu Hamed.* Desp. Jan. 25, Sept. 30, 98.
12th Battalion (Soudanese)	Brev.-Maj. C. V. F. Townshend, C.B.	I.S.C.	Brev.-Lieut.-Col.	Brev.-Lt.-Col. C. V. F. Townshend, C.B.	I.S.C.	Desp. May 24, Sept. 30, 98.
,, ,,	Capt. R. S. Webber	R. Wel. F.	4th Medjidie.	Brev.-Maj. A. K. Harley, D.S.O.	I.S.C.	Wounded at Athara. Desp. May 24, '58. 4th Medjidie.
,, ,,	Lieut. H. C. B. Hopkinson	Sea. High.	....	Capt. G. H. Ford-Hutchinson	Conn. Rng.	Desp. May 24, Sept. 30, 98.
,, ,,	....	....	....	Capt. A. de S. McKerrell	Cam. Hdrs	
,, ,,	....	....	....	Capt. Hon. C. E. Walsh	Rif. Brig.	*Abu Hamed*, on Gen. Hunter's Staff. Desp. Jan. 25, '98. Wounded at Athara. Desp. May 24, 98. 4th Medjidie.
13th Battalion (Soudanese)	Maj. J. Collinson	North. R.	Brev.-Lieut.-Col.	[Brev.-Lt.-Col. J. Collinson]	North. R.	See O.C. 4th Brigade, above.
,, ,,	....	....	....	Brev.-Lt.-Col. H. L. Smith-Dorrien, D.S.O., p.s.c.	Derb. R.	Joined July, 98. Desp. Sept. 30, 98.

APPENDIX I

Battalion	Officer	Notes		Regt.	Remarks
13th Battalion (Soudanese)	Capt. V. T. Bunbury		Leic. R.	Bedf. R.	*From Brig.-Maj., 3rd Brig.,* q.v. Desp. May 24, '98.
,,	Capt. C. E. Keith-Falconer	Invalided to England, Aug. '96.	Nrth. Fus.	Cold. Gds.	See Brig.-Maj., 2nd Brig., above.
,,	Lieut. H. H. F. Farmar	Died at Suarda, July 20, 96.	60th Rifles	Linc. R.	Desp. Sept. 30, '98.
,,				E. Lanc. R.	Desp. Sept. 30, '98.
,,	Capt. T. Capper, p.s.c.			R. War. R.	Joined June, '98. Desp. Sept. 30, '98.
,,	Capt. R. D. Whigham				
14th Battalion (Soudanese)	Brev.-Maj. H. P. Shekleton, p.s.c.	Native officers.		S. Lanc. R.	*From 2nd Bn. E.A.*, q.v. Wounded at Atbara. Desp. May 24, '98. 4th Osmanieh. Desp. Sept. 30, '98.
,,	Maj. H. I. W. Hamilton			R.W.S.R.	Desp. May 24, Sept. 30, '98.
,,	Capt. G. E. Matthews			R.M.L.I	Desp. May 24, Sept. 30, '98.
,,	Capt. E. G. T. Bainbridge			Buffs.	*From 1st Bn. E.A.*, q.v. On gunboats Aug. '97. Desp. Jan. 25, '98. Remained at Geneinetti with half of 5th battalion E.A. April, '98. Desp. Sept. 30, '98.
15th Battalion	*Maj. W. R. P. Wallace*	4th Osmanieh.		Worc. R.	Commanded attack on Shendy. Desp. May 24, Sept. 30, '98.
,,	*Capt. S. Willcock*		Glouc. R.	Glouc. R.	Desp. Jan. 25, May 24, Sept. 30, '98.
,,	Lieut. E. B. North			R. Fus.	Desp. Sept. 30, '98.
,,	Lieut. J. M. A. Graham			R. Lan. R.	Desp. Jan. 25, '98. Orderly Offr. at Atbara, to O.C. and Brigade, E.A. Desp. Sept. 30, '98.
16th ,,	Capt. A. G. Dwyer	Raised in 1897		E. Sur. R.	At Kassala.
17th ,,	Brev.-Maj. V. T. Bunbury	,, ,, ,,		Leic. R.	*From 13th Battn. E.A.*, q.v. Commanded 11th Bn. E.A. at *Abu Hamed*. Desp. Jan. 25, '98.

† See footnote, p. 295.   ‡ See footnote, p. 295.

EGYPTIAN ARMY—continued

Egyptian Army.	DONGOLA EXPEDITION, 1896.			NILE EXPEDITION, 1897—8.		
	Name.	British Regt.	Remarks, Honours, after Dongola Expedition.†	Name.	British Regt.	Remarks, Honours, &c.‡
INFANTRY—cont.						
17th Battalion	Raised in 1897			Capt. F. E. P. Curzon	R. Ir. Rif.	
18th "	" "			Capt. E. S. Herbert	Bk. Watch	Desp. Sept. 30, '98.
" "	" "			Captain H. G. K. Matchett	Con. Rgrs.	
" "	" "			Lieut. F. Burges	Glouc. R.	
Kassala Irregulars	" 1898			Capt. E. B. Wilkinson	Linc. R.	} At Kassala.
" "				Lieut. H. M. A. Hankey	War. R.	
DEPARTMENTS.						
Commissariat Dept.						
Director of Supplies	See Headquarter Staff			See Headquarter Staff		
Director of Stores	See Headquarter Staff			See Headquarter Staff		
General Duty	Lieut. C. E. G. Blunt	A.S.C.	4th Medjidie.	Capt. F. J. L. Howard	A.S.C.	Desp. Sept. 30, '98.
" "	Lieut. F. J. L. Howard	A.S.C.		Lieut. H. G. A. Garsia	A.S.C.	
" "				Lieut. W. S. Swabey	A.S.C.	
Transport Dept.						
Director of Transport	See Headquarter Staff			See Headquarter Staff		
General Duty	*Capt. L. C. Sherer*	Leic. R.		*Capt. E. C. J. Williams*	Buffs	Desp. May 24, '98.
" "	*Sec. Lt. T. H. Healey*	Cam. Highrs.		Sec. Lt. T. H. Healey	Cam. Highrs.	*Abu Hamed*, in command of transport. Desp. Jan. 25, May 24, '98 (Lieut. May, '98).
" "				Sec. Lt. C. McKey	Middx. R.	Promoted from ranks, after Dongola. Desp. May 24, Sept. 30, '98.

APPENDIX I

General Duty	Sec. Lt. S. K. Flint		R. Ir. Rif.	Promoted from ranks after Dongola. Desp. Sept. 30, '98.
Medical Dep.				
Principal Medical Officer	See Headquarter Staff			
General duty	Surg.-Maj. G. D. Hunter	D.S.O.	R.A.M.C.	
,,	Capt. R. H. Penton, D.S.O.		,,	Desp. Jan. 25, May 24, Sept. 30, '98. *Abu Hamed*, Desp. Jan. 25, May 24, Sept. 30, '98.
,,	Surg.-Capt. R. H. Penton	D.S.O.	,,	
,,	Capt. H. E. Hill Smith		,,	
,,	Surg.-Capt. H. E. Hill Smith	4th Medjidie.	,,	*Abu Hamed*, Desp. Jan. 25, May 24, Sept. 30, '98.
,,	Capt. C. S. Spong		,,	
,,	Surg.-Capt. C. S. Spong	4th Medjidie.	,,	Desp. May 24, '98. 4th Medjidie. Sept. 30, '98.
,,	Capt. P. H. Whiston	4th Medjidie.	,,	
,,	[Surg.-Capt. A. H. Whiston]		A.M.S.	
,,	Capt. G. A. T. Bray	See "Suakin" District, above.	R.A.M.C.	Desp. Sept. 30, '98.
,,	Capt. J. W. Jennings.		,,	Desp. Sept. 30, '98.
,,	Surg.-Capt. H. N. Dunn, M.B.		,,	Desp. May 24, Sept. 30, '98.
,,	Capt. H. N. Dunn, M.B.	Died at Kosheh, July 26, '96.	,,	
,,	Surg.-Capt. J. E. Trask		,,	See "Suakin" District, above.
,,	[Capt. C. C. Fleming, M.B.]		,,	
,,	Lieut. C. F. Wanhill		,,	
Veterinary Dep.				
Prin. Vet. Surg.	See Headquarter Staff			
General duty	*Vet.-Lieut. W. D. Smith.*		A.V.D.	
,,	Vet.-Lieut. A. H. Lane.		,,	
,,	Vet.-Lieut. T. E. W. Lewis		,,	4th Medjidie. Desp. Sept. 30, '98.
Otherwise Employed.				
General duty	Capt. J. R. O'Connell		Shrop. L.I.	Joined July, '98.
,,	*Capt. R. S. Webber*		R. W. Fus.	Desp. Sept. 30, '98.
,,	Capt. C. H. M. Doughty		R. W. Fus.	Joined May, '98.
,,	Capt. R. C. L. Battley		Essex R.	Desp. Sept. 30, '98.
,,	Capt. F. M. B. Hobbs		R.M.L.I.	On gunboats. Desp. Sept. 30, '98.
,,	Lieut. N. T. Borton		Welsh R.	
,,	Lieut. H. H. S. Morant		Durh. L.I.	
,,	Lieut. C. E. Wilson		E. Lanc. R.	Joined July, '98.

† See footnote, p. 295.   ‡ See footnote, p. 295.

BRITISH TROOPS IN THE DONGOLA EXPEDITION, 1896.

NOTE: All the North Staffords, Departmental troops attached to them, and the details on the gunboats (with the exception of those invalided to Cairo and those left behind at Kosheh), received the Dongola medal, and clasp for Hafir. Those left at Kosheh and the Indian Contingent received medal without clasp.

1ST. BATTLN. NORTH STAFFORDSHIRE REGIMENT (64TH).

Left Cairo for Soudan, March 1896, leaving Depot at Citadel. Present at the Battle of Hafir. Returned to Cairo, Sept. 1896

Name.	Remarks, Honours, &c.	Name.	Remarks, Honours, &c.
Lieut.-Col. T. A. Beale...	Invalided to England, July '96, h.p.	Lieut. B. I. Way	4th Medjidie.
		[Lieut. W. H. Goldfinch.]	With Maxim Battery, E. A. q. v.
Maj. T. Currie...............	Lieut.-Col. vice Beale, 14 Sept. '96. Desp. 3 Nov. '96., C.B., 3rd Medjidie.	Lieut. A. R. C. Rew......	Died at Cairo, May '97.
		Lieut. M. H. Knaggs ...	
		Lieut. J. Wilson...........	
Maj. H. B. Mortimer.....	Desp. 3 Nov. '96.	Lieut. A. W. Foote........	Invalided to England, Dec. '96.
Capt. H. Marwood, *Adjt.*	Desp. 3 Nov. '96. Brev.-Major 4th Medjidie.	Lieut. E. V. Fox...........	
		Lieut. F. E. Johnston....	
		Lieut. H. W. M. Down..	
Capt. R P. Stuart.........		Lieut. J. J. B. Farley....	
Capt. L. B. Scott, ...		Lieut. H. S. L. Alford....	
Quartermaster Acting	4th Medjidie.	Lieut. T. A. Andrus......	Remained at Kosheh, 12 Sept. '96
Capt. C. W. Crofton.......			
Capt. J. Rose	Died at Cairo, Oct. '96.		
		2nd-Lieut. A. W. Ralston	
Capt. S. J. Astell............	Remained at Kosheh, 12 Sept. '96.	2nd-Lieut. W. D. Sword.	
		2nd Lieut. L. J. Wyatt...	Remained at Kosheh, 12 Sept. '96.
[Lieut. R. S. Hutchison.]	With Maxim Battery, E. A. q. v.		

DEPARTMENTAL OFFICERS ATTACHED TO NORTH STAFFORDSHIRE REGIMENT.

Name.	Remarks, Honours, &c.	Name.	Remarks, Honours, &c.
Lieut. G. E. Elkington, R.E., Detachment R.E.	Desp. 3 Nov. '96. 4th Medjidie......	Surg.-Major C. J. Holmes M.D., A.M.S...............	
Capt. H. Morgan, A.S.C.	Desp. 3 Nov. '96. 4th Medjidie.	Surg.-Capt. W. H. Pinches, A.M.S..........	4th Medjidie
Rev. R. Brindle, C.F. (R.C.)........................	Desp. 3 Nov. '96. 3rd Medjidie.	Surg.-Capt. H. Carr, A.M.S.	Invalided, July, '96.
Rev. A. B. Watson, C.F. (C.E.)........................	Remained at Kosheh, 12 Sept. '96.	Quar.-Mast.(Hon. Lieut.) A. Short, A.M.S., Detachment A.M.S.........	5th Medjidie.
Surg.-Major A. T. Sloggett, A.M.S.	Desp. 3 Nov. '96. Promoted Lieut.-Col. 4th Osmanieh	Capt. C. M. Mathew (Durh. L.I.), O.S.C....	Desp. 3 Nov. '96.
		Capt. A. G. Smith (Worc. R.), A.P.D.	Remained at Koshed, 12 Sept. '96.

APPENDIX I 307

ON THE GUNBOATS

Boat.	Name.	—	Remarks, Honours, &c.
Tamai	Commander Hon. S. C. G. Colville	R.N.	Wounded at Hafir. Desp. 3 Nov. '96. Post-Capt., C.B.
El Teb	Commander C. H. Robertson, C.M.G.	R.N.	Desp. 3 Nov. '96. 4th Osmanieh.
Metemmeh	[Capt. H. Oldfield]	R.M.A.	E.A. q. v. (Art.)
Abu Klea	Lieut. D. Beatty	R.N.	Desp. 3 Nov. '96, D.S.O.
,,	[Capt. C. H. de Rougemont].	R.A.	Attached to E.A. q. v. (Art.).

INDIAN CONTINGENT AT SUAKIN.

For officers of the Egyptian Army at Suakin, see "Egyptian Army—Suakin District" above.

Appointment.	Name.	Regt.	Remarks, Honours, &c.
Commanding Contingent...	Col. (Brig.-Gen.) C. C. Egerton, C.B., D.S.O.	I.S.C.	Appointed A.D.C. to the Queen.
D.A.A. and Q.M.G.	Maj. E. A. Travers	I.S.C.	Brev.-Lieut.-Col.
Intelligence Dept.	Capt. A. Bower	I.S.C.	Brev.-Major.
Brigade Major	Maj. E. de Brett	I.S.C.	Brev.-Lieut.-Col.
Brigade Transport Offr.	Capt. Steele	I.S.C.	
Chief Commissariat Offr.	Maj. Bond	I.S.C.	
Asst. ,, ,,	Capt. Palm	I.S.C.	
,, ,, ,,	Lieut. Dickson	I.S.C.	
Field Engineer	Maj. S. Grant	R.E.	4th Osmanieh.
Asst. Field Engineer	Lieut. Bremner	R.E.	
,, ,, ,,	Lieut. Gardiner	R.E.	
Prin. Med Offr.	Surg.-Capt. Calthrop	A.M.S.	
,,	Lieut.-Col. E. L. Elliot, D.S.O.	I.S.C.	C.B.
,,	Brev.-Maj. C. E. Benson	R.A.	4th Osmanieh.
,,	Capt. R. G. Egerton	I.S.C.	Brev.-Major.
,,	Capt. Cadell	I.S.C.	Brev.-Major.

THE INDIAN CONTINGENT WAS COMPOSED OF :—

    1ST BOMBAY LANCERS.
    5TH BOMBAY MOUNTAIN BATTERY.
    26TH BENGAL INFANTRY.
    35TH SIKHS.

308   THE EGYPTIAN SOUDAN

BRITISH TROOPS IN THE NILE EXPEDITIONARY FORCE, 1898.

ORGANISATION OF THE BRITISH BRIGADE AT THE BATTLE OF THE ATBARA. APRIL 8TH, 1898.

British Brigade.	Name.	Regt.	Remarks, &c.
			NOTE. — For "Honours," see "Divisional Staff," &c. under "Final Advance on Omdurman," below.
STAFF.			
Attached, as D.A.A.Gs. to the Headquarter Staff of the Sirdar, Commanding Expeditionary Force	Capt. Sir H. S. Rawlinson, Bart.	Cold. Gds.	
	Maj. C. a'Court	Rifle Brig.	
	Capt. E. E. Bernard	A.S.C.	Not present at Atbara (at Berber).
Commanding Infantry Brigade	Maj.-Gen. W. F. Gatacre, C.B., D.S.O.		
A.D.C.	Capt. R. G. Brooke	7th Hrs.	
Brigade-Major	Maj. T. D'O. Snow	R. Innis. Fus.	
Chaplains	Rev. R. Brindle (R. C.)		
,,	Rev. J. M. Simms (Pres).		
,,	Rev. A. W. B. Watson (C.E.)		
Prin. Med. Offr.	Brig.-Surg.-Lt.-Col. W. H. McNamara	A.M.S.	
Senr. Ordn. Store Offr.	Lieut.-Col. T. Heron	A.O.D.	Not present at Atbara.
Chief Paymaster	(Hon.) Lieut.-Col. R. M. Ireland	A.P.D.	Not present at Atbara.
Asst. Paymaster	(Hon.) Capt. A. G. Smith	A.P.D.	
Vet. Surg.	Vet.-Lieut. W. Russell	A.V.D.	*See* ¹ , *Regimental Lists, below.*
Staff Officer	Capt. J. G. Fair	21st Lrs.	
,, ,,	Lieut. G. E. Pigott	A.S.C.	
TROOPS COMPOSING THE BRIGADE.			
R.A. (Det. 16th Co., E. Div.*)			
R.E. (Det. 2nd Co. Fortress)			
1st Bn. Royal Warwickshire Regt.	For names of officers see Regimental Lists under "Final Advance on Omdurman."		
1st Bn. Lincolnshire Regt.			
1st Bn. Seaforth Highldrs.			
1st Bn. Cameron ,,			
A.S.C. (Detachment)			
A.M.S. ,,			

* With six Maxims.

APPENDIX I

ORGANISATION OF THE BRITISH DIVISION IN THE FINAL ADVANCE ON OMDURMAN. AUGUST AND SEPTEMBER, 1898.

ATTACHED TO THE HEADQUARTER STAFF OF THE SIRDAR COMMANDING EXPEDITIONARY FORCE.

British Brigade.	Name.	Regt.	Remarks, &c.
D.A.A.G.	Capt.Sir H. Rawlinson, Bart.	Cold. Gds.	4th Medjidie. Desp. May 24, Sept. 30, '98.
,, ...	Capt. E. E. Bernard	A.S.C.	Desp. Sept. 30, '98.
P.M.O.	Surg.-Gen. W. Taylor, M.D.	R.A.M.C...	Desp. Sept. 30, '98.
Secretary to P.M.O.	Maj. E. M. Wilson	R.A.M.C...	Desp. Sept. 30, '98.
Sen. Ord. Store Officer	Lieut.-Col. T. Heron	A.O.D. ...	
Sen. Veterinary ,, ...	Vet.-Capt. L. J. Blenkinsop	A.V.D.......	Desp. Sept. 30, '98.
General Duty	Maj. L. G. Drummond	Sco. Gds....	Desp. Sept. 30, '98.
,, ...	Capt. E. W. Blunt	R.A.	
TROOPS ATTACHED TO HEADQUARTER STAFF.			
21st Lancers.....................			
32nd Field Battery, R.A....			
37th Field Battery, R.A. ...			
5-in Howitzer Battery........	*See Regimental Lists, below.*		
2 40-pr. Armstrong guns ...			
A.S.C. detachment............			
A.O.C. ,, ...			
R.A.M.C. ,, ...			

DIVISIONAL STAFF.

Appointment.	Name.	Regt.	Remarks, Honours, &c.
Commanding British Division	Major-Gen. W. F. Gatacre, C.B.	—	Desp. May 24, Sept. 30, '98.
A.D.C.	Capt. R. G. Brooke............	7th Hrs. ...	Desp. May 24, Sept. 30, '98.
Extra A.D.C.	Lieut. E. Cox	Sea. Hghrs.	Desp. Sept. 30, '98.
Orderly Officer	Lieut. W. D. Ingle............	Middx. R.	Desp. Sept. 30, '98.
D.A.A.G	Maj. F. S. Robb................	h.p.	Desp. Sept. 30, '98.
,, ...	Maj. H. M. Sargent...........	A.S.C.	Desp. Sept. 30, '98.
Chaplains	Rev. R. Brindle (R.C.) ...	C.F........	Desp. May 24, Sept. 30, '98.
	Rev. J. M. Simms (Pres.) .	,, ...	Desp. May 24, Sept. 30, '98.
	Rev. A. W. B. Watson(C.E.)	,, ...	Desp. May 24, Sept. 30, '98.
	Rev. O. S. Watkins	,, ...	Desp. Sept. 30, '98.
P M.O.	Lieut.-Col. McNamara	R.A.M.C.	Desp. Sept. 30, '98.
Chief Paymaster	Maj. W. C. Minchin...........	A.P.D.	
Asst. ,, ...	Capt. A. G. Smith	A.P.D. ...	Desp. May 24, '98.
DIVISIONAL TROOPS.			
R.A.; Det. 16th Co., E. Divn., with 2 Maxims.	*See Regimental Lists, below.*		

1ST BRIGADE STAFF.

Appointment.	Name.	Regt.	Remarks, Honours, &c.
Commanding 1st British Brigade	Col. (Brig.-Gen.) A. G. Wauchope, C.B............	Blk. Watch	Desp. Sept. 30, '98.
A.D.C.	Capt. J. G. Rennie......... ...	Blk. Watch	Desp. Sept. 30, '98.
Brigade-Major	Maj. T. D'O. Snow.........	R. Innis. F.	Desp. May 24, Sept. 30, '98.
P.M.O	Lieut.-Col. Sloggett............	R.A.M.C. .	Wounded at Omdurman. Desp. Sept. 30, '98.
TROOPS OF 1ST BRIGADE. R.A.; Det. 16th Co., E. Divn., with 4 Maxims. R.E.; Det. 2nd Co. (Fortress). 1st Bn., R. Warwickshire Regt. 1st Bn., Lincolnshire Regt.. 1st Bn., Seaforth Highlanders. 1st Bn., Cameron Highlanders.	*See Regimental Lists, below.*		

2ND BRIGADE STAFF.

Appointment.	Name.	Regt.	Remarks, Honours, &c.
Commanding 2nd British Brigade	Col. (Brig.-Gen.) Hon. N. G. Lyttleton, C.B...............	—	Desp. Sept. 30, '98.
A.D.C.	Capt. D. Henderson............	Arg. and Sth. High.	Desp. Sept. 30, '98.
Orderly Officer	Lieut. H. M. Grenfell.........	1st L.G.	Desp. Sept. 30, '98.
Brigade-Major.................	Maj. C. a'Court...............	Rif. Brig....	Desp. May 24, '98.
P.M.O...........................	Lieut.-Col. G. A. Hughes....	R.A.M.C.	Desp. Sept. 30, '98.
TROOPS OF 2ND BRIGADE. R.E.; Det. 2nd Co. (Fortress). Det. 1st Bn. R. Ir. Fus., with 4 Maxims. 1st Bn. Grenadier Guards. 1st Bn. Northumberland Fusiliers. 2nd Bn. Lancashire Fuslrs. 2nd Bn. Rifle Brigade.	*See Regimental Lists, below.*		

APPENDIX I

NAVAL DETACHMENT ON THE GUNBOATS.

Boat.	Name.	Corps.	Remarks, Honours, &c.
Sultan	Lieut. W. H. Cowan	R.N.	Desp. Sept. 30, '98.
Melik	Maj. W. S. Gordon	R.E.	Egyptian Army, from Headquarter Staff. Desp. Sept. 30, '98.
Sheikh	Lieut. J. B. Sparks	R.N.	Desp. Sept. 30, '98.
Fatteh	Lieut. D. Beatty, D.S.O.	R.N.	Desp. Jan. 25, Sept. 30, '98, 4th Medjidie.
Nasir	Lieut. Hon. A. Hood	R.N.	Desp. Jan. 25, Sept. 30, '98, 4th Medjidie.
Zafir	Commander Colin Keppel, D.S.O	R.N.	Commandant Nile flotilla. Desp. Jan. 25, May 24, Sept. 30, '98.
	Brev-Maj. Prince Christian Victor of Schleswig-Holstein	60th Rif.	Desp. Sept. 30, '98.
Tamai	Lieut. H. F. G. Talbot	R.N.	Desp. Sept. 30, '98.
El Teb	Lieut. C. M. Staveley	R.N.	Desp. Sept. 30, '98.
Abu Klea	Lieut. A. G. Stevenson	R.E.	Egyptian Army. Desp. Sept. 30, '98.
Metemmeh	Lieut. Kemble	R.N.	

Capt. F. M. B. Hobbs, R.M.L.I., and Lieut. Newcombe, R.E. (both Egyptian Army, *q.v.*), were also temporarily attached for duty on the gunboats. The Naval detachment under Engineers E. Bond (4th Medjidie) and R. Poole, R.N. (despatches Sept. 30, '98) included 3 engine-room artificers and 3 leading stokers of the R.N., and 9 N.-C.O.'s (gunnery instructors) of the Royal Marine Artillery.

REGIMENTAL LISTS.

21ST LANCERS.

Left Cairo for Soudan, July, 1898, leaving Depot at Abbassyieh. Present at the Battle of Khartoum. Returned to Cairo, Sept., 1898.

Name.	Remarks, Honours, &c.	Name.	Remarks, Honours, &c.
Brev.-Col. R. H. Martin	Desp. Sept. 30, '98.	(Hon. Capt.) W. H. King, (Rg. Mr.),	
Maj. W. G. Crole-Wyndham, p.s.c.	Desp. Sept. 30, '98.	(Hon. Capt.) G. L. Graham, Quartermaster	
Maj. H. Finn	Desp. Sept. 30, '98.		
Maj. J. Fowle	Desp. Sept. 30, '98.	*Attached to 21st Lancers.*	
Capt. W. M. Doyne			
Capt. F. H. Eadon	Desp. Sept. 30, '98.		
Capt. T. H. E. Dauncey			
Capt. J. G. Fair	Staff Officer to Gen. Gatacre, at Atbara. Desp. May 24, 1898.	Lieut. J. C. Brinton, 2nd Life Guards	Wounded at Omdurman. Desp. Sept. 30, '98.
Capt. W. W. Cordeaux		Lieut. J. Vaughan, 7th Hussars	
Capt. P. A. Kenna	Desp. Sept. 30, '98.	Lieut. A. M. Tabor, 3rd Hussars	
Lieut. C. J. Clerk		Lieut. F. W. Wormald, 7th Hussars	
Lieut. Hon. R. H. L. J. de Montmorency	Desp. Sept. 30, '98.	Lieut. T. Conolly, Scots Greys	
Lieut. A. M. Pirie, *Adjutant*	Wounded at Omdurman. Desp. Sept. 30, '98.	Lieut. Hon. R. F. Molyneux, R. Horse Guards	Wounded at Omdurman. Desp. Sept. 30, '98.
Lieut. R. N. Smyth	Desp. Sept. 30, '98.		
Lieut. A. H. M. Taylor	Desp. Sept. 30, '98.	Lieut. W. L. Spencer Churchill, 4th Hussars	
Lieut. A. D. Champion			
Lieut. E. H. Lewis		Lieut. R. S. Grenfell, 12th Lancers	Killed at Omdurman, Sept. 2, '98.
Lieut. H. B. Protheroe Smith			
Lieut. D. Maclachlan	Wounded at Omdurman. Desp. Sept. 30, '98.	[Vet.-Lieut. W. D. Smith, A.V.D.]	See A.V.D. below.
2nd Lieut. C. S. Nesham			
2nd Lieut. O W. Brinton			

32ND FIELD BATTERY, ROYAL ARTILLERY.

Left Cairo for Soudan, July, 1898. Present at the Battle of Khartoum. Returned to Cairo, Sept., 1898.

Name.	Remarks, Honours, &c.	Name.	Remarks, Honours, &c.
Major W. H. Williams...	Desp. Sept. 30, '98.	Lieut. W. H. C. Despard	
Capt. E. J. Duffus.........		2nd Lieut. F. D. Logan...	
Lieut. G.W. H. Nicholson	Desp. Sept. 30, '98.		

37TH FIELD BATTERY, ROYAL ARTILLERY.

Left Cairo for Soudan, July, 1898. Present at the Battle of Khartoum. Returned to Cairo, Sept., 1898.

Name.	Remarks, Honours, &c.	Name.	Remarks, Honours, &c.
Maj. F. B. Elmslie.........	Desp. Sept. 30, '98.	Lieut. H. A. L. H. Wade	
Capt. G. F. Milne		2nd Lieut. H. R. W. M. Smith...............	
Lieut. W. A. S. Gemmell			

DETACHMENT, No. 16 COMPANY, E. DIVISION, ROYAL ARTILLERY.*

Left Cairo for Soudan, Jan., 1898. Present at the Battles of Atbara and Khartoum. Returned to Cairo, Sept., 1898.

Name.	Remarks, Honours, &c.	Name.	Remarks, Honours, &c.
Maj. W. C. Hunter-Blair	Desp. May 24, '98.	Lieut. C. H. W. Owen ...	With Maxims. Desp. May 24, Sept. 30, '98.
Capt. C. O. Smeaton......	With Maxims. Desp.Sept.30,'98.	2nd Lieut. G. F. Clayton	With Maxims. Desp.Sept.30,'98.
Lieut. E. G. Waymouth...	Desp. Sept. 30, '98.		

* Two 40-pounders, under Lieut. Waymouth, and six 5in. B. L. Howitzers firing 50lb high explosive Lyddite shells, were attached to this detachment.

MAXIM BATTERY, DETACHMENT 1ST BATTLN. ROYAL IRISH FUSILIERS.

Left Cairo for Soudan, July, 1898. Present at the Battle of Khartoum. Returned to Cairo, Sept., 1898

Name.	Remarks, Honours, &c.
Capt. D. W. Churcher.....................	Desp. Sept. 30, '98.
Lieut. M. Wilson	

APPENDIX I

DETACHMENT, 2ND COMPANY (FORTRESS), ROYAL ENGINEERS.

Left Cairo for Soudan, Jan., 1898. Present at the Battles of Atbara and Khartoum. Returned to Cairo, Sept., 1898

Name.	Remarks, Honours, &c.
Maj. L. B. Friend	Desp. Sept. 30, '98.
Maj. L. A. Arkwright	Desp. Sept. 30, '98.
Lieut. D. A. Friedrichs, p.s.c.	Desp. Sept. 30, '98.

1ST BATTN. GRENADIER GUARDS.

Left Cairo for Soudan, July, 1898. Present at the Battle of Khartoum. Returned to Cairo, Sept., 1898

Name.	Remarks, Honours, &c.	Name.	Remarks, Honours, &c.
Col. Villiers Hatton	Desp. Sept. 30, '98.	Lieut. C. E. Corkran	Desp. Sep.. 30, '98.
Maj. F. Lloyd	Desp. Sept 30, '98.	Lieut. Hon. E. D. Loch	
Maj. H. Goulburn		Lieut. Hon. F. C. Stanley	
Maj. Hon. G. Legh		Lieut. E. H. Trotter	
Maj. W. A. L. Fox-Pitt		Lieut. G. S. Clive	
Capt. Hon. W. L. Bagot	Wounded at Omdurman.	Lieut. Hon. J. F. Gathorne-Hardy	
Capt. W. G. H. Marshall		Lieut. H. F. Crichton	
Capt. G. Dalrymple-White		Lieut. F. L. V. Swaine	
Capt. Hon. W. E. Cavendish		Lieut. J. A. Morrison	
		2nd Lieut. G. D. Jeffreys	
[Capt. (Brev.-Maj.) Lord E. H. Cecil] with Headquarter staff, E.A., q.v.		2nd Lieut. M. Gurdon-Rebow	
		2nd Lieut. E. Seymour	
Capt. E. G. Verschoyle		2nd Lieut. H. St. L. Stucley	
Lieut. W. Murray-Threipland	Desp. Sept. 30, '98.	2nd Lieut. G. B. A. Russell	
Lieut. G. L. Derriman		2nd Lieut. Sir R. M. Filmer, Bart.	
Lieut. W. R. A. Smith		Quartermaster (Hon. Lt.) G. Powell	
Lieut. F. E. W. Hervey-Bathurst			
Lieut. E.F.O. Gascoigne, *Adjutant*	Desp. Sept. 30, '98.		

For Medical Officers, see R.A.M.C., below.

1ST BATTN. NORTHUMBERLAND FUSILIERS (5TH).

Left Cairo for Soudan, July, 1898, leaving Depot at Citadel, Cairo. Present at the Battle of Khartoum, Sept., 1898.

Name.	Remarks, Honours, &c.	Name.	Remarks, Honours, &c.
Lieut.-Col. C. G. C. Money	Desp. Sept. 30, '98.	[Lieut. C. M. A. Wood]	With Irregulars, E.A., q.v.
Maj. Hon. C. Lambton	Desp. Sept. 30, '98.	Lieut. H. T. Crispin	
Maj. E. W. Dashwood		Lieut. B. T. Buckley	
Capt. E. B. Eagar		Lieut. H. S. Toppin	
Capt. J. H. L. White		Lieut. H. G. Lynch-Staunton	
Capt. C. H. L. James		Lieut. R.C.B. Lethbridge	
Capt. D. Sapte		Lieut. R. W. M. Brine	
Capt. G. L. S. Ray, *Adjutant*	Desp. Sept. 30, '98.	Lieut. H. C. Hall	
Capt. S. H. Enderby		2nd Lt. A. C. Girdwood	
Capt. F. C. Turner		2nd Lt. W. A. L. Hale	
Capt. S. C. Ferguson		2nd Lt. F. L. Festing	
Lieut. A. J. B. Percival		2nd Lt. H. V. Fison	Died at Cairo, Oct. 5, '98.
Lieut. C. E. Fishbourne		2nd Lt. F. R. Coates	
Lieut. E. M. Moulton-Barrett		2nd Lt. C. W. Brown	

1st Battn. ROYAL WARWICKSHIRE REGIMENT (6th).

Left Alexandria for Soudan, January, 9, 1898, leaving Depot at Ras-el-Ten (Alexandria). Present at the Battles of Atbara and Khartoum. Returned to Alexandria, Sept. 1898.

Name.	Remarks, Honours, &c.	Name.	Remarks, Honours, &c.
Col. Longbourne	Left for England, Feb, 24, '98.	Lieut. MacG. Greer	Wounded at Atbara. Desp. May 24, 1898. [Capt. June, 1898]. Left for 3rd battn. on promotion.
Lt.-Col. W. E. G. Forbes	Joined Apr. 7, took command Apr. 10. Attached to Gen. Gatacre's Staff at Atbara. Desp. Sept. 30, '98.	Lieut. W. D. Sanderson	Not at Omdurman.
Lt.-Col. M. Quayle Jones	Commanded regt. on march thro' Berber, and at Atbara, and left for 2nd Bn., Apr. 10, '98. Desp. May 24, '98.	Lieut. A. Vincent.	Mar. '98 at Alexandria.
		Lieut. H. G. A. Moore	
		Lieut. A. S. Toogood	
		Lieut. F. G. Skipwith	
		Lieut. A. Y. Spearman	May, '98, at Korti.
Maj. H. E. Irwin	Joined May, '98. Desp. Sept. 30, '98.	Lieut. C. E. Etches.	Mar. '98, at Korti (detachment). Wounded at Omdurman. Desp. Sept. 30, '98.
Maj. C. de C. Etheridge	March, 1898. At Korti (detachment).		
Maj. C. J. Cockburn, p.s.c.		[Lieut. H. M. A. Hankey].	With Kassala Irregulars, E.A., q.v.
Maj. H. J. S. Landon	Desp. May 24, '98.		
Capt. O. A. Chambers	March, 1898. At Korti (detachment). Left for 2nd Brig., May 1898, on promotion to majority.	Lieut. G. N. B. Forster.	
		Lieut. W. C. Christie.	Orderly officer at Atbara to Col. Wauchope. Desp. Sept. 30, '98.
		Lieut. J. B. R. Bacchus.	Joined May, '98.
Capt. H. R. Blyth	Not at Atbara (sick, England).	Lieut. R. H. W. Brewis.	
Capt. C. C. East		Lieut. H. P. Creagh-Osborne	
Capt. G. Caldecott	Killed at Omdurman, Sept. 2, '98.	Lieut. D. A. L. Day	
		Lieut. R. F. Meiklejohn.	
Lieut. W. M. L. Lee	March, 1898. At Korti (detachment). Left for 3rd Bn., May, '98, on promotion.	Lieut. P. E. Besant	Joined May, '98.
		Lieut. F. A. Jackson	Joined May, '98.
		(Hon.) Lieut. and Qr.-Mr. Dixon	Desp. Sept. 30, '98.
Lieut. F. A. Earle, Adjutant	[Capt., Apr. 6, '98]. Desp. May 24, Sept. 30, '98.		

APPENDIX I

1ST. BATTN. LINCOLNSHIRE REGIMENT (10TH).

Left Cairo for Soudan, January, 1898, leaving Depot at Citadel, Cairo. Present at the Battles of Atbara and Khartoum. Returned to Cairo, Sept., 1898.

Name.	Remarks, Honours, &c.	Name.	Remarks, Honours, &c.
Col. T. E. Verner..........	Wounded at Atbara. Desp. May 24, '98. Left battn., on half pay, May 11, '98.	Lieut. P. M. Peters	At Depot (Cairo).
		Lieut. H. E. R. Boxer...	Wounded at Atbara. Desp. May 24, '98. Not at Omdurman.
Lieut.-Col. F. R. Lowth.	Joined from other battn. May. Desp. Sept. 30, '98.	Lieut. E. A. Plunkett......	Desp. Sept. 30, '98
		Lieut. E Tatchell............	Desp. May 24, '98.
		Lieut. C. J. Rennie.........	Wounded at Atbara.
Maj. C. R. Simpson, p.s.c.	Desp. May 24, Sept. 30, '98.	Lieut. R. H. G. Wilson...	
		Lieut. R. d'E. Hill..........	Not at Omdurman, at depot (Lincoln).
Maj. H. B. Mainwaring.	Desp. May 24, Sept. 30, '98.		
Capt. V. G. R. Johnson..	Desp. Sept. 30, '98.	Lieut. L. A. Burrowes....	
Capt. R. P. Maxwell......		Lieut. H. Hodgson..........	Joined May, '98.
Capt. J. Forrest.............	Desp. May 24, '98.	2nd Lieut. F. W. Greatwood.	
Capt. A. E. Hubbard.....			
Capt. R. O. Cumberland.		2nd C. E. Hollins.	
Capt. J. R. M. Marsh, Adjutant....................	Desp. May 24, Sept. 30, '98.	2nd Lieut. A. N. Johnson.	Not at Omdurman (sick).
Capt. Barlow.................	Left for 2nd bn. after Atbara.	2nd Lieut. R. N. King...	Not at Omdurman, (at Atbara with details).
Lieut. S. FitzG. Cox......	[Capt. May '98]. Divisional Signalling Officer.	2nd Lieut. E. E. Woodcock................................	
Lieut. L. Edwards..........	[2nd bn., temporarily attached].	(Hon.) Lieut. and Qr.-Mr. P. Woodrow...............	

2ND. BATTN. LANCASHIRE FUSILIERS (20TH).

Left Cairo for Soudan, July, 1898, leaving Depot Kasr-en-Nil (Cairo). Present at the Battle of Khartoum. Returned to Cairo, Sept., 1898.

Name.	Remarks, Honours, &c.	Name.	Remarks, Honours, &c.
Lieut.-Col. C. G. Collingwood	Desp. Sept. 30, '98.	Lieut. G. H. B. Freeth...	
Maj. C. J. Blomfield......	Desp. Sept. 30, '98.	Lieut. G. M. Stewart.	
Maj. F. Hammersley, p.s.c		Lieut. T. G. C. Bliss......	
Maj. F. Amber...............		Lieut. J. V. Timmis..	
Capt. C. M. Brunker......		Lieut. H. H. Wilson.......	Desp. Sept. 30, '98.
Capt. E. C. Tidswell......		Lieut. J. R. Mallock ..	
Capt. W. F. Elmslie.......		Lieut. H. Shaw	
Capt. O. C. Wolley-Dod.	Desp. Sept. 30, '98.	Lieut. A. J. Allardyce....	
Capt. J. N. Whyte.........		2nd Lieut. R. R. Willis...	
Capt. H. V. S. Ormond...		2nd Lieut. R. S. Wilson.	
Lieut. G. J. Farmar.......		2nd Lieut. R. J. Dennis.	
Lieut. W. B. Pearson.....		2nd Lieut. T. J. Marrable	
Lieut. R. B. Blunt Adjutant........................		2nd Lieut. H. M. Farmar.	
		(Hon). Capt. and Qr.-Mr. J. S. Cameron	Desp. Sept. 30, '98.

1st Battn. SEAFORTH HIGHLANDERS (72nd).

Left Cairo for Soudan, Mar. 1898. Present at the Battles of Atbara and Khartoum. Returned to Cairo, Sept. 1898.

Name.	Remarks, Honours, &c.	Name.	Remarks, Honours, &c.
Brev.-Col. R. H. Murray, C.B.................		Lieut. W. T. Gaisford....	
	Wounded at Atbara. Desp. May 24, Sept. 30, '98.	[Lieut. E. Cox]..............	Extra A.D.C. to G.O.C. Brit. Divn., q.v.
Maj. J. A. Campbell......	Desp. May 24, Sept. 30, '98.	Lieut. N. A. Thomson....	Wounded at Atbara.
Maj. S. B. Jameson........	Desp. May 24, '98.	Lieut. A. C. B. Alexander	
Capt. G. G. A. Egerton..	Desp. May 24, '98. [Maj. June.]	Lieut. K. W. Arbuthnot..	
		Lieut. C. P. Doig..........	
Capt. A. A. Spottiswoode.	Desp. Sept. 30, '98.	Lieut. A. J. McNeill......	Desp. Sept. 30, '98.
Capt. A. C. D. Baillie....	Wounded at Atbara, and died at Cairo, May 16, '98. [Desp. May 24, '98.]	Lieut. F. J. Marshall.....	
		Lieut. F. E. Ll. Daniell..	Desp. May 24, '98.
		Lieut. C. I. Stockwell	
		2nd Lieut. D. H. Graeme	[Lieut. May.]
		2nd Lieut. E. Campion..	[Lieut. June.]
Capt. N. C. Maclachlan..	Wounded at Atbara. Desp. Sept. 30, '98.	2nd Lieut. D. A. Carden.	
		2nd Lieut. L. Holland....	
Capt. E. R. Bradford.....		2nd Lieut. G. W. Murray	
Capt. A. B. Ritchie........	Joined May, '98.	2nd Lieut. R. A. Gore....	Killed at Atbara, April 8, '98.
Lieut. R. S. Vandeleur...	Wounded at Atbara. Desp. May 24, '98. [Capt. May.]	2nd Lieut. W. M. Thomson..............................	
		(Hon.) Capt. and Qr.-Mr. G. W. Anderson	Desp. Sept. 30, '98.
Lieut. C. J. Ramsden, *Adjutant*.................	Desp. May 24, Sept. 30, '98.		

1st Battn. (QUEEN'S OWN) CAMERON HIGHLANDERS (79th).

Left Cairo for Soudan, Jan. 1898, leaving Depot at Kasr-en-Nil (Cairo). Present at the Battles of Atbara and Khartoum. Returned to Cairo, Sept. 1898.

Name.	Remarks, Honours, &c.	Name.	Remarks, Honours, &c.
Brev.-Col. G. L. C. Money, D.S.O., A.D.C.	Desp. May 24, Sept. 30, '98.	Lieut. A. Chancellor.......	
		Lieut. H. R. Brown	
Maj. T. F. A. Watson-Kennedy...................	Desp. May 24, Sept. 30, '98.	Lieut. N. J. G. Cameron	Desp. Sept. 30, '98.
		Lieut. G. C. M. Sorel-Cameron...................	
Maj. R. F. L. Napier.....	Wounded at Atbara, and died at Cairo May 23. [Desp. May 24, '98.]	Lieut. A. D. Nicholson...	Wounded at Omdurman. Desp. Sept. 30, '98.
		Lieut. R. L. Adlercron ...	
		Lieut. Hon. A. H. Maitland............................	
Maj. F. Hacket-Thompson	Desp. Sept. 30, '98.	2nd Lieut. W. M. Stewart.	[Lieut. May 19.]
Maj. B. C. Urquhart......	Killed at Atbara, April 8, '98.	2nd Lieut. St. C. M. G. MacEwen	
Capt. C. Findlay	Killed at Atbara, April 8, '98.	2nd Lieut. D. N. C. C. Miers..............................	
Capt. J. S. Ewart, p.s.c...	Desp. Sept. 30, '98.	2nd Lieut. Hon. R. A. Campbell........................	
Capt. Hon. A. D. Murray	Desp. May 24, Sept. 30, '98.	2nd Lieut. J. W. Sandilands............................	Desp. Sept. 30, '98.
Capt. F. A. MacFarlan ..	Desp. Sept. 30, '98.	2nd Lieut. A. Horne.......	
Capt. A. F. Egerton.......		2nd Lieut. A. J. C. Murdoch	
Capt. S. S. S. Clarke......	Wounded at Omdurman. Desp. Sept. 30, '98.	2nd Lieut. G. I. Fraser....	Joined May, '98.
Capt. A. C. McLean		2nd Lieut. P. W. N. Fraser............................	Joined May, 1898.
Capt. J. D. McLachlan...	Joined June, '98.		
Lieut. J. Campbell, *Adjt.*	Desp. May 24, Sept. 30, '98. [Capt. May 19.]	(Hon.) Capt. and Qr.-Mr. A. P. Yeadon	Desp. Sept. 30, '98.

APPENDIX I

2ND BATTN. RIFLE BRIGADE.

Left Cairo for Soudan, July, 1898. Present at the Battle of Khartoum. Returned to Cairo, Sept. 1898.

Name.	Remarks, Honours, &c.	Name.	Remarks, Honours, &c.
Brev.-Col. F. Howard, C.B., A.D.C.	Desp. Sept. 30, '98.	Lieut. J. Harington	
Maj. G. Cockburn	Desp. Sept. 30, '98.	Lieut. G. B. Byrne	
Maj. G. F. Leslie		Lieut. Hon. H. Dawnay.	Desp. Sept. 30, '98.
Capt. C. D. Shute, P.S.C.		2nd Lieut. A. J. Markham	
Capt. S. Mills		2nd Lieut. G. C. D. Fergusson	
Capt. A. V. J. Cowell		2nd Lieut. L. W. Nelson.	
Capt. G. H. Thesiger, *Adjutant*	Desp. Sept. 30, '98.	2nd Lieut. R. W. Pearson	
		2nd Lieut. L. D. Hall	
Capt. R. B. Stephens		2nd Lieut. S. Davenport.	
Capt. H. D. Ross		2nd Lieut. A. R. Harman	
Lieut. J. E. Gough		2nd Lieut. Hon. E. G. Boyle	
Lieut. G. Paley		2nd Lieut. C. D'A. B. S. Baker-Carr.	
Lieut. J. D. Heriot-Maitland			
Lieut. C. H. G. M. Clarke			

DETACHMENT ARMY SERVICE CORPS.

Present at the Battles of Atbara and Khartoum.

Name.	Remarks, Honours, &c.	Name.	Remarks, Honours, &c.
Lieut.-Col. L. A. Hope	Joined August, '98. Desp. Sept. 30, '98.	Capt. M. Coutts	
		Lieut. K. Macdonald	
Maj. H. G. Morgan, D.S.O.	Joined August, '98. Desp. Sept. 30, '98.	Lieut. G. E. Pigott	Staff officer, at Atbara, to Gen. Gatacre. Desp. May 24, Sept. 30, '98.
[Capt. H. M. Sargent]	*See Divisional Staff.*		
[Capt. E. E. Bernard]	*See Headquarter Staff*	Lieut. F. Hunnard	
		Quar.-Mast. (Hon. Lt.), H. Chase	
Capt. A. K. Seccombe	Commanding Det., A.S.C.		

Attached to Det. A.S.C. for Transport Duties.

Capt. R. M. de Berry, Royal Irish Fusiliers, joined August, '98.
Capt. S. Bird, Royal Fusiliers, joined August '98. Desp. Sept. 30, '98.
Capt. A. B. Hamilton, K.O. Sco. Bord., joined August, '98. Desp. Sept. 30, '98.

DETACHMENT, ROYAL ARMY MEDICAL CORPS.

Arranged according to distribution during advance on Omdurman. Those present at Battle of Atbara are indicated.

British Division.	Name.	Regt.	Remarks, Honours, &c.
P.M.O. Headquarter Staff.	Surg.-Gen. Taylor, M.D. ...	R.A.M.C...	⎫
,, Secretary to do. ...	Maj. Wilson, C.M.G............	R.A.M.C...	⎬ See Staff Lists, above
,, British Division ...	Lieut.-Col. Macnamara	R.A.M.C...	
,, 1st Brigade(British)	Lieut.-Col. Sloggett............	R.A.M.C...	
,, 2nd ,, ,,	Lieut.-Col. Hughes	R.A.M.C...	⎭
1ST BRIGADE.			
Attached, R. Warwicks Rg.	Maj. J. M. Irwin, M.B.......	R.A.M.C...	
,, Lincolnshire ,,	Maj. H. M. Adamson, M.B.	R.A.M.C...	[Atbara.] Desp. May 24, Sept. 30, '98.
,, Cameron Highls.	Capt. H. B. Mathias	R.A.M.C...	[Atbara.] Desp. May 24, Sept. 30, '98.
,, Seaforth ,,	Lieut. E. W. Bliss	R.A.M.C...	[Atbara.] Desp. May 24, Sept. 30, '98.
No. 1, Sect. Field Hosp.[1] ..	Maj. E. H. Myles, M.B. ...	R.A.M.C...	
,, 2, ,, ,,	Maj. C. A. Webb................	R.A.M.C...	Desp. Sept. 30, '98.
,, 3, ,, ,,	Maj. G. W. Robinson.........	R.A.M.C...	[Atbara.]. Desp. Sept. 30, '98.
,, 4, ,, ,,	Maj. D. Wardrop, M.B. ...	R.A.M.C...	Desp. Sept. 30, '98.
,, 5, ,, ,,	Maj. A. Dodd	R.A.M.C...	Desp. Sept. 30, '98.
2ND BRIGADE.			
Attached, 1st Grenadier Gd.	⎰Maj. C. R. Kilkelly, M.B....	R.A.M.C...	Desp. Sept. 30, '98.
	⎱Capt. J. H. E. Austin.........	R.A.M.C...	
,, Northbld. Fuslrs.	Lieut. R. D. Jephson	R.A.M.C...	
,, Lancashire ,,	Capt. A. J. Luther	R.A.M.C...	
,, Rifle Brigade......	Capt. D. M. O'Callaghan ...	R.A.M.C...	Desp. Sept. 30, '98.
No. 6, Sect. Field Hosp.[1]...	Maj. T. F. MacNeece.........	R.A.M.C...	
,, 7, ,, ,,	Maj. F. T. Wilkinson.........	R.A.M.C...	
,, 8, ,, ,,	Maj. J. R. Stuart, M.B. ...	R.A.M.C...	[Atbara.]
,, 9, ,, ,,	Maj. H. N. Thompson, M.B.	R.A.M.C...	
,, 10, ,, ,,	Maj. F. W. C. Jones, M.B.	R.A.M.C...	
CAVALRY.			
Attached, 21st Lancers	Maj. W. H. Pinches	R.A.M.C...	[Atbara.] Desp. Sept. 30, '98.
No. 11, Sect. Field Hosp...	Maj. R. H. S. Sawyer,M.B.	R.A.M.C...	
ARTILLERY.			
Attached, Artillery.............	⎰Capt. T. H. F. Clarkson ...	R.A.M.C...	
	⎱Lieut. F. J. Gaine	R.A.M.C...	
No. 12, Sect. Field Hosp...	Maj. R. W. Barnes	R.A.M.C...	Desp. Sept. 30, '98.
COMMUNICATIONS.			
Convoy Boat. A[2]	Maj. G. D. Hunter, D.S.O.	R.A.M.C...	
,, B................	Capt. A. Y. Reily, M.B......	R.A.M.C...	[Atbara.] Desp. Sept. 30, '98.
,, C..............	Capt. W. A. S. J. Graham...	R.A.M.C...	
,, D..............	Lieut. W. E. Hudlestone	R.A.M.C...	
,, E..............	Maj. H. Carr, M.D............	R.A.M.C...	[Atbara.] Desp. May 24, 1898.
,, F..............	Capt. J. Thomson, M.B......	R.A.M.C...	
,, G..............	Capt. H. S. Peeke	R.A.M.C...	
,, H	Lieut. P. McKessack, M.B.	R.A.M.C...	

[1] Each Sectional Field Hospital contained 25 beds.
[2] Each convoy boat (barge) contained 25 beds. On each boat was 1 officer, 1 compounder, 1 sergeant, and 4 or 5 privates of the R.A. Medical Corps.

APPENDIX I

DETACHMENT, ROYAL ARMY MEDICAL CORPS—continued.

British Division.	Name.	Regt.	Remarks, Honours, &c.
STATIONARY HOSPITALS.			
Atbara Hospital [1] (200 beds)	Lieut.-Col. N. Leader.........	R.A.M.C...	[Atbara.] Desp. Sept. 30, '98.
,, ,,	Maj. G. F. A. Smythe.........	R.A.M.C...	
,, ,, ...	Maj. W. G. Birrell, M.B......	R.A.M.C...	
,, ,, ...	Lieut. S. A. Archer.............	R.A.M.C...	
,, ,, ...	Lieut. C. H. Hopkins.........	R.A.M.C...	
Abadieh ,, (300 beds).	Lieut.-Col. J. A. Clery, M.B.	R.A.M.C...	
,, ,, ...	Maj. A.O. Geoghegan, M.D.	R.A.M.C...	
,, ,, ...	Maj. J. Battersby, M.B......	R.A.M.C...	
,, ,, ...	Capt. E. S. Marder	R.A.M.C...	
,, ,, ...	Maj. S. G. Allen	R.A.M.C...	[Atbara.] Desp. May 24, Sept. 30, '98.
,, ,, ...	Maj. M. O'D. Braddell, M.B.	R.A.M.C...	
,, ,, ...	Maj. J. R. Burrows, M.D...	R.A.M.C...	
,, ,, ...	Capt. J. Girvin....................	R.A.M.C...	
,, ,, ...	Capt. A. L. Borradaile, M.B.	R.A.M.C...	
,, ,, ...	Lieut. M. P. Corkery	R.A.M.C...	
,, ,, ...	Lieut. S. L. Cummins, M.B.	R.A.M.C...	[Atbara.] Desp Sept. 30, '98.
,, ,, ...	Lieut. J. McArdle, M.B.....	R.A.M.C...	
,, ,, ...	Lieut. H. G. F. Stallard......	R.A.M.C...	
Wady Halfa Hosp. (50 beds)	Maj. H. T. Baylor	R.A.M.C...	
,, ,, ...	Capt. G. F. Alexander, M.B.	R.A.M.C...	
Shellal Hospital (50 beds)...	Capt. J. Hayes....................	R.A.M.C...	
,, ,, ...	Lieut. L. J. C. Hearn, M.B.	R.A.M.C...	

[1] Built of mud bricks, the walls were some 3 feet thick, the roof was lofty, and the ceilings were formed with matting and thickly thatched with dhurra straw. This hospital could, if necessary, accommodate more than the *minimum* number of 200 patients, and the provision could be raised to meet the needs of 300 patients, if necessary, by means of tents.

DETACHMENT, ARMY ORDNANCE DEPARTMENT.

	Name.	Regt.	Remarks, Honours, &c.
Sen. Ord. Officer...............	[Lieut.-Col. T. Heron]........	—	*See Headquarter Staff, above.*
Ord. Officer, 4th Class.......	Capt. C. Hall......................	Conn. Rang.	
,, ,, ...	Capt. C. M. Mathew	Durh. L.I.	Desp. Sept. 30, '98.
D.C. of Ord......................	Hon. Capt. D. E. Collins. ...	—	

DETACHMENT, ARMY VETERINARY DEPARTMENT.

	Name.	Honours, Remarks, &c.
Sen. Vet. Surg.	[Vet.-Capt. L. J. Blenkinsop]	*See Headquarter Staff, above.*
Asst. ,, ,, ...	Vet.-Capt. F. B. Drage, R.H.G....	Desp. Sept. 30, '98.
,, ,, ,, ...	Vet.-Lieut. W. Dunlop Smith	With 21st Lancers. Desp. Sept. 30, '98.
,, ,, ,, ...	Vet.-Lieut. W. E. Russell	Desp. May 24, Sept. 30, '98.

N.-C. O.'S AND MEN, MENTIONED IN THE SIRDAR'S DESPATCHES, ETC.

Mentioned in Despatches, November 3, 1896:—

Egyptian Army:—Sergeant Bailey (promoted 2nd Lieut. E. Lanc. Regt.).
Sergeant McKey (promoted 2nd Lieut. Middx. Regt.).
Sergeant Flint (promoted 2nd Lieut. R. Irish Rifles).

Mentioned in Despatches, May 25, 1898:—

Egyptian Army:—Sergt.-Maj. Blake (17th Lancers).
Cr.-Sergt. Kelbam
Cr.-Sergt. Sheppard (R. W. Kent Regt.).
Sergt. Scott-Barbour (Gordon Highrs.).
Sergt. Handley (K. O. Yorks L. I.—wounded at Atbara).
Sergt. Hilton (wounded at Atbara).
Lance-Sergt. Russell.
Seaforth Highlanders:—Cr.-Sergt. McIver, Corp. Lawrie.
Cameron Highlanders:—Cr.-Sergt. Fisher, Pte. Cross (since deceased), Pte. Chalmers.
Army Service Corps:—Staff-Sergt. Wyeth.

Mentioned in Despatches, September 30, 1898:—

Egyptian Army, and on Staff Employment:—
Squadn. Sergt.-Major Blake (17th Lancers).
Sergt. Russel (Scots Guards).
Cr.-Sergt. H. Sheppard (R. W. Kent Regt.).
Sergt. Handley (K. O. Yorks L. I.).
Divnl. Staff-Sergt. Jack (Middlesex Regt.).
Drill Instructor Sergt. Donald McLeod (Seaforth Highrs.).
Sergt. Scott-Barbour (Gordon Highrs.).

21st Lancers:—
　Corp. Swarbrick.
　Pte. Ayton.
　Pte. Brown (wounded).
Royal Artillery:—
　Sergt. Howard.
　Corp. Kelly.
Royal Engineers:—
　Coy. Sergt.-Maj. Bennett.
　Sergt. G H. Rawlinson.
　Second Corp. A. Jones.
　Sapper F. Bird.
　Sapper H. Brown.
Grenadier Guards:—
　Qr.-Mr. Sergt. Chamberlain.
　Sergt.-Master-Cook Brooke.
　Sergt.-Instructor Lewis.
　Sergt. J. Phillips.
Northumberland Fusiliers:—
　Cr.-Sergt. T. Burdett.
　Sergt.-Drummer J. Cordeal.
　Sergt. A. Bannerman.
Royal Warwickshire Regt.:—
　Sergt. Girling.
　Corp. Darnley.
　Lce.-Corp. Marsden.
Lincolnshire Regt.:—
　Sergt.-Major W. Church.
　Serg. G. Stevens.
　Sergt. J. Wogan.
Lancashire Fusiliers:—
　Cr. Sergt. Evans.
　Corp. Porter.

Seaforth Highlanders:—
　Cr.-Sergt. D. Mackie
　Cr.-Sergt. McEwen.
　Cr.-Sergt. Robertson.
　Sergt. Murray.
Cameron Highlanders:—
　Sergt.-Major Donald McLeod.
　Cr.-Sergt. A. Fisher.
　Cr.-Sergt. F. Mackenzie.
　Pte. A. Cameron.
Royal Irish Fusiliers (Maxim battery):—
　Cr.-Sergt. J. Teaque.
　Corp. M. Mullin.
Rifle Brigade:—
　Sergt.-Maj. E. Bull.
　Qr.-Mr.-Sergt. J. Alldridge.
　Cr.-Sergt. J. Nicholas.
A. S. C.:—
　Qr.-Mr.-Sergt. Osburn.
　Staff-Sergt. Beville.
　Sergt. Parsons.
　Sergt. A. Titterell.
　Sergt. J. Topliss.
　Sec. Corp. Pawley.
　Shoeing-Smith P. Smith.
　Pte. Darling.
R. Army Med. Corps.:—
　1st Cl. S.-Sergt. A. Benson.
　1st Cl. S.-Sergt. F. Crooke.
　1st Cl. S.-Sergt. Hoist.
　Sergt. Scrase.
　Lce.-Sergt. A. P. Mears.
　Pte. A. Davidson.
Army Vet. Dep.:—
　Farrier-Major Escreet.

AWARDS OF ROYAL HUMANE SOCIETY.

Seaforth Highlanders:—Pte. A. Greenwood (Bronze Medal), for saving Pte. Lupton and Private Ainslie, in the Nile, on April 21, 1898.
Ptes. R. Jaggard, H. Allkins, and B. Bates (Bronze Medals), for saving Pte. Hawkshaw, at Nagh Hamadis.

APPENDIX II

ROLL OF BRITISH OFFICERS, WARRANT OFFICERS, NON-COMMISSIONED OFFICERS AND MEN WHO LOST THEIR LIVES DURING THE CAMPAIGNS ON THE NILE 1896—8.

DONGOLA EXPEDITION, 1896.

WADY HALFA.

Lieut. R. Polwhele, R. Eng.
Sergt. J. Brewster   ,,
Band-Sergt. F. Piper, 1st N. Stafford Regt.
Lce.-Corp. J. Baker   ,,   ,,
,,   ,,   E. Tucknall   ,,   ,,
Pte. H. Allen   ,,   ,,
,, W. Allsopp   ,,   ,,
,, J. Banks   ,,   ,,
,, D. Bollington   ,,   ,,
,, G. Bradshaw   ,,   ,,
,, F. Croft   ,,   ,,

Pte. E. Green, 1st N. Stafford Regt.
,, G. Haddon   ,,   ,,
,, J. Hadfield   ,,   ,,
,, W. Liggins   ,,   ,,
,, C. Moran   ,,   ,,
,, J. Wood   ,,   ,,
Staff-Sgt. L. Whitwell, A.S.C.
Sergt. J. Ross-Smith, M.S.C.
Pte. J. Morris   ,,
,, J. Park   ,,

GEMAI.

Armr.-Sergt. T. Lees, 1st N. Stafford Regt.
Sergt. J. Rixon   ,,   ,,
Corp. J. Dunwiddie   ,,   ,,
Lce.-Corp. T. Ash   ,,   ,,
,,   ,,   H. Clayton   ,,   ,,
,,   ,,   M. Plant   ,,   ,,
Pte. A. Bellamy   ,,   ,,
,, S. Beresford   ,,   ,,
,, J. Blackwell   ,,   ,,
,, T. Connolly   ,,   ,,
,, P. Dooley   ,,   ,,
,, W. Emery   ,,   ,,

Pte. J. Gould, 1st N. Stafford Regt.
,, A. Green   ,,   ,,
,, G. Hall   ,,   ,,
,, G. Hunter   ,,   ,,
,, P. Johnson   ,,   ,,
,, L. Jones   ,,   ,,
,, E. Skitt   ,,   ,,
,, J. McTighe   ,,   ,,
,, M. Turner   ,,   ,,
,, F. Weatherby   ,,   ,,
,, H. Wilding   ,,   ,,
Sergt. H. Vick, A.P.D.

AMBIGOL.

Brev.-Maj. E. R. Owen, Lancashire Fus. (E.A.), D.S.O.

KOSHEH.

Surg.-Capt. J. E. Trask, A.M.S. (E.A.).

SUARDEH.

Lieut. H. H. Farmar, K.R.R.C. (E.A.).

FAREIG.

Pte. J. Harvey, 1st North Stafford Regt.

HAFIR.

Sapper W. H. Abbott, R. Eng.
Pte. W. Doran, 1st North Stafford Regt.

Armr.-Sergt. W. Richardson.

DONGOLA.

Pte. H. Dale, 1st North Stafford Regt.

ASSIUT.

Sergt.-Maj. E. Cunningham, 1st N. Stafford Regt.

CAIRO.

Capt. J. Rose, 1st N. Stafford Regt.
Corp. B. Williams „ „
Lce.-Corp. A. Banes „ „
„ „ T. Farndon „ „
„ „ W. Wickstead „ „
Pte. C. Ault „ „
„ S. Bailey „ „
„ H. Bradshaw „ „
„ W. Bull „ „
„ T. Busby „ „
„ H. Davis „ „
„ J. Doughty „ „

Pte. G. Egerton, 1st N. Stafford Regt.
„ J. Ford „ „
„ J. Garton „ „
„ A. Harper „ „
„ J. Herriman „ „
„ R. Jeffs „ „
„ C. Johnson „ „
„ S. Micklewright „ „
„ J. Saunders „ „
„ H. Trotman „ „
Staff-Sergt. Maj. F. E. Page, A.S.C.

NILE EXPEDITION, 1897.

WADY HALFA.

Lieut. E. H. S. Cator, R.E. (E.A.)

KILLED AT ABU HAMED.

Brev.-Major H. M. Sidney, D.C.L.I. (E.A.) | Lieut. E. FitzClarence, Dorset Regt. (E.A.

NILE EXPEDITION, 1898.

KILLED AT THE BATTLE OF THE ATBARA.

Sergt. J. Malone, Lincolnshire Regt.
Pte. T. Hale, R. Warwickshire „
„ G. Howling „ „
„ M. Lee „ „
2nd Lieut. P. Gore, Seaforth Highlanders
Lce.-Corp. D. Martin „ „
Pte. W. Bowman „ „
„ A. Daper „ „
„ J. Derlin „ „
„ J. McNeal „ „
Maj. B. C. Urquhart, Cameron Highlanders
Capt. C. Findlay „ „
Lce.-Corp. T. Cullen „ „

Lce.-Corp. A. Micklethwaite, Cameron Hldrs
Piper F. Stewart „ „
Pte. W. Bartlett „ „
„ F. Chesworth „ „
„ G. Denaghan „ „
„ J. Fleming „ „
„ W. Galloway „ „
„ R. McKee „ „
„ F. Markham „ „
„ J. Taylor „ „
„ R. Wilkinson „ „
„ W. Williamson „ „

CAIRO.

*Major R. F L. Napier, Cameron Highdrs. | * Capt. A. D. C. Baillie, Seaforth Highdrs.
Lieut. H. V. Fison, 1st Northumberland Fusiliers.

* From wounds received at the Atbara.

WADY HALFA (near, at No. 6 Station).

Sapper D. Macpherson, R.E.

ABADIEH

Sapper F. Wythe, R.E.

APPENDIX II

DARMALI.

Sapper R. Allsopp, R.E.
Pte. J. Ansell, Lincolnshire Regt.
" J. Brannon " "
" W. Clayden " "
" A. Dawson " "
" G. Ellis " "
" W. Gage " "
" W. Gamwell " "
" H. Gillogley " "
" J. Holland " "
" — Johnston " "
" J. Kelly " "
" G. Maltby " "
" F. Rushby " "
" W. Warriner " "
Sergt H. Doughty, R. Warwickshire Regt.
" A. Strafford " "
Lce.-Corp. A. Mitchell " "
Drummer — Cox " "
Pte. J. Close " "

Pte. W. Dutton, R. Warwickshire Regt.
" F. Gardner " "
" J. Hubbard " "
" H. Hunt " "
" H. Jones " "
" H. Pettipher " "
" E. Wilson " "
Lce.-Corp. — Lowson, Seaforth Highlanders.
Pte. B. Ellis " "
" W. Newman " "
" J. Patterson " "
" J. Rae " "
" J. Stephen " "
Bandsman W. Cuthbert, Cameron Highdrs.
Pte. W. Cooper " "
" T. Cross " "
" D. Kearton " "
" P. McLeod " "
" G. Stagpole " "
" T. Jackman, A.S.C.

ATBARA.

Mr. Henry Cross (Correspondent, *Manchester Guardian*)
Driver J. Clark, 32nd F.B., R.A.

Pte. A. Whidby, 1st Grenadier Guards
Pte. G. Howling, 1st Warwickshire Regt.

JEBEL ROYAN.

Shoeing Smith G. Evans, 32nd F.B., R.A.
Pte. W. Allen, 1st Grenadier Guards
" G. Baker, 1st North. Fusiliers
" G. Clayton, 1st R. Warwickshire Regt.
" C. Gibbons " "
" J. H. Blomley, 2nd Lancashire Fus."

Pte. E. Mather, 2nd Lancashire Fus.
" D. Mackenzie, 1st Cameron Highdrs.
Clr.-Sergt. W. H. Yates, 1st R. Ir. R. (E.A.
Sergt. J. Bowden, Rifle Brigade
Pte. G. Willsher, A.S.C.
" H. Livett, R.A.M.C.

KILLED AT THE BATTLE OF KHARTOUM (*Omdurman*).

Lieut. R. Grenfell, 12th Lancers (attached to 21st Lancers)
Sergt. R. Allen, 21st Lancers
" E. Carter " "
Lce.-Sergt. A. Grantham "
Lce.-Corp. J. Weller "
Lce.-Corp. F. W. S. Elliot "
Corp. I. Woods " "
Pte. H. Borthwick " "
" H. Bradshaw " "
" W. Etherington " "
" T. Hannah " "
" E. Hatter " "
" H. Hunt " "

Pte. F. J. Kelly, 21st Lancers
" T. Miles " "
" F. Morhall " "
" W. Oldbury " "
" F. J. Rawle " "
" A. Roberts " "
" J. S. Scattergood " "
" C. Wright " "
Capt. G. Caldecott, 1st R. Warwickshire Regt.
Pte. J. Johnstone, 1st Seaforth Highlanders
Corp. A. Allan, 1st Cameron "
" A. B. Millar " "
Pte. J. Smith, 2nd Rifle Brigade
Hon. H. Howard (*Times*), Correspondent

OMDURMAN.

Corp. D. Peables, 1st Cameron Highlanders.

From wounds received in the battle.

Pte. G. Rayner, 1st Lincolnshire Regt. | Pte. H. Mullin, 1st Seaforth Highlanders.

INDEX

INDEX

The names in italics are of the officers who took part in the Expeditions (1896-8).

ABABDAS (tribe), 60
Abadar, 205
Abadieh, 237
Abbas (Khedive, '48), 4
Abbas II. (Khedive of Egypt), 49, 132, 230, 282
Abbassyieh, 38, 48
Abdul Azim (Sheikh), 102
Abdullah (*see* Khalifa)
Abdullah, Wad Saad (Jaalin), 161
Absárat, 107
Abu Delek, 173, 229
Abu Dis, 196, 200
Abu Fatmeh, 162
Abu Hamed, capture of, part iii., chap. i.; 153 164
Abu Klea, battle, 17; 153, 244
Abu Kru, 244
Abu Simbel [ruins], 56
Abyssinians, 29, 31, 195, 238
Adams, Capt., 137
Adarama, 170-1, 204, 229
Adowa, battle, 41
Ahmed Bey, Khalifa (Sheikh), 169
Ahmed Fedl, 173, 180, 286
Akasheh, 43, 59 66
Aliab, 201, 203
Ali Digna (Emir), 204
Ali Wad Helu (Emir), 245
Allah-ed-Deen, death of, 11
Ambigol Wells, 60, 66
Arabi Pasha, 37
Arduan Is., 119
Argo Is., 134
Arguin, battle, 32
Aroda (Sheikh), 186
Assabala (Sheikh), 186
Assiut, 151
Assouan, 50, 151

Atbara, 169, 206; battle, part iv., chap. iii.; fort, 236, 241

BAGGARA (tribe), 161
Bahr-el-Ghazal, 6, 8
Baillie, Capt., wounded at Atbara, 222; death of, 226
Bainbridge, Capt., 168, 203
Baker, Sir Samuel, 4
Baker, Valentine, 12, 13
Balliana, 50
Bara, 10
Baring, Capt. Hon., 205
Baring, Sir Eveyln, 16
Barji, 117, 119
Batn-el-Hagar, 75, 97
Beale, Lieut.-Col., 48, 95
Beatty, Lieut., R.N., 126, 168, 175, 181, 206
Bedouin (tribe), 60
Beni Amir (tribe), 186
Berber, 8, 14, 15, 152; occupied by Sirdar, 169, 237
Beresford, Lord Charles, 19
Bishara (*see* Wad-el-B.)
Bishara Redy (*see* Redy)
Blunt, Lieut. (A.S.C.), 103
Blunt, Lieut. (Conn. R.), 89
Boats : Cooks, 51, 151
 Gordon's (and afterwards Dervish), 128, 130, 132, 164, 279, 283
 gunboats, 54, 104, 107, 110, 126, 136, 149, 152, 153, 167, 169, 175, *et seq.*; 199, 202, 206, 237, 248, 251, 284
 gyassas and nuggars, 103, 121, 130, 131, 134, 142
 postboats, 54, 104, 110, 126, 284
 sternwheelers, 54, 104, 281
Boxer, Lieut., wounded, 222

INDEX

Brindle, Rev. Father, 51, 226
Brinton, Lieut., wounded, 226
Broadwood, Capt. (Brev.-Lieut.-Col.), 64, 66, 85, 202, 210, 248, 260
Brooke, Capt., 219
Burn-Murdoch, Maj., 64, 87
Burnaby, Col., killed at Abu Klea, 18

Cairo, part ii., chap. i.; 152, 239, 240
Caisse de la Dette, 43
Caldecott, Capt., killed at Omdurman, 259
Cameron Highlanders, 23, 78; leave Cairo, 197; from Wady Halfa to Berber, 200, 201; arrive at Kunur, 201, 202; advance to Ras el Hudi, 203; to Mutrus, part iv., chap. ii.; at the battle of the Atbara, part iv., chap. iii., 216, 218–224; casualties at Atbara, 227; Darmali, 231, 238, 239; Wad Hamed, 243, 245; advance to Egega, part iv., chap. vi.; at the battle of Omdurman, part iv., chap. vii; casualties, 278; return to Cairo, 282; one company to Fashoda, 284; to Cairo, 285
Capper, Capt., 261
Carr, Surg.-Capt. (Maj.), 51
Cataracts (description), part ii., chap. vii
  See Assouan (1st), Wady Halfa (2nd), Semneh, Tanjore, Ambigol, Dal, Kaibar, Hannek (3rd), Merawi (4th), El Umar(5th),and Shabluka(6th)
Chermside, Col., 29
Clarke, Capt., wounded, 259
Cochrane, Col., 50, 153
Coetlogon, Col., 11
Collinson, Maj. (Lieut -Col.), 59, 247, 251
Colville, Commander, 126, 127, 140, 151
Correspondents, War, Dongola, 82, 83, 139
  Nile Expedition, 1897, 172, 231
  Nile Expedition, 1898, 239, 240, 259, 274, 283.

Cross, Pte., gallantry of, 222
Currie, Lieut.-Col., 95

DAL (Cataract), 102
Darfur, 4, 8, 10, 29
Dar Monassir (cataracts), 21, 168
Dar Shagiyeh, 102. (*See* Shagiyeh)
Darmali, 231, 238, 241
de Montmorency, Lieut., 265
de Rougemont, Capt., 263
Debbeh, 15, 152, 162
Dervishes, definition, 25; army, 92; distribution, &c., 61, 86, 173, 196, 199, 207, 253, 278
Dongola, 3, 4, 8, 14; evacuated by British, 23; expedition, 1896, part ii., capture of, part ii., chap. x.; the town, part ii., chap. xi.; the province, 156 and 158–161
Doran, Capt., 202
Doyle, Dr. Conan, 53
Drage, Hon. Capt., 63
Dulgo, 112.

Earle, Gen., killed at Kirbekan, 20
Ed Damer, 169, 198
Edfoo, 53
Egega, 253
Egerton, Col., 73
Egyptian Army, 37—39; at Cairo, 48, 49; Wady Halfa, 60; Akasheh, 66; Ferket, 93; Kosheh, 100; start south, 109, 115—117; casualties, 154; occupy Merawi-Debbeh frontier, 153; casualties Dongola campaign, 154; at capture of Abu Hamed, 167; distribution (Berber, &c.), 195, 201; Kunur and Atbara, 202; Hudi, 203; Mutrus, part iv., chap. ii.; Wad Habeshi, 241; Wad Hamed, 243; brigades of Egyptian army, 246; Omdurman, part iv., chaps. vii. and viii.; casualties, 278.
El Atta Wad Ussul (Emir), killed at Atbara, 227
El Fasher, capture of, 186
El Gemuaia, 258
El Hajir, 250
El Obeid, 8, 10, 243
El Sofieh, capture of, 198

INDEX

El Teb, battle, 13
El Umar (5th Cataract), 241
Elkington, Lieut., 51, 107
Emin Pasha, 28
Emir, definition, 25, 93
Equatorial Provinces, 4, 28
Er'-kowit Hills, part ii., chap. iii
Es Sillem, 238
Esneh, 53

Fakri Wad Oman (Sheikh), 164
Fareig, 114—118
Farmar, Lieut., death of, 99
Farshut, 52
Fashoda, 283—4
Fenwick, Capt., 69; gallantry at Khor Wintri, 71; death of, 99
Fergusson, Capt., 69
Ferket, 61, 64, battle, part ii., chap. v
Fincastle, Lieut. Lord, 64
Findlay, Capt., killed at the Atbara, 220
Fitton, Capt., 64, 168, 212
FitzClarence, Lieut., killed at Abu Hamed, 166
Foggara (tribe), 60
Friendlies, 60, 118, 169, 190, 198, 248; *see* Ababdas, Bedouin, Beni Amir, Bishara, Foggara, Hadendowad, Jaalin, Kababish, Shagiyeh, and Shukrieh tribes

GAKDUL Wells, 167
Galabat, battle, 31
Garrett (Correspondent), 99
Gatacre, Maj.-Gen., 197, 202, 212, 217-219, 222, 239, 245
Gedaref, 173, 187, 229, 285
Gemai, 96
Gemaizah, battle, 31
Gessi, 6
Gineinetti, 203, 238
Ginniss, battle, 23, part iii
Girouard, Lieut., 61
Goldfinch, Lieut., 89
Gondokoro, 4
Gordon, Capt., 48, 237, 242
Gordon, General Charles, 5-7, 13 *et seq.*; death of, 19; his funeral service, 281
Gore, Lieut., killed at the Atbara, 221

Graham, Gen. Sir Gerald, 13, 21
Graham, Lieut. J., 206
Greer, Lieut., wounded, 222
Grenadier Guards, leave Cairo for front, 239, 240; reach Atbara, 241; Wad Hamed, 243, 245; advance to Egega, part iv., chap. vi.; at the battle of Omdurman, part iv, chap. vii.; casualties, 278; return to Cairo, 282
Grenfell, Gen. (Sir Francis), 23, 30.; wins battle of Toski, 33; visits Omdurman, 285
Grenfell, Lieut., killed at Omdurman, 265
Gubat, battle, 18

HADENDOWA (tribe), 68, 204
Hafir, battle, part ii, chap. ix.; 125, 139
Halfa, *see* Wady Halfa
Hamuda (Emir) 61, 86
Handoub, part ii, chap. iii
Handoub, battle, 30
Hannek (3rd Cataract), 121, 149
Harar, 4, 8
Harasab, part ii, chap. iii
Harley, Lieut., wounded, 222
Harrington, Lieut., visits Menelik, 238
Hebbeh, 164
Heygate, Major, 69
Hewett, Admiral, 12
Hickman, Brev.-Major, 206
Hicks Pasha, 10; death of, 11; relics of his force, 130, 276
Hobbs, Capt., 237
Holmes, Surg.-Capt. (Major), 51
Hopkinson, Lieut., wounded, 261
Hood, Lieut., (R.N.), 168, 175, 181, 183, 206
Hosh Ben Naga, 205
Howard, Hon. H.(Correspondent), killed at Omdurman, 274
Hudi, 203
Hunter, Col. (Maj.-Gen.), 58, 84, 156; captures Abu Hamed, 164; occupies Berber, 169; and Adarama, 172, 202; reconnoitres Mahmud's position, 206-7 and 209, 210; 218, 222, 273, 285
Hunter, (Surg.-) Major, 62

INDIAN Troops at Suakin, part ii, chap. iii
Italy (and Kassala), 41, 184 *et seq.*

JAALIN (tribe), 161, 171, 205, 206
Jackson, Maj., 65, 153, 171, 227, 263
Jebel Barkal, 2, 163
Jebel Royan, 242, 250
Jehadia (tribe), 89
John (King of Abyssinia), 27; killed at Galabat, 31
Judge, Capt., 68
Junker, Dr., 28

KABABISH (tribe), rise against Khalifa, 26, 60, 198
Kaderma, 112, 113
Kaibar (Cat.), 113
Karnak [ruins], 52
Kashgal, battle, 11
Kassala, 14, 41, 172 ; acquisition of, part iii., chap. iii ; 285
Keith-Falconer, Capt., 181
Keneh, 49
Kenna, Capt., 265, 266
Keppel, Capt. Colin, 168, 175, 181, 199, 206, 248, 284
Kerma, 23, 102, 125, 162
Kerreri, 252, 260
Khalifa (Abdullah). (*See also* 'Dervishes'), 23, part i., chap. iii. ; 153, 161, 173-4, 199, 209, 243, 244, 261 ; escapes from Omdurman, 274
Khartum, 4, destroyed by Khalifa, 25 ; sighted by the Sirdar's army, 242 ; battle of, part iv., chap. vii. ; occupied by the Sirdar, part iv., chap. ix.
Khedive. *See* Abbas II
Khor Shambat, 268, 270, 276
Khor Wintri, part ii., chap. iii.
Kincaid, Brev.-Major, 209
Kirbekan, battle, 20
Kitchener, Lt.-Col., 202
Kitchener, Colonel (Maj.-Gen.), Sir Herbert H. (the Sirdar). *See also* Egyptian Army for Headquarters, &c. Commandant at Suakin, 29, 30 ; his career, 39 ; leaves Cairo for front, 50 ; arrives Wady Halfa, 58 ; at Ferket, 92 ; at Hafir, 131 ; reviews army at Dongola, 146 ; visits Merawi, &c., 153 ; returns to Cairo, 154 ; continues policy in 1897, 162 ; reviews army at Kunur, 202 ; frustrates Mahmud's schemes, 207 ; at the Atbara, 224 ; interviews Mahmud, 228 ; formal entry into Soudan, 231 ; returns to Cairo, 238 ; reviews army at Wad Hamed, 245 ; at battle of Omdurman, 261, 263 ; enters Omdurman, 271 ; visits Khartum, 280 ; hoists British flag at Fashoda, 284 ; and at Sobat, 284 ; returns to Cairo, 285
Knowles, Maj.-Gen., 48, 76
Kokreb, 42
Kom Ombo [ruins], 53
Kordofan, 4, 8, 27, 243
Korosko, 56
Korti, 17, 153
Kosheh, 100, 107, 110, 111, 150
Kosseir, 49
Kunur, 198, 201

LADO, 8
Lancashire Fusiliers, leave Cairo for front, 239, 240 ; reach Atbara, 241 ; Wad Hamed, 243, 245 ; advance to Egega, part iv., chap. vi. ; at the battle of Omdurman, part iv., chap. vii. ; casualties, 278 ; return to Cairo, 282
21st Lancers, leave Cairo for front, 239, 240 ; reach Atbara, 241 ; Wad Hamed, 243, 245 ; advance to Egega, part iv., chap. vi. ; at the battle of Omdurman, part iv., chap. vii. ; casualties, 278 ; return to Cairo, 282
Laurie, Capt. (Brev.-Major), 87, 89, 206, 263
Le Gallais, Maj., 210
Legge, Capt., 91
Lewis, Maj. (Brev.-Lt.-Col.), 86, 122, 202, 212, 214, 241, 261
Lincolnshire Regiment, leave Cairo, 197 ; from Wady Halfa to Berber, 200 ; arrive at Kunur, 201, 202 ; advance to Ras el Hudi, 203 ; to

INDEX

Mutrus, part iv., chap. ii. ; at the battle of the Atbara, part iv., chap. iii. ; 216, 219, 220, 223 ; casualties, 227 ; Darmali, 231, 238, 239 ; Wad Hamed, 243, 245 ; advance to Egega, part iv., chap. vi. ; at the battle of Omdurman, part iv., chap. vii. ; casualties, 278 ; return to Cairo, 282

Lloyd, Lt.-Col., 68, part ii., chap.iii.
Long, Lt.-Col., 202, 217
Luxor, 52, 151, 240
Lyttleton, Col. (Brig.-Gen.), Hon. A. G., 239, 245, 263

Macdonald, Maj. (Brev.-Lt.-Col.), 86, 153, 202, 212, 214 ; at the battle of Omdurman, 261, 263
Maclachlan, Capt., wounded at the Atbara, 222
Mahdi, the (Mahomed Ahmed), part. i., chap. ii. ; death of, 23
Mahmud, 161, 174 ; crosses Nile at Metemmeh, 198, 201 ; reaches Atbara, 203 ; taken prisoner, 228
Mahomed Ahmed. *See* Mahdi.
Mahomed Ali (Khedive), 3
Mahomed El Khair (Emir), occupies Dongola, 23
Mahomed Zein (Emir), 166
Mahon, Capt., 101
Manifold, Lieut., 62, 286
Marchand, Maj., 284
Martin, Col., 264
Matchett, Capt., 69
Mathew, Capt., 51
Maxwell, Maj. (Brev.-Lt.-Col.), 87, 202, 212, 214, 261, 263, 270, 272
McNeill, Gen. Sir John, 21
McNeill's zariba, battle, 21
Menelik (King of Abyssinia), 31, 195
Merawi (4th Cat.), 2, 152, 153, 158, 162, 163, 241
Metemmeh, 17, 161 ; part iii., chap. ii. ; 198, 244
Micklem, Lieut., wounded, 267 *n.*
Mitford, Maj., 281
Moghrat Wells, 60
Molyneux, Lieut., 266

Moncrieff, Capt., death of, 12
Money, Col., 224
Morgan, Capt., 51
Murat Wells, 42, 61
Murray, Capt. the Hon., 284, 285
Murray, Col., 217 ; wounded, 221
Musa Pasha, 4
Mutrus, the advance of the Anglo-Egyptian army to, part iv., chap. ii.

NAKHEILA, 203
Napier, Maj., wounded at the Atbara, 221 ; death of, 227
Nason, Maj., 263
Nasri, Is., 241
Nejumi, Wad el (Emir), 26; killed at Toski, 33
Nepata [ruins], 2, 163
Nesham, 2nd Lieut. C. S., wounded at Omdurman, 265
Neufeld, Charles, 275
Nicholson, Lieut., wounded, 260
Nile, Expedition, 1884, 1885, part i, chap. ii., pp. 16 *et seq*
1897, part iii.; 1898, part iv.
Scenery, etc., 54—56, 60, 104, 114, 162—163, 164, 168, 171, 242-3
North Staffordshire Regt. leaves Cairo, 50 ; arrives Wady Halfa, 57 ; at Halfa, part ii., chap. iv. ; moves to Gemai, 96 ; Cairn, 100 ; at Sarras, 108; starts south from Kosheh, 111 ; at the battle of Hafir, part ii., chap. ix. ; strength on leaving Hafir, 133 ; at the capture of Dongola, part ii., chap. x. ; addressed by the Sirdar, 146 ; leaves Dongola, 149 ; arrives Cairo, 152 ; casualties, 152 ; Sirdar's despatches, 154
Northumberland Fusiliers, moved to Egypt, 1897 ; leave Cairo for front, 239-240 ; reach Atbara, 241 ; Wad Hamed, 243, 245 ; advance to Egega, part iv., chap. vi. ; at the battle of Omdurman, part iv., chap. vii. ; casualties, 278 ; return to Cairo, 282
Nubia, 8

O'DONOVAN (correspondent), death of, 11
Ohrwalder, Father, escapes from Omdurman, 34
Oldfield, Capt., 126, 152
Omdurman, 15, 19; takes the place of Khartum, 25, 153, 253; battle of, part iv., chap. vii.; capture of, part iv., chap. viii.
Om Waragat, Slatin defeated at, 10
Osman Azrak (Emir), 61, 75, 120
Digna (Emir), 12, 29, 30, 33; part ii., chap. iii.; 170, 173-4 196, 198, 227, 229
Osobri, capture of, 186
Owen, Maj. "Roddy," death of, 98

Pain, Major Hackett, 153
Parsons, Col., 128, 153; takes over Kassala from Italians, part iii., chap. iii.; captures Gedaref, 285, 286
Peake, Capt., 171, 207, 263
Penton (Surg.) Capt., 63
Persse, Capt., 64, 205, 210
Peyton, Capt., 217
Philae [ruins], 53
Pinches, Surg.-Capt. (Major), 51, 265
Pink, Major, 169
Pirie, Lieut., wounded, 266
Polwhele, Lieut., 61, death of, 99
Power, Mr., 15

RAILWAY (Cairo-Assouan), 50, 53, 196, 240
reaches Moghrat Wells, 62; Ambigole, 66; Akasheh, 93; Ferket and Kosheh, 102; Kerma, 158
new line commenced from Halfa, 163; *reaches* Abu Hamed, 183; Abu Dis, 196
Ras el Hudi, 204
Rashed Bey, 10
Rauf Pasha, 10
Rawlinson, Capt. Sir H., 209
Red Sea littoral. *See* Suakin.
Redy, Bishara (Emir), killed at Atbara, 227
Reily (Surg.), Capt., 51
Rennie, Lieut., wounded, 222

Rhodes, Col. (Correspondent), wounded at Omdurman, 259
Rifle Brigade, leave Cairo for front, 239, 240; reach Atbara, 241; Wad Hamed, 243, 245; advance to Egega, part iv., chap. vi.; at the battle of Omdurman, part iv., chap. vii.; casualties, 278; return to Cairo, 282
Robertson, Commander, 126
Rodd, Mr. Rennell, 195
Rose, Capt., 100; death of, 152
Rundle, Col. (Maj.-Gen.), 58

SADEK, 120, 123
Safir (boat), 20
Said Pasha, 4; death of, 10
Samincatelli, Count, 185, 190
Sarras, evacuated by British, 23; battle, 29, 49, 51
Sayal, 252
Seaforth Highlanders, moved to Egypt, 197; leave Cairo for Assouan, 197; from Wady Halfa to Kunur, 202; advance to Ras el Hudi, 203; to Mutrus, part iv., chap. ii.; at the battle of Atbara, part iv., chap. iii., 216, 220, 222; casualties, 227; Darmali, 231, 238, 239; Wad Hamed, 243, 245; advance to Egega, part iv., chap. vi.; at the battle of Omdurman, part iv., chap. vii.; casualties, 278; return to Cairo, 282
Semneh, 59
Sennâr, 4, 8, 14, 27
Shabluka (6th Cat.), 242
Sheikh Nib, 252
Shekleton, Brev.-Maj., 153, 222
Shellal, 54, 151, 240
Shendy, 8, 176, 198, 206
Shereik (railhead), 200
Shukrieh (tribe), 68, 186
Sidney, Maj., 69; killed at Abu Hamed, 166
Sillem, Capt., 90
Simms, Rev. Mr. 226
Sinket, massacre, 12
Sirdar, definition, 37
See Sir Evelyn Wood, Sir Francis Grenfell, Sir Herbert Kitchener.

INDEX 335

Sitwell, Maj., wounded, 202, 206
Slatin Pasha, 10, 20; escapes from Omdurman, 34; starts up Nile, 50, 77, 146; enters Omdurman with the Sirdar, 271, 284
Sloggett, Surg.-Capt. (Maj.), 51; wounded, 267 *n*.
Sloman, Capt., 206
Smith, Hon. Capt., 51
Smith, Col. Holled (Commandant Suakin), 33
Smith-Dorrien, Lieut.-Col., 273
Smyth, Lieut., 209
Sobat, 284
Soudan, The, definition, 1
   its extent prior to sway of Mahdi, 8
   prior to its recapture, part i.
Souter, Capt., 68
Sparkes, Capt. (Maj.), 90, 172
Special Correspondents. *See* Correspondents.
Stanley, H. M., 28
Stanton, Capt., 168
Staveley, Lieut. R.N., 281
Stern-wheelers. *See* Boats.
Stephenson, Gen., 23
Stevenson, Lieut., 61
Stewart, Col., 15, 164
Stewart, Gen. Sir H., 17; killed at Gubat, 19
Stewart, Piper, gallantry of, 223
Stuart-Wortley (as Lieut.), 19; (as Maj.), 181, 248, 250
Suakin, 8, 21, 30, 33; part ii., chap. iii.; route to Berber reopened, 172
Suarda, 101, 102, 107
Suleiman (son of Zobeir), 7
Sururab, 253
Swarbrick, Corp., gallantry at Omdurman, 265

TAMAI, 21
   battle, 13
Tambuk, part ii., chap. iii.
Tanjore, 60
Telegraph, 62; *reaches* Suarda, 93; Absárat, 107; Dongola, 149; Omdurman, 282; Kassala, 285
Tel-el-Kebir battle, 37
Teroi Wells, part ii., chap. iii.
Tewfik Bey, death of, 12

Tewfikieh, 76, 95
Thebes [ruins], 52
Thompson, Lieut., wounded, 222
Tokar, massacre at, 12; battle, 12, 33
Tokar, fight at, 34; part ii., chap. iii.
Toski, battle, 33
Townshend, Major (Lieut.-Col.), 87
Trask, Surg.-Capt., death of, 99
Trombi, Count, 66
Tudway, Capt. (Brev.-Maj.), 87, 167, 261
Tumbus, Is., 123, 126
Tuti, Is., 272

UM TEREF, 250
Umdabia, 211, 229
Urquhart, Maj., killed at the Atbara, 221

Vandeleur, Lieut. R.S., wounded, 222
Vandeleur, Lieut. C.S. (E.A.), wounded, 263
Verner, Col., wounded, 122

WAD (EL) BISHARA (Emir), 61, 125, 129, 137; killed at Atbara, 227
Wad (el) Bishara (place), 249
Wad (el) Habeshi, 241
Wad (el) Nejumi. *See* Nejumi.
Wad (el) Obeid, 251
Wadai, annexed by Khalifa, 32
Wadib Gerub, 164
Wady Amur, 200
Wady Atireh, 59
Wady Halfa (2nd Cat.), British withdraw to, 23, 49, 59; part ii., chap. iv., 200, 241
Walsh, Capt., wounded, 222
Walter, Capt., wounded, 222, 263
Warwickshire Regt. (Royal) leaves Cairo, 197; from Wady Halfa to Berber, 200; arrives at Kunur, 201, 202; advance to Ras el Hudi, 203; to Mutrus, part iv., chap. ii.; at the battle of the Atbara, part iv., chap. iii., 216, 219, 220, 122; casualties, 227; Darmali, 231, 238, 239; Wad Hamed, 243, 245; advance to

Egega, part, iv., chap. vi., at the battle of Omdurman, part iv., chap. vii., casualties, 278; return to Cairo, 282
Watson, Capt., A.D.C., 281
Watson, Rev. A. W., 51, 226
Wauchope, Col. (Brig.-Gen.), 239, 245, 263
Welch, Capt., 49
Whitla, Capt., 64
Wilkinson, Capt., 153
Williams, Maj., 259
Wilson, Sir Charles, 18
Wingate, Maj. (Col.), 50, 77, 275, 284
Wodehouse, Col., 32
Wolseley, Lieut., 169

Wolseley, Gen. Lord, 16, 22, 37, 282
Wood, Gen. Sir Evelyn, 12
Wood, Lieut., 248

YACOUB (Emir, Khalifa's brother), 258, 263
Young, Capt. (Brev.-Maj.), 87, 126, 206
Yussef, Pasha, 10

ZABDERAT, 191
Zeki, Osman Mahomed (Emir), 169; killed at Atbara, 227
Zobeir, Pasha, 4
Zowerat, 134, 135

THE END

www.ingramcontent.com/pod-product-compliance
Lightning Source LLC
Chambersburg PA
CBHW070834160426
43192CB00012B/2191